UnEldered

Françoise Elvin

Dear Mia
Thanks for your dedication 2 your path ♡x
Françoise

Honeybee Books

Published by Honeybee Books
www.honeybeebooks.co.uk

Printed in the UK using paper from sustainable sources

ISBN: 978-1-913675-43-1

www.elephant.intheroom.is

Author portrait on back cover by Pete Smollett

Disclaimer

The information provided in this book is intended for a lay audience, and is not to be used as a clinical resource. The author offers no warranty in regards to accuracy or suitability of the material for any specific purpose. The author does not assume and hereby disclaims any liability to any party for any loss, damage, disruption, or distress caused by errors or omissions, whether such errors or omissions result from accident, or any other means.

For
the Ancestors
and the Youth

May the wheel
come
Full circle

Contents

Preface

This book started as an exploration of the one-time role of Elders in traditional collectivist societies (the pre-communist version of course): their importance in making, shaping and maintaining 'Culture'. It describes the 'technology' of Elderhood - discussing initiation and the power of the circle: - that highly social shape, assumed by cells of humanity for untold stretches of time, before the advent of QR codes and clocks. What's written here is also a testament of my own evolving Elderhood; what life has taught me - in both formal and informal settings - from sitting in rows; circles; facing the wall even, as in the Zen tradition. It's a compilation of lessons learned, including the 'school of hard knocks'; a curated bundle of what seems to me to be worth passing on. What started off as a book about mental, emotional and spiritual health grew to include memoir - I felt compelled to make myself visible, sometimes in a very personal way. Turbulent Teenage Times prompted the risk of exposure; and with the benefit of hindsight, I realise how badly I needed the support I never got at the time. In no small part my impetus for writing is an attempt to rescue the lost teenager who lives inside me still. Looking around me, I see young people needing emotional holding - now more than *ever* - so this is a kind of ad-hoc manifesto, or plea, for the Elder's Return.

I started writing in the first year of the pandemic, and felt immediately that what was unfolding was not really about health or well-being, but the rolling out of vested interests on a global, unprecedented scale. So the book morphed to encompass a deep dive into geo-politics, economic and historical realities. I tie those in with questions of ethics, morality and leadership; since an Elder, or anyone tasked with 'curating' mental health; has to be responsible for wielding *the power* of that role: – Meaning, amongst other things, eyes wide open to reality... Thinking of leadership qualities, an ostrich with its head in the sand is probably not the first image that comes to mind. As we will see though, personal bias is inevitable; the challenge is to learn our 'confirmation biases', now more than ever with the echo chambers we live inside of, and to notice how they affect our behaviour. Using our lens to 'Zoom out'; becoming aware of the 'meta-perspective' asks us to carefully consider all angles, and to recognise we base most of our *opinions*, and even *actions*, on second or third hand information these days. The first duty of the Elder is to act as 'Radar-to-Our-Meta-Predicament' – you could say – which is no mean feat in a post-truth era.

I was unpleasantly surprised by the levels of compliance I saw in the institutions I was a part of between 2020 & 22: – University; a Meditation Centre I attended regularly; a School of Social Entrepreneurs I mentored with; The stance of the BACP – The British Association of Counselling and Psychotherapy – who I witnessed at close quarters via their monthly journal, with a circulation of 50,000. All of these institutions are charged with the mental health and well-being of society in some capacity. Throughout the pandemic, *why* weren't they questioning the mandates that forced us deeper into isolation and unprecedented levels of regulation, whilst *reducing* humane, face to face encounters? Why didn't they seek to measure the collateral damage caused by government – to the economy and the individual? Why didn't they question the vested interests behind the 'science' and the 'statistics'? Why so much blind faith? Why sweep so much under the carpet and mindlessly comply? You'll find two chapters of investigative journalism in the book dedicated to answering these questions. The *compliance*, for me, has been the most shocking thing about the 'pandemic' years... The over-arching recurrent concern throughout the book is: ***'Why do we give up our freedoms so readily, and fail to question the mainstream narrative: – What has become of our innate wisdom, resilience and sovereignty?'***

It's difficult to calibrate loss – to detect what's missing. Western culture – for all it's shiny packaging – seems deeply flawed – we've traded community for comfort in a Faustian bargain of sorts that was never properly explained – perhaps with many tracks deliberately erased. It's possible no one understands the full extent of sleights of hand centuries, if not Millennia, deep – yet many seem to experience a visceral unease, and to recognise that we're 'in deep'; up over our heads even, with the exponential rate of change having us treading water much of the time. In order to create resilience to the 'New World Order' – there's a whole chapter on this – we need to understand the forces of control, and then find creative ways to avoid becoming their sitting targets – assuming it's not too late. Can we band together, against all the odds; somehow reinventing structures from the ground-up that allow us to distinguish fact from fiction, enabling purpose, connection and authentic wellness to take centre stage once more?

This is an opportunity and a time like no other: – so much is at stake – from literally our human DNA, to what remains of our fragmented communities, our freedoms, and our health. Yuval Noah Harari has ominously referred to the human race as 'hackable animals'... At this turning point in our history, we need to decide if that's a definition we like, and if not, resist it with all our might! Many are calling this time a 'fork in the road', meaning the path we take now will irrevocably influence the trajectory of humanity for a very long time to come... This book lays out in depth, and in detail, some of the most profound and pressing choices we currently face... It offers maps, tools and insights gathered from wisdom traditions, neuroscience, psychology and contemporary culture, weaving together a journey that is personal and universal in scope. It's my hope that you will find a place in the pages where you feel 'at home'; where an Elder is walking alongside you on the long-discovery-road; pointing out traps and tricks as well as waterholes and places to rest. It's my genuine wish for you to feel safer, freer, better informed, inspired and empowered from reading the contents herein. May these pages somehow offer a hand to hold, and a wry wrinkled smile, in this strange place and in these strange times: – at least for a while.

Chapter One

Elderhood: Then and Now

As people age in the West, we don't seem to have a role for them; Youth is worshipped as 'where it's at', for obvious reasons - health, beauty, strength, 'relevance'. Getting older feels like getting hitched to the conveyor belt with 'scrap heap' stamped on our foreheads... If you're lucky, you have involvement with family and community in advanced years; finding ways to create connection, comfort, purpose and peace; and because we're living longer, some are even able to carve out second or third careers and new hobbies. Yet we seem to have lost touch with the ancient system where 'Elders' were held up as Teachers, Guardians of Culture and Makers of Maps of Meaning - a precious living lexicon of how to live well and understand our place in the larger scheme of things. Elders gave a certain kind of structure to the societies that honoured them - providing verifiable, direct Wisdom Lineages passed from generation to generation. With those lineages came an embodied, 'site specific' way of knowing the world, rather than the 'remote' screen learning we mostly rely on today, which imparts 'opinion' rather than depth of understanding, and hijacks our attention towards outward-focussed representations of the 'real world'. We don't fully understand how this might be impacting consciousness; the book explores this in later chapters, including the power and import of awareness itself, and how it is being shaped and manipulated in our times.

Today's supra-rational culture automatically questions the 'Wisdom' concept. In doing so, we neglect to notice we worship 'rationality' at a cost - noticeably in distancing ourselves from the natural world we depend on for survival, and in doing so, from the 'contemplative impulse', that the Greeks (who invented 'logic') said was a necessary compliment. *Going inside*, according to Aristotle, was a way to connect to Inspiration and Insight, and recognise *the limits of logic* in orienting us to Reality.[1] For Greek philosophers, contemplation was *superior* to logic; which was seen to be in the service of Truth, meaning we had to use intuition and an interior way of connecting the dots to reach deeper understanding.

Yet the 'wisdom project' has always been *interactive* as well as intuitive... Elders were the guides who helped young initiates in the task of catalysing 'knowledge' into 'wisdom'. Founder of communication training organisation Reaching People, David Charalambous, in a podcast with Aubrey Marcus,[2] remarked that in today's world, it is as if we're eating one meal after another without taking the time to digest. That's the effect of being 'passive consumers' of information. The traditional way of making sense of our world was actively hands-on, including dialogue and contemplation in a process that enabled us to 'digest as we go'. This bathed our nervous systems in real-time stimulation and reward, called 'co-regulation' in neuroscience, through conversation and emotional engagement, providing a felt sense of safety and belonging.[3]

Belonging and the Nervous System

It's only through developing an intimate relationship with people, place, and even, over time, the natural forces that govern our inner and outer worlds, that *safety* and *belonging* come; and with them; the beginnings of *thriving*. Wisdom in the context of traditional Elderhood was about studying the patterns and indivisibility of the natural world - *and thus* learning to thrive within limits; knowing how to stress test wood, water, winter; how to develop *rapport* with resource and one another; how to adapt, and learn to interact fruitfully with the natural world. Women tended the hearth, whilst men hunted farther afield;

---

1. Jeremy Naydler, Living in the Shadow of the Machine (Temple Lodge Books, 2018): p. 76
2. Aubrey Marcus. "Fighting Back Against Divide & Conquer w/ David Charalambous | Aubrey Marcus Podcast", YouTube, 1:55:24, June 23, 2022, https://youtube.com/watch?v=cr1ypyA_z1o
3. Primary care giver and infant forge healthy neural circuitry – termed co-regulation in the neuro-science of attachment – a life-long process.

communal endeavours of foraging, fashioning and adornment informed life as it was daily lived. Children were woven into the fabric of living; rather than being ferried about to be 'looked after', and so they learned by observing and copying, and through play; embedded in the very heart of daily activity, where singing was common. Those too old to do much hunting and foraging would still have had a place, helping with childcare; still very much part of the community. Have any of us, I wonder, glimpsed the *sweetness* in this way of living?... Nature might have been harsh at times, at other times bountiful as swelling mares' bellies in early spring; berries in autumn, or the familiar scent of a loved-one's skin...

The rhythm, routine and variety of communal lifestyles was very beneficial to our sense of well-being - soothing and comforting one another in lives of close proximity, priming the nervous system for 'secure attachment' also called 'ventral vagal dominance'. This bottom-up system (meaning the brain takes readings from the body) informs 'all is well' when appetites are sated and closeknit community prevails; allowing the frontal cortex of the brain, responsible for advanced communication skills, to develop and dominate. Modern day research confirms our nervous systems were forged in this way, because we are now able to study the problems arising downstream of losing social networks, where their loss causes long-term damage to the bio-psycho-social organism. In the 'Neuroscience, Nurture and Narcissism' chapter we will study bonding mechanisms and the Autonomic Nervous System (ANS) in more detail. We should never seek to deny there was brutality and hardship in prehistory, but having a well-developed safe social system to return to ensured emotional trauma could be metabolised, and optimal functioning restored.

Belonging as birthright: tribal living adapted over tens or even hundreds of thousands of years of human evolution, was eventually dismantled by the gradual development of modern agriculture around 5,000 years ago. The accumulation and storing of food as wealth effectively began to tear us out of the emotional sense of security that came from sharing resources equally with all, as was the case in close knit cultures living as hunting and foraging bands. Developments in farming led to an increase in the population, which led to competition over land. Dynasties and Empires rose and fell, the most import being the Roman Empire which developed close ties with the Hohenzollerns in Europe who excelled at taxing their serfs, thus ending up acting as pawn brokers to the Holy Roman Emperor Sigismund.[4]

Bearded natives shown with their hands tied behind their backs and kneeling at the feet of the clean shaven Roman victors. From the Antonine Wall, built around AD 142 and spanning from the Clyde in Glasgow to the Firth of Forth in Edinburgh, Scotland. On permanent display at the Hunterian museum in Glasgow university. This wall marked the edge of the Roman Empire. The Calendonii tribes to the north in what is now Scotland remained unconquered.

Warfare played its part: also according to Will Zoll: The Teutonic Knights acquired their land by conquering the pagan tribes of the region, slaughtering them to the point of genocide... This was known as the 'Northern Crusade', responsible for bringing to birth the Prussian Empire, explored elsewhere in this volume.

4. *Will Zoll. "Shiny Toys, KlownShows and the War for Happiness", Prussia Gate, last modified November 29, 2023, https://prussiagate.substack.com/p/shiny-toys-klownshows-and-the-war*

Of course, ideology and religion played a part in these developments. According to the 'Guru Papers', the development of religion fed into the stratification of Authoritarian culture.[5] The invention of a Transcendent God who punished bad and rewarded good behaviour made it ok for some to be wealthy and others poor, justified by the idea that those at the top of the Hierarchy were emissaries 'chosen' by God, and justifiably privileged. Whereas once 'security' as a well-regulated nervous system and sense of belonging were common property, now 'Status' had to be earned, and hard work required in maintaining it...

The pain entailed in putting up with a new stratified and oppressive social order was justified with the notion of original sin – that if we toiled and kept our heads down, a special reward might come in the 'afterlife'. The burning of the witches in medieval Europe helped ensure that none remained to profess direct contact with the healing power of nature, destroying vestiges of pagan, tribal and even matriarchal culture. Intermediaries – Priests – were now needed to interpret and convey the will of an Abstract God out of reach of the common people.

Perhaps paradoxically, Eden must describe the magical place of belonging we *all* knew before Authoritarian religion, feudalism, the rule of Kings and Queens, Enlightened Despotism and modern politics came to steal away sovereignty and a felt sense of belonging? We speak now of the 'social contract' born of the European Enlightenment, but never was this idea developed in consultation with the common people! No one ever signed the fictitious paperwork, yet the notion presupposes that we willingly relinquished, and relinquish still, our freedoms to reap the rewards offered by modern day society and the Nation State. This rests on a large amount of 'good faith' on the part of the citizenry, whose knowledge of other available options has been totally obliterated! Perhaps in our 'collective unconscious' we long to return not to the Eden described in the bible but to the lives we lived in pre-history, deeply inscribed in DNA and bone

5. Joel Kramer and Diana Alstad, The Guru Papers: Masks of Authoritarian Power (Frog Books, 1993)

marrow...? Our modern pursuit of limitless growth shows how seriously we have taken on the 'status' challenge, whilst our failure to connect with 'healthy boundaries' reflects our disconnection from the natural world: our foundation for survival even now.

... We seem to have supplanted the infinite inner world of the imagination and connection to the ultimately mysterious forces of nature with an obsession for unbridled 'economic growth'. We have transposed an inner quest onto materialism, 'science' and wealth; instead of regarding life's journey as primarily spiritual, where limits can be tolerated, *loved, even,* as ways to belong; as portals: – Thresholds that lead to new approaches or understandings... Think of *Wisdom* as learning to listen to, resonate with, and *revere* the living web that holds us all; finding our place within it, whilst developing communication skills that enable us to get the most from our relationships, and you might start to understand the Flame Traditional Elders kindled in the hearts of their peoples.

Becoming a Useful Human Being

Elderhood once constituted the foundations of a society; Foundation and Scaffold for ethics, healing, arbitration, cosmic and natural Law[6], even whilst setting bench-marks of endurance and proficiency. Elders were deeply embedded in a system that served all – not as puppets or prophets throwing their weight about; true Elders guarded against Narcissism, rather than encouraging it – helping younger members of the culture to fit in, and find their true place. Elderhood was never about posturing or proselytising. Rather, initiated, experienced, seasoned adults would assemble, and in some places, assemble still, based on the understanding that the psychic health and wholeness of young people depended and depends on them being there. Initiation consciously choreographed was an intense experience – a gateway – acting as preparation for adulthood, involving severance with the past and the assuming of new perspectives that go with new roles and responsibilities... Rites of Passage guide, author and

6. Australian Aboriginal academic explores these: Tyson Yunkaporta, Sand Talk: How Indigenous Thinking Can Save the World (HarperOne, 2020)

story teller Dr Martin Shaw[7] speaks of this process when he describes the three stages of initiation as *leaving the village,* the *initiatory adventure,* and *the return.* Each part of the process is equally important and significant. The return allows us to be seen in a new light by other members of the clan, and when it's done well, enables us to digest and integrate the raw power of the initiatory journey itself.

Imagine how it might be to live in a culture that maps multiple stages of life, giving each one a name. The oldest members of the Clan recognise patterns of emerging, blooming, ripening, fruiting and decay; time for play and celebration, as well as great solemnity, rest and letting go... These life stages are able to cohere by being witnessed in communal settings. People with close knit community ties are able to see, feel, touch and hold the immediacy of each individual life in all its phases and stages - moments of pain as well as glory are witnessed via ritual markers helping to metabolise emotion - returning us to a place of equilibrium.

Elders' availability and 'quality of attention' was and *still is* pivotal to the way children and adults learn to value and see themselves evolving through life's many iterations... When, as adults, our lives resemble a rich tapestry of victory and defeat forged in the fire of daring, success, disappointment, restitution and repair, we might become *useful human beings,* characterised as possessing resilience, self-knowledge and great inter-personal skills. Even in the modern day, our trials bring insight and build in us the capacity to become 'holding containers' for others to explore their own journeys. This long-term process is the inner alchemical journey, referred to in the modern day as developing 'touch stones' of meaning in the person-centred counselling approach.[8] Moments of deep meaning are woven in to the fabric

---

7. Dr Martin Shaw is a Story teller, mythologist, writer, and rites of passage leader living in the south west of England. I took part in a year-long training with him at the West Country School of Myth and Story Telling.

8. Mick Cooper explores the idea that key life experiences, once they have been metabolised and integrated, are 'touch stones' that enable therapists (one time Elders) to help others, building an internal frame of reference for the task of meaning-making in the client-therapist relationship. David Mearns and Mick Cooper, Working at Relational Depth in Counselling and Psychotherapy (SAGE Publications, 2017)

of a life well lived, and have a seamless quality, forming coherent life-narratives that carry us from cradle to grave...

Elders Once Taught Endings Too

The wonderful reciprocity offered by Elders, from a modern-day vantage point, gets labelled 'primitive'. Not only has the onetime pivotal role disappeared from our societies in the west, the way the older generation depart this life in the modern age must give us cause for reflection. In his book, Stephen Jenkinson[9] explores how modern medicine and the 'helping' professions have made it harder (not easier) for the elderly to go through the process of ageing and dying with dignity. Not all modern medicine is bad, of course, but what seems to gets lost in 'institutionalised dying', is the opportunity to approach the experience for all concerned, especially the dying person, as primarily a grieving process, where death remains a mystery - a Deity even, that none shall overcome. Seen from this perspective - the dying person needs to be allowed - facilitated - if you will - in turning away from this life. The effort expended in 'keeping people alive' with drugs and medical interventions impedes this very natural and necessary process. In so doing, it robs us all - the dying person as well as extended family and society - of the opportunity of giving ourselves mentally, emotionally, psychologically, and spiritually, to the task of dying, in an appropriate, sober yet mystical fashion. It robs us perhaps of the deepest, most meaningful practice we could use to simultaneously celebrate and mourn our Elders, and of being able to grasp the profound import of the end stages of a person's life...

It wasn't always thus. Death and Life, once upon a time, were aspects of the same indivisible journey... one where the institution of Elderhood provided a lynch pin that held people and purpose together. When an Elder had performed his or her Sacred Duty in terms of guiding and training young people, he or she might feel more ready and willing to leave, at peace in the knowledge of

---

9. He worked in palliative care in Canada for 14 years, and tellingly describes it as 'working in the death trade'. Stephen Jenkinson, Die Wise: A Manifesto for Sanity and Soul (North Atlantic Books, 2015)

having 'done their bit' for culture and community. In times like ours, perhaps Elders are the ones able to see through the sugar-coating of consumer culture – and teach the young discernment; giving them the confidence to connect with their inner impulses and resources, rather than being hood-winked by the 'engineered consent' so prevalent in our tech and ad saturated environments. Elders can provide reference points youth can trust, and courageously call out the corruption that has infiltrated the heart of our institutions – those arenas young people are often required to engage as they attempt to carve out their futures.

This book makes a case for the rediscovery of Elderhood, and for ramping it up to a new level, as part of a quest that involves us all in seeking our true humanity in an age when it has never been under so much assault from all sides: media, pharmaceutical companies, Big Tech; – the robbing of our livelihoods by robots, the removal of inalienable human rights by puppet politicians. It might be that we need to form a new 'people's movement', as described by Vaclav Benda's paper in 1977 – the 'Parallel Polis', that helped overthrow the repressive post-War Czechoslovak Communist government.[10] Is it possible that young visionaries and older people with experience could combine to form a 'parallel culture' free from the lying, manipulative systems that seek to enslave and deceive? Vaclav Benda[11] described the parallel polis as 'a sort of embryonic prototype or symbolic micro-model of future political structures. The 'parallel polis' notion built a culture that embraced the arts as vehicles for protest and change, promoting human and civil rights, as enshrined in the 1975 Helsinki Accords.[12] We will come back to this in the last chapter, and acknowledge for now how important it is to feel a sense of

10. James F. Pontuso. "F. Flagg Taylor, Ed., The Long Night of the Watchman: Essays by Václav Benda 1977-1989. Translated by Barbara Day," Society 56, no. 1 (2019): 99.
11. Michael Martin' "The Parallel Polis, or How to Beat the Technocracy", The Center for Sophiological Studies, last modified August 31, 2021, https://thecenterforsophiologicalstudies.com/post/the-parallel-polis-or-how-to-beat-the-technocracy
12. The Helsinki Accords were between European nations, the USA, and Canada. Articles include sovereign equality, refraining from threat or use of force, inviolability of frontiers, territorial integrity, respect for human rights and freedoms, including freedom of thought, conscience, and religion. "Helsinki Accords", Wikimedia Foundation, last modified December 11, 2023, https://en.wikipedia.org/wiki/Helsinki_Accords

hope in the possibility of treading in the footsteps of those who came before, facing similar challenges to the ones we face now.

Holding the Line

... *I had a dream last night that humans weren't REAL any more. It was a dystopian nightmare of a dream – you could tell the human was a fake by looking him or her in the right eye. In the dream, if I saw the fakery sign in the eye, I lunged forward and stuck my finger in it, eviscerating fakery; pulling the eye out...* If we combine forces to resuscitate the tradition of Eldering, 'pulling out fakery' might be part of the job description, although perhaps not in such a literal fashion as in the dream: – *if it sounds harsh, it possibly is.*

That is perhaps why parents don't make good Elders of their own children, as Stephen Jenkinson[13] has pointed out – an Elder is not always 'nice'; and the message he or she brings is unlikely to be 'convenient', because Elders are committed to the well-being of the Whole, not any one individual. Elders are guardians, representatives and rescuers of Culture – that always comes first, and so 'cutting through the crap' – eviscerating fakery – being able to tell apart the trans-human and true human – is the Order of the Day when Elders are about... *Lest we forget*, developing refined *courtoisie* is also a necessary skill and emblem of Elderhood elaborated by Jenkinson in his latest book 'Come of Age'. I realise my dual Scots-French heritage has added a certain feisty slant to the task that might be rather off-putting for the more mild-mannered here. *There's room for everyone!*

While discernment might be an essential quality of the Elder in our days of simulacra; Elders also exhibit care, and are informed by an abiding love for the entire web of life. Love accompanies authenticity; showing up; being willing to go the extra mile on *'the road less travelled'...* On the personal level, Elders scrutinise the contortions and consequences of our actions, helping the misshapen to take up its natural form again; holding up tough mirrors and smiling wryly. *In a Distorted World, Elders are tasked*

13. Elder, Author, performer, and one time palliative care front-line worker, holds Masters degrees in Theology from Harvard, and in Social Work from the University of Toronto. Stephen Jenkinson, Come of Age (North Atlantic books, 2018)

with remembering what things in their natural habitat, assuming their honest shapes, once looked like. Whilst adaptability has always been *the* key skill that's enabled humanity to survive, thrive, and reach the top of the food chain, Elders hold the moral compass. They tell us when we've crossed the line - when our reliance on technology and our bending under the weight of the 'social contract' becomes enslavement and addiction, *torture* even - They notice the cusp we're on right now, as technology invades our minds, hearts and bones, and they ***hold the line***. Not the easiest job description, clearly - perhaps an Elder in these days of hyper-change needs to be slightly crazy to consider the undertaking. Elders are *way-markers* who help calibrate the pace of change, and ethically evaluate whether 'changes' real, necessary, proposed, or imagined, have beneficial or disastrous consequences. Who else is engaged in this type of Fundamental, Necessary Calculation? It sounds daunting - and it is - as part of the task of loving humanity in unprecedented times.

Truly Independent Fact Checkers

... Of course, there are hosts of people who are paid to 'measure' and 'evaluate' change, including 'journalists', although it seems the profession has been taken over by vested interests, more so since the Covid-19 debacle.[14]

Most, if not all, paid 'change commentators' have their parameters set out strictly, and part of the deal is to discount certain factors. Elders have no such strictures, and therefore are free to measure *anything* and *everything*. Being the unpaid, self-appointed Keepers of the Remnants of what Matters to us as a Society, their opinion can't be bought, sold, or tarnished. Elders are in fact the only Independent Fact Checkers worth their salt in today's post-truth Era. Given this role, the company Elders keep becomes vitally important. If an Elder is to act as a kind of cultural barometer - *who* should he or she associate with? - *How* should an Elder profitably spend his or her days? Which pulses should Elders have their fingers on?

---

14. Some so-called fact-checkers are merely husband/wife teams at home, paid by vested interests to 'de-bunk' inconvenient truths, and smear the efforts of credentialed physicians. Plandemic: Indoctornation, directed by Mikki Willis (London Real, 2020), 1:24:03

... As wide a variety as possible, no doubt, and yet sifting information from this kind of broad remit, especially in our days of fake news and overload, swiftly becomes impossible, bringing a need for triage. We are not talking here about Elders as disseminators of yet more 'information'; reinventing the wheel by creating some kind of 'political' or even 'spiritual' 'manifesto', no matter how compelling; it's more engaged, personal and *emotional* than that. Elders need to reach out with wisdom and empathy, stealth and nous, being those with whom the young might *take shelter;* as people who have tussled, hustled and survived. Extensive life experience ensures Elders possess depth and breath, encouraging wide ranging conversations, whilst a long life's neural networks in the brain lend a tree-like quality to their cognition and bearing:

'Come in, they said, we'll Give you Shelter from the Storm...'

Elders are *connoisseurs* of life; pirate-scientist-grandfather-entrepreneur mash-ups; or grandmother-alchemist-researcher-artisan hybrids. They have a Warrior's presence and precision, able to look in the right eye of a trans-human, sense the fakery and, without hesitation, lean in to take it out; those with something at once new and old to offer the world in disturbing times. How do we evolve that kind of courage and discernment, bearing in mind that one without the other is no good? ... Perhaps 'Elder Material' is someone who has had their heart broken open; who has reached too close for the sun, much like Icarus, and never-the-less retains a certain limping dignified swagger; possessing a good pinch of 'salt of the earth' and fairy dust, for sprinkling alternately on the crown of a young person's head when needed. The Elder has also hopefully garnered one or two accolades for fronting up to the judges and juries of life; a crumpled striped ribbon or two bearing insignia-embossed glittering discs commemorating battles won.

Fulfilling a Sacred Duty

In each life phase, wisdom accrues. The perspective shift that comes from having navigated the demands of life cultivates in the Elder the skill and capacity to help the younger person find clarity and encourage faith in their own potential. This kind of mentoring means the hearts of both parties are nourished. The

Young feel seen and validated, whilst the Old experience the Exchange as the Fulfilling of a Sacred Duty. Each side Gifts the Other. Of course, the Elder role might look like it is the most giving role of the two, but in reality, the old need to stay connected with young hearts to avoid withering and buckling under the weight of Nostalgia!

Memoir: Reciprocity

If we do a good enough job, and are deemed 'worthy' by the young, they might offer up the immediacy and potency of their experience as Gift.

... I was at a bare-foot dance a couple of years ago, in the Totnes part of Devon, renowned for gatherings of this sort. There was a long-haired, graceful woman in her 30s dancing soulfully who I connected with – her movements fluid, agile, somehow seeking to express the feminine power of her erotic nature; the walking a tight-rope quality when women show up as embodied and sensual in our culture was apparent to me... I stayed with her dance moment-to-moment, never taking my eyes off her, attempting to meet and breathe and mirror her movements – the grace and courage of her aliveness and vulnerability entwined in the dance. Afterwards, when the dancers sat in a circle this woman came spontaneously and bowed down in front of me weeping. I hadn't asked for anything and hadn't announced myself as 'Elder' (as if I could!) It unfolded wordlessly – as an exchange where my presence seemed to invite her to bring more of herself – to feel her edges and trust and let go more fully into the precious moment of the still, steady witnessing process.

More recently a young counselling client pulled out a frame drum at the end of a session and sang me one of her own songs. First she told the story of the making of the drum: the horse's belly skin stretched over the wooden hoop, and then she wove a haunting soundscape for me with lyrics woven from red threads, ancestors and Mythic Time. She reflected back to me via the gift of her voice and the steady beat of the drum the ancient world I seek to conjure between the pages of this book. I was silenced; humbled, it felt like a full circle of sorts – my attempted gift returned.

The Elder receives and reflects back the often visceral rawness of youth, in an Act that helps them process Uncertainty at the many Beguiling Cross Roads of life. According to the Book of Miracles – 'Giving and Receiving are the Same.' Life is built on Reciprocity: I am because you are. In the relationship between Elder and Younger, each gives meaning and purpose to the other's life, no less. For one; the struggle has not been in vain; for the other, they are no longer alone in their Quest of Becoming, but deeply Seen; Honoured; Upheld.

ACTIVITY: Time Line

You should take at least an hour for this exercise – maybe two or three. You can share your findings with a friend (who might participate) or therapist; Take a big piece of paper, or tape a couple of smaller pieces together. Draw a long line across the paper horizontally

– Write 'zero' to represent your birth on the LHS of the line, and 'now' at the opposite end of the long line you've drawn. Think of key moments in your life – they might be births or deaths of relatives, peak experiences, or catastrophes. Moving house, travel, divorce, marriage, significant relationships, episodes in the classroom or at work, your first job, getting promoted, starting a business, reaching a goal, bankruptcy, giving birth to a child, your first sexual experience, being ridiculed or targeted, moments of achievement, recognition, failure or rejection. Plot these events on your timeline. You can use a bubble diagram if it seems more natural. Doodle and draw images and icons on the paper if you like – some represent positives and others negatives – if it appeals, use coloured pens. Maybe plot 'positive' experiences above the line, and 'negative' ones below... Ask yourself – was anyone around to support or recognise your challenge, achievement or defeat, or notice the threshold you crossed? – Make notes by each event. Write names of people who played a significant part in these important events, or maybe write 'no one' if you felt there was an absence of support or witnessing. Then describe the difference having support or recognition made to the experience, or would have made, at the time. If you didn't receive support at a crucial time in your life – ask yourself how that feels now, and consider whether you might be able to find someone still to help gain recognition or support with one of your threshold, defining moments... Grieving the absence of support might be appropriate in this exercise, as would celebrating yourself and any support that was present.

This is not just a mental exercise. You might find yourself becoming deeply emotional when you consider significant life events in the light of these questions. If feelings surface – allow them space. You may like to take notes after giving them space, defining what they meant then and now. If you want to go farther with the exercise, consider what the learnings have been from key life events – how might you now describe them as 'touchstones' in your life now – how have certain experiences coloured your views? Which feel integrated, and which are still raw? How could you use these experiences to give you wisdom and empathy when holding space for someone else who might describe a similar situation? How have these experiences shaped your sense of self, and your view of humanity? You may have other questions... After this review, be sure to have some down time, go for a walk, or have a long bath so you can process or integrate more fully the thoughts and feelings that have come up. Ideally, find someone you trust who you can share some of this exercise with...

Developing Strength of Character

Elders were the ones to conduct rites of passage ceremonies for the young, during gatherings where strength, endurance, mental fortitude, and being a good team player counted. In today's world, in developing these qualities youth learn to stand up for themselves in situations at home, college, or even in the workplace. A bit different to the 'hear and obey' mentality inculcated at school! In the absence of self-esteem and resilience-building experiences, how much more often does Youth get subsumed, ignored, or condescended to in conflict scenarios? What about the pseudo-corrective processes that exist to right wrongs within our modern-day institutions? Of course, there's such a thing as 'pecking order' and insubordination, and I'm not about encouraging the latter. It seems, though, there's a mental health epidemic amongst young people in our times, and that standing up for oneself is a life skill that needs to be taught. I have inside experience of speaking truth to institutionalised power... At best, if someone is very lucky and persistent; respect and restitution may be achieved. More likely, a posse of vested interests prevails, going through the motions of meting out 'justice' whilst colluding and counterfeiting openness and impartiality in a bid to protect their own backs.

Elders have no such agendas - they teach the young to stand up for themselves. Having *no vested interests* is one of their defining traits, meaning they freely follow moral imperatives, enabling them to shape humanity for the better. Their remit is passing on skills and knowledge in a challenging and yet nurturing environment. Elders must be robust, wise, and wild, having undergone their own rites of passage over decades in different contexts. Of course, it's easier said than done for would-be Elders in our time to step up to the high bar required. Eldering, as a project, is a perfect vehicle for 'honing the ego', making us think more deeply beyond the confines of self-centredness. *Polishing ourselves as Elders is a job that is never done!* In Native American culture, 'Honouring the Children's Fire' was at the centre of decision-making processes; meaning the well-being of the young was put first; and consequences of actions were considered seven generations deep.[15] Continuity of culture, meaning, responsibility, and care wove shining silver threads through sinew and synapse of a People when Elderhood was still an embodied part of daily living.

Today's culture is begging for a certain breed of adult to step forward and offer themselves as guides, mentors and witnesses for the young. It's not just way-off-the-rails youth who need input via social work departments, therapists, and police. All could benefit from mentoring and guidance. In fact, if there's an evolved version of the 'contrary gene' in you as potential Elder, that might be just what's needed, to help young people wake up to a system that is becoming more oppressive by the year. Never before in human history have we seen the type of *global* takeover emerging, as the neo-feudal Technocracy takes hold. These are

15. I heard this from Mac McCarthy - one time business coach, author, story teller and founder of Embercombe - eco-project and adult education centre in the West Country in England. He spent much time apprenticing as a Dog Soldier with Amer-Indian teachers.

themes we'll fully explore in the chapters 'New World Order' and 'Psychological Warfare'.

It might seem counter-intuitive, as we tend to think the older we get, the more conservative we become; yet Elders, as Guardians of Culture, have a role to play as 'interrupters' of the NWO, which is fast becoming the 'new normal'. We are going to have to dust down the *Rebel* Archetype, as we fight to conserve something of the pre-Covid Olde Worlde Charm, and dig deeper to unearth some of the ancient tribal roots and routes that Eldering is steeped in. Another perhaps counter-intuitive point to remember is that modern education makes us *more*, not *less* susceptible to being duped... It is a function of the State; a way to condition and prime for Obedience - if we are to preserve and develop resilience, we need to embrace multiple 'wisdom streams' including face-to-face embodied learning, remembering *where we come from*, as a necessary antidote to where we might be headed.

The Symbiosis of Eldering

Much in the same way as forests are now being seen as interwoven and inter-communicating intelligent networks of roots, fungi and leaves; so Elders, when assembled together in groups, offer a Woven Wisdom Web; the best we have, to offer a coherent field of meaning to the young who are lucky enough to step into the latticed canopy and fecund ground offered by this system. Elders need Eldering for their own mental health, to know and be known in cultural contexts that honour their experience and knowledge; we need each other as much as we need a younger generation to hold in our hearts and minds, whilst we act to encourage and support them. If the more extreme versions described here are not for you; there are surely any number of iterations Eldering can take, since together we are stronger; and able to offer more to those in need, with a plurality of voices emerging in circles or 'Clan gatherings' being a closer approximation to the truth than any one of us can individually express. The danger might be that Eldering becomes a talking shop for the ideology of Elderhood, rather than a crucible into which the young can enter. How might we guard against this and ensure we gather to serve the needs of the young?

Most young people are infatuated with technology. Imagine if Elders took a collective stand, inviting, by means fair and foul (bribery/rewards!) young people to step away from their screens, to engage in face-to-face contact, and to explore the natural world. Elders could set up Technology Detox Retreats for the young; help them to reconnect and reacquaint themselves with nature, whilst also explaining the darker sides of technology as the emergent Technocratic State – which we explore later on.

We need to re-learn the art of simplicity; cutting our cloth according to the parameters of our exquisite, finite, regenerative planet. There are so many skills to be learned and things to discover in the multi-dimensional physical Universe. Retreats could explore practical ways to reduce our carbon footprints and increase biodiversity, simultaneously re-wilding the psyche and the landscape as an antidote to the excesses of consumer culture rapidly exporting itself to all corners of the globe. It is precisely because of the urgency of the situation, with 'Technocracy' instead of 'Sovereignty' being offered up as the solution by the likes of the UN and WEF, that we need to rediscover our core values and pit them against the NWO. Having mentors to encourage and shape the aspirations of the young in real-time, face-to-face encounters brings stability, hope, strength, and direction. Perhaps more than ever, young people are in need of core values, as they struggle to navigate a world where, for many, their 'virtual' presence has become more powerful and immediate to them than flesh-and-blood reality.

It may seem hypocritical to expect youth to put their faith in us... Perhaps we need to take a long hard look in the mirror and be willing to eat humble pie... To apologise for the blindness and recklessness of our own culture's Ways, of our own moral bankruptcy, before we can expect them to set any store by the 'guidance' we may wish to offer. None of this is comfortable to contemplate. And as stated before, Elders are not all about comfort. So, if we wish to see the young grow in substance by setting challenges, then we need to live with the same courage and willingness to step out of our comfort zones which we expect of them. Can we help them get down and dirty in the messy, fleshy, dusty, scary 'real world'? Unless we take a stand, we face a dystopian world where fact and fiction become indistinguishable, and tracking and tracing the norm; now that freedom of speech is confabulated with 'conspiracy theorising', and where the Technocratic Global Government makes most choices for us most of the time. For Gen Z, much of this description of life may already feel 'normal', or at least not 'out of place'.

Eldering the Elder

You will have had your own initiation experiences, with the guidance of teachers, masters and mentors. Sometimes the Devil Himself was the main protagonist; Elders will be able to look back on many trials by fire - deliberate, accidental or inevitable they somehow survived. Maybe scarred, humiliated, rejected, taken for a ride; but on the Other Side they used the experience to evolve a canny, quirky resilience; to navigate new pathways, unearth hidden talents, and hold themselves with more accountability, dignity, respect and self-love. Trials by fire are in themselves initiations; they have a habit of breaking us down so we find new ways to reinvent ourselves; a distillation process that we can offer up to the young, if only in homoeopathic doses. Even as we recognise the urgency of the situation; it is wise to proceed with caution; to acknowledge that none of us have been Eldered properly ourselves; that we're all making it up as we go along; and that our wounds can and do and *will* trip us up; often.

How do you find out if you have what it takes to Elder? You get yourself Eldered even as you seek to Elder. You show up in groups of all sorts and observe how you behave. You should be more interested in the people who bug you than the ones you get along with. Most likely they hold 'disowned' aspects of self crying out for healing and integration. When you can sit in a circle that is tasked with a mission larger than anything any one of you could accomplish alone; and when you can contribute humbly to the mission, seeking neither to dominate nor disappear, for the sake of a higher cause you believe in, rather than for Glory; then you might be on the way to Elderhood.

Perhaps a voluntary fundraising project would be a good starting point? Pay close attention to conflicts of interest and power struggles. Scrutinise yourself in these situations to find out how you navigate a collective effort. These are the dynamics of the circle, and the circle is the first and last iteration of meaningful, participatory democracy. Can you help calm power struggles within a group - turning conflict into collaboration? Our nervous systems evolved over thousands of years in the 'Eldered Container' of small tribal groups of around 150 people, according to British anthropologist Robin Dunbar.[16] These small groups possessed internal consistency and emotional depth by virtue of the continuity of contact which characterised their daily existence. When we seek out these group experiences; they inform and impel us to grow still, even though we may hit a 'chaos field' early on in the experience because we haven't benefitted from the harmonising effect of the collectivist cultures of the past.[17]

Ongoing Practices of Eldering

So often we speak about 'Tribalism' whilst conjuring the notion of cycles of violence and partisan allegiances. Perhaps the opposite is true - that in order to successfully navigate collective lives, and peaceful times, we need and needed ample skills and discipline in the arts of cooperation, organisation, foresight, sharing, and communication. There is evidence - cited in 'The Master and his Emissary' by Iain McGilchrist[18] - to support the idea that we learned to sing before we learned to talk, suggesting that living together was a joyful, rather than a harsh experience, once-upon-a-time, in the depths of pre-history. Interestingly, Robin Dunbar

---

16. Anthropologist and evolutionary psychologist Robin Dunbar FBA FRAI is professor Emeritus of the Social and Evolutionary Neuroscience Research Robin Dunbar, The Human Story (Faber and Faber, 2004)

17. Collectivist culture emphasises the importance of social harmony, respectfulness, etc. Self is defined as interdependent; alignment of personal and communal goals; greater consideration of social norms than individual attitudes. In contrast western citizens tend to think in terms of the 'curtailment of our liberty', rather than noticing the compromising of our neurobiology brought about by the hyper-private modern society. Charlotte Nickerson. "Understanding Collectivist Cultures: Overview & Examples", SimplePsychology, October 16 2023, https://simplypsychology.org/what-are-collectivistic-cultures.html

18. Iain McGilchrist, The Master and his Emissary (Yale University, 2019)

cites the three practices that keep communities strong as singing, dancing and eating together – in that order. Perhaps communal living was a recipe for mental health, whereas modern societies in the west spawn a plethora of mental health disorders that we need to pay 'professionals' to diagnose and treat: – professionals who have replaced extended family, Elders and healers that we could access for free in traditional societies. The modernisation of 'mental health' in this fashion, allows for the cynical of the profession to pathologise healthy emotional responses to care deficits, whilst profiting from 'treating' wounded, stressed victims of today's atomised cultures.

It's difficult to know which way round the cart and the horse sit sometimes. Whilst certain care deficits result in changes in the architecture of the brain that may be impossible to heal (I explore this in the chapter on narcissism) there is a strong case to be made for the importance of developing self-love across the board. 'Self-parenting' as an aspect of self-love helps us rewire the brain for secure attachment. The jury is still out as to whether 'self love is enough', and if it can be developed at all in certain extreme cases of neglect and abuse... The question has something to do with the territory where psychology and spirituality intersect... Perhaps this is a good time to introduce myself to the reader, revealing something of the formative experiences that shaped me as someone interested in asking questions like the one above.

Memoir: Ferment

'Essence needs to be seen in order to be developed – A. H. Almaas.[19]

With self-love, there are layers and phases of it, I find. That layer: 'I love you no matter what' is a kind of foundational layer, and I'm imagining it's also the final layer, the alpha and omega of the self-love layer cake. What about the in between bits? I need to do all the things I need to do to thrive, as acts of self love. Sometimes this might entail putting a lot of energy into ensuring I have social contact. At other times, it's about cultivating self-discipline and following through with plans and projects. Even as self-love might sometimes be about 'letting oneself off' the proverbial hook; as often as not; it's about skillfully keeping oneself hooked; becoming fisher woman, fish and hook, in fact. This for me, at any rate, proves to be a subtle art. Swallowing the bait and hook: no problem... that could be seen as the initial phase... Ideas and inspiration have always come easily to my over-active (over-educated?) mind. However, landing, clubbing, gutting, frying and eating the fish (apologies to vegans): – sticking with the idea through the phases of refinement, prototypes, tests and tribulations, to completion – that's another kettle of fish – if you'll excuse the pun!

Holding a steady compass internally while I am assailed with doubts and fears is a regular challenge – requiring me to raise my game, adapt my game, reframe my game, somehow camouflage from the Fish that I am also the Fisher Woman... In effect: calling my own bluff! (Call an ambulance you say!) Although to be fair to myself, writing this book has revealed to me that I can focus and put doubt to one side – in spite of some self-diagnosed ADHD tendencies. That's actually relatively easy. A sense of impending danger is not so easy to dismiss, because there are two chapters of contentious material in this book; 'polarising content', some would say: 'inconvenient truths' even. It's possible I'm making myself a target. And there's little I can do about that... Well maybe I could do something, but a 'nom de plume' just doesn't sit right with a project that's about rebuilding social cohesion from the ground up – and it would probably just raise my anxiety levels, making the

19. A. H. Almaas is a Kuwaiti author and spiritual teacher, who Gabor Maté considers an important mentor

(perceived) need (?) to hide more real. **Then** *– I set the bar so damn high. I can't write a book unless it's an encyclopaedia. I can't engage thought without having, as an ambition, a stitching together of all the worlds of psychology, spirituality, sociology and anthropology.*

It started young. My Father worked long hours and my Mother, left to her own devices, could act out just like her father before her in the best French tradition of 'Authoritaire'. Things at home sometimes felt hard. I needed more attention to thrive, and was beset with a gnawing sense of lack from an early age which my mum labelled 'demanding'!

At secondary school, my English teacher, my **Redeemer;** *he saw grace and grandeur in me where my parents, alongside plenty of other preoccupations and concerns, saw only inconvenience and unruly behaviour. Maybe there is such a thing as benevolent neglect, maybe some kids, some of the time, thrive. In our first house, where the kids played outside together in the relatively car-free street, I did thrive for a time, especially with the care of the kindly neighbours Carol and Terry at Number 5. And then we moved, and my world shrank and the seamless quality of a life I'd known folded itself up and languished in a drawer of memory.*

Main roads and bullies and teenage hormones and a longing to be found, seen and saved somehow set in. And my English teacher did some of these things for me in his own inimitable way – for a while – introducing me to Metaphor and Myth, Sylvia Plath, George Orwell, Shakespeare, Animal Farm and Catcher in the Rye. I made a silent inner pact with him I only discovered last year at the University of Aberdeen studying person-centred counselling. I believed if I somehow sewed together a cloak magnificent enough to link all the new, high-faluting, sophisticated, wise worlds he was introducing me to, I would be able to claim him as my Own... Earning myself a Cosmic Father with a Comb-Over who would Protect me from Thorns; Adore the Ferment in me, turning me patiently in his cool cellar to remove sediments and impurities. For him, as my femininity developed as a suggestion of froth and foam towards the neck of my glass-enveloped form, there would only be celebration, continuation; an encouragement to develop the bouquet of my becoming with complex combinations of laughter, movement, metaphor and song... With his encouragement, I hoped to make fine champagne from the crazy complexity of troubled teenage times.

I sought to please him with 'Exquisite' Renditions of Erudition in the classroom – my arm perpetually in the air to answer each and every question – hoping to receive his Undying Reverence and Respect. I realise now in my half-centenary, that I never stopped playing this game – never stopped believing that if I join up enough dots, sew a big enough patchwork quilt of interwoven experience, insight, and received wisdom from the farthest edges of the humanities, the arts and the spiritual traditions I have pursued, then He Will Be There. Resplendent. Permanent. Complete. An Elder of Elders. And so the bar of this writing gets set incredibly high... And Yet He Comes Not... Consigned to the disjointed vault of memory, I still have two tiny dictionaries he gave me – one a dictionary of Greek Myth, and the other a pocket Robert Burns. Part of the task of writing about Elderhood is being able to Discern and Name Absences in our Lives. How do we measure the loss of what we've never received? What I know from Mr Caw is that it's vital for the young to have someone who notices and believes in them.

And then, how does loss or absence make itself manifest...? Maybe it is betrayed in a certain kind of brittleness sometimes in social interactions; feeling lost – character flaws that are difficult to discern because they are mine. Rabby Burns has a fine line for that... In Scots it sounds like this: 'Wud the Lord the Grace Tae Gie us, Tae see Oorsel's as Uthers see us'... In English it's: 'Would the Lord Give Us Grace to See ourselves the Same Way Others See Us...'

As a sign of my dislocation in this world, I remember dreaming, many years ago now, that my home was a caravan blown into a tree by a hurricane, where it lodged, perched between two large branches; a symbol of how 'not at home' I felt in this world. Even as Elders can challenge, they serve to welcome, to receive new life, and to make that 'emerging, tender life' feel planted, rooted and admired – right where it is. I remember running across a car park when my son was tiny, his head shaking vigorously so I could show him to Jean, a horse-drawn woman with a gypsy bow top wagon I'd met when I was heavily pregnant at an 'alternative' style festival in Wales. I needed for him to be smiled at, for someone to gently pinch his cheek, and there were so few people around me at the time who could do that. His father's family were traditional farming stock, and I was disapproved of. 'Too young, too, well....' – it was before the term 'tin-foil hat wearer' had been invented! Our relationship didn't last and by the end of the summer I blew into another Welsh town where some of the 'Rainbow Circle' camp people I'd met lived. A single parent on welfare for a while, in spite of a good education; a university dropout who left a degree course to go and milk goats, grow vegetables, and learn to be self-sufficient on a small holding in Corsica. I was looking for answers and longing to be held.

A kind of Jekyll and Hyde character I was back then, maybe still am now. Painfully shy and afraid of being rejected and judged, I covered it up ineptly with a thick layer or rebelliousness. Trapped between the four walls of a flat in a small town in Wales with my young son, I lurched though the days longing for a different world. I read the 'Great Cosmic Mother' by Monica Sjoo... That stirred the ferment, but maybe not in a good way. Everything was wrong with the world, compared to the Matriarchal lives we had once lived peacefully, close to the elements, supporting each other, woven into the cycles of nature and our own femininity, according to her analysis. The 'New Age' hippies of the summer had packed away their Rainbow Circle dream for the winter. I was lost, lonely, angry and out of kilter with the world around me.

... It started way younger than that when I was a child. My mum seemed always to be busy studying, or spending time with her French friend; my dad a newly qualified charter surveyor. They were like so many young married couples, just trying to do their best for the family, pulling themselves up by the bootstraps, propelled by the dream of being 'upwardly mobile', and bending over backwards under the weight of economic pressure which has only got worse for families in the intervening years. My dad was brought up in a tenement in central Edinburgh – there was still a blacksmith's forge across the road where horses were shod for delivering coal and milk around the city; two adults and four kids in a two-bedroomed flat. His elder sister used to take him across the road to see the horses – he remembers looking up at them – Huge Beasts that made him feel so small. He was born during the war; sometimes there were only cornflakes for breakfast, lunch and tea, although his dad had an allotment that was part of the 'dig for victory' campaign. My dad went on to send all three of his kids to private school, and I respect him for that – both mum and dad, in fact. Like so many

families where the parents are on an 'upwardly mobile treadmill', or even just struggling to make ends meet, the kids can get left behind. I remember feeling no one had much time for me. I acted out: getting caught shop lifting, drinking, and being promiscuous from my early teens. 'Jumping out of the frying pan and into the fire,' I think it's called!

*I remember my mum and her best friend (both originally from France) seemed thick as thieves together – **'Refugees!'** a therapist exclaimed once when I described how close they had seemed to me at the time – that helped explain the context to me somewhat – but it didn't do anything to change how 'shut out' I felt. Later there was the Vietnamese boat people family mum helped, who arrived in the UK with nothing. Both my parents befriended them and assisted them in setting up a business making tofu in the bath of their council house, where the local welcome included stink bombs through their letter box, and having the roof of their car jumped on; Yet the bravest thing my mum and dad did was take in my mum's parents, who both came to live with us. My grandfather had leukaemia and needed regular complete blood transfusions, and my grandmother suffered from senile dementia, and could be found on the street outside our Edinburgh home, totally disorientated, saying she was 'going home' to the small town in North East France where she was born.*

I tell my story here because the conspicuous lack of the right kind of adult support in my life in my younger years left scars that are difficult to heal. If I'm honest, my 'becoming fully human' project feels like a process rather than a destination, and so I'm not sure if I'll ever be able to say I'm totally 'over' my youth. The one word title of this book 'UnEldered' is the encapsulation of too many years of my life. Something happens when loneliness sets in; we so easily internalise the cause; imagining it's somehow all our own fault. The sense of shame, withdrawal and fear of further rejection easily create a self-fulfilling prophecy. Isolation begets isolation. We need to learn social skills and co-regulation from our family of origin. In spite of the private school education I had for about five years of my life until I left home at 18, there were glaring gaps in terms of what I needed to become a successful adult in the modern world.

It's not all been bleak! I received much from several therapists, counsellors, mentors and group facilitators as an adult; the combined package going some way to replace what I missed in teenage years. My own counselling training in four settings has added to the process, bringing skills that enable me to hold space for others on their journey, whilst allowing me insights into critical life junctures of my own. With awareness comes healing, and better self-care... This book seeks to fill gaps that are increasingly hazards of modern times. As we'll see, it's my contention the Youth need Elders- and vice versa - and even everyone in between needs to pitch in, take a stand, and lend a hand, in times like these...

Chapter Two

Initiation

This chapter attempts to discuss and describe the parameters of initiation; 'beating the bounds', if you will; piecing together fragments from story tellers and rites of passage leaders like Dr Martin Shaw[20] and Mac McCarthy[21], the late Robert Bly[22], Shivam O'Brian[23] and Hugh Lupton[24] who keep and kept an ear to the ground and an eye on the horizon; seeking to accomplish a transfusion of Old Worlds into New Places using the time-honoured Oral tradition... *'They're all men!' 'Sssh! ... I know.'*

During my immersion in this material, spanning decades, there have also been many women-led retreats and several study groups, Landmark Education, a Property mastermind programme, lasting a year or longer, and countless workshops and circles, encompassing Kabbalah, Tantra, ISTA, the art of 'Sacred Relationship' with the late John Welwood and his wife Jennifer, and last but not least Zen – to which I devote a whole chapter: 'Non-Duality'. This chapter is also loosely based on anthropology and depth psychology texts by white westerners, ethnographies by indigenous peoples; counselling training in four settings and receiving my own therapy; encounters with

---

20. I apprenticed for a year with Dr Martin Shaw and colleagues at the West Country School of Myth and Storytelling in 2010, the year my son left home. It helped metabolise the grief that came with his departure.

21. He apprenticed for many years with Amer-Indians, and was given substantial corporate funding to start a centre 'Embercombe' in Devon where Ecological awareness and the Mytho-poetic tradition inform the curriculum. I've listened to him speak and tell stories several times.

22. His book 'Iron John' is credited with starting the Men's movement... He is also responsible for translations of the Persian mystical poet Rumi. I was lucky enough to witness both Coleman Barks and Robert Bly's recitations in Devon, UK, at various Storytelling festivals.

23. Founder of 'Spirit Horse' camps in the wilds of West Wales.

24. I heard him tell tales of apples and horses; buried treasure under trees; and the cadence and soulfulness of his telling; the webs he wove with words, cast a thick, portentous spell upon me – why I include him here

Medicine people from Central America, and random forays in the imagination and on the trail with motley meaning-seeking crews[25]... These ingredients are somewhat haphazardly flung into a cauldron of a chapter that's Mytho-Poetic in parts. We'll agitate and scry the brew for glyphs and signs; seeking patterns and portents in rising smoke and steam; perhaps rediscovering some of the Beauty and Grace of a largely forgotten world in the process.

We'll also examine some of the nefarious forces in today's world contributing to the dismantling of a culture that could and can support and sustain the 'initiatory impulse'. As a woman *existing* (deliberately chosen word) in the modern western world; I confess to feeling the poverty of the *absence* of Initiation. That's not to say I don't also recognise my vast privilege. I have food, shelter, a surplus of money (recent achievement!), a car, an ancient laptop, a mobile phone, a passport, my country isn't presently being bombed, I have access to some free medical care, I used to have access to free dentistry, the potholes in the roads are mostly navigable, I can afford to heat my home (just about), I can jump on a train close by that will take me all over the country, I have easy access to more food than even my grandmother's generation ever dreamed of, and no one is drilling for oil or mining precious metals in my back yard, nor am I required to work down a poorly lit hole in the ground, without adequate props, no health and safety and no compensation for my family if I die...

And yet - I live in one of the most *hyper-private* civilizations that has ever existed, contributing to my UnEldered, UnInitiated status. In this chapter, we'll cast our imaginations far back in time; way back before the beginnings of recorded history, painting in broad brush strokes *of necessity* and returning to an era when Initiation was still a *thing*, and 'division of labour' widespread. This meant women, including breast feeding ones, hung out together lots... If we go back far enough, before the nuclear, or even *extended* family rose to ascendency as the building block

---

25. Landmark Education. "We are meaning making machines." Facebook, 2018, 9 May, https://facebook.com/profile.php?id=100063579968340

of society, women spent most of their time together, somewhat 'bathed' in oxytocin, the bonding hormone produced by breast feeding mothers.

At that time, resources were shared equally amongst all, and safety was *felt and known* as a clan-wide, clan-deep phenomenon... Imagine, if you will, that status and private property, as we know them today, hadn't yet been invented. It was 'all for one and one for all' - *literally!* - meaning there was a greatly *reduced* need for jealousy, possessiveness and *competitiveness*. In this time, we can imagine that women formed a kind of 'sisterhood' together, and men a 'brotherhood', which likely provided the foundation for the scaffold of Initiation to rest upon... We look further at the science behind bonding, also known as 'co-regulation' in the chapter 'Neuroscience, Nurture and Narcissism'.

Women's initiatory experience might best be described as an 'immersion in the feminine collective' - one governed by a very different neuro-biology to that of men. Perhaps we can visualise female initiatory experience as 'turning inside out' the notion of the tests of strength, or 'Hero's Journey' more typical of men's experience. The feminine foundation thus was: safe, sociable, stable, trusting, interwoven. In those days, we didn't have to worry about kids getting squashed under cars or carted off by paedophiles - or any other of the numberless ruptures to the envelope of communal living - occasioned by millennia of change... Of course there were *multiple* natural dangers - but they didn't stop kids playing together outdoors. Children were and remain the leaven in life's bread - enlivening the world of adults in innumerable, unpredictable, heart-gladdening ways - Strange times indeed that we need *reminding!* Additionally-no clocks meant no rushing... This might seem like a detail, but it's not. Clocks and schedules create stress, which activate the fight or flight system, which suppresses the production of the bonding and bliss hormone oxytocin. Whilst awareness of falling testosterone levels among men is widespread, 'oxytocin deficit' doesn't seem to be on our radars, perhaps because it has a low base line and doesn't persist for long in the body – ergo: *we need to be topping it up all the time* – in relaxed, connected and safe life situations!

We'll return to this woman's world in a bit; but lest the men are getting restless, let's look at Initiation in a way that could apply across time and space, and genders, attempting to make sense of it in a down-to-earth way. In simple terms, Initiation rites were often designed for teenage boys, amongst other things as a kind of *endurance test,* one involving moving from the known to the unknown; leaving comfort zones to confront challenges (big or small) – and cross thresholds: gathering skill sets, depth and maturity in the process, as opposed to simply gathering 'knowledge' or 'opinion'... A life well lived potentially involves *this* type of initiation as a kind of constant: one where we open to new experiences and unfamiliar challenges.

Life seems to have a habit of supplying us with 'initiations' of one kind or another, whether we like it or not, and when it doesn't, we might sense sterility casting a pall over our days. Humans seem to need challenge to thrive, and often these events come unbidden, turning the day-to-day upside down and forcing us to learn new skills. In a modern day context it might look like: standing up to bullying or discrimination, being forced to flee one's country of origin, learn a new language, fit into a new environment, even accept a new diagnosis, or learn to live with chronic pain. The difference between the 'life well lived' and 'tortuous' versions depends to some extent on our resources – social networks, finances and other forms of resilience, as well as the attitude we adopt in the face of adversity. I've often heard: 'we can't choose what happens to us – but we *can* choose how we respond' – maybe that's from a privileged western perspective – and *maybe not*. Even in concentration camps, the ones who best tolerated the intolerable were those who salvaged shreds of dignity, continuing to wash, or practice small ritual 'acts of meaning' amid the unimaginable suffering and chaos.[26]

---

26. Michael Aharony, Hannah Arendt and the Limits of Total Domination (Routledge, 2015)

As well as a test of strength and adaptability, in different times and places, initiation was understood to be a spiritual process of sorts; an alchemical opportunity to burn off dross, karma, shame, or 'impediments to flight', depending on which lens, or tradition, we look though. But lest this observation incline the reader towards imagining it's all about 'getting rid' of the things we don't like about ourselves, quite the opposite is true:

> "You have to remember that duality is a sham, and that these shadowy aspects of ourselves that we'd rather not look at are not bad, or wrong, or shameful, or tragic. They just *are*. But human beings are programmed to demonize the shadow, which is totally ass-backward, given that the shadow is the one that is patiently holding on to this stuff for us, waiting for us to stop pretending it's not there, and to stop distorting our consciousness in the face of the ruse, and to start taking responsibility for our junkery, regardless of how gross we judge it to be".[27]

Along with confronting *'the shadow'*, consciously choreographed initiation is about increasing capacity; alchemising challenge into opportunity; finding ways to work within strict parameters, discovering diamonds in the dirt, even. *'Limitation is the foundation of creativity'*, a Chinese proverb informs us; making of Initiation a passing through the eye of the needle: never a *comfortable passage,* but one that has us recalibrate our relationship to self and world. Skilful others, who encourage, witness, and mirror back to us our new understandings and capabilities on the other side, turn a potentially traumatic episode into an Initiation. Orchestrating such journeys, as we saw in the previous chapter, was the remit and purview of Elders in traditional cultures.

Because initiations are multi-dimensional, they often include opportunity to recover and reclaim fragmented aspects of the psyche. In modern day psychotherapy we refer to 'internal emotional damage' creating 'amnesiac barriers' and 'dissociation'. In Jungian depth psychology we refer to 'shadow

---

27. Shaman Durek, Spirit Hacking (Yellow Kite books, 2019), p. 190

work' as a necessary aspect of 'individuation'; and in cultures where Initiation persists, we might speak of 'Soul Retrieval'. All traditions conceptualise **integration, increased capacity, acceptance and empowerment** as products of the Initiatory journey of Youth. Rather than simply holding space for youth to transition to Adulthood, Elders experience (often unsought) Initiations of their own - **gathering a depth of experience and wisdom, one hopes, whilst simultaneously finding ways to accept the loss of cultural norms of 'beauty' and physical prowess; the deterioration of the body; and loss of loved ones and 'cultural mores' we might have assumed would 'see us out'.**

For Youth; when the 'small self' travels into the unknown and *returns enlarged and more fully cognisant that apparent opposites are part of a larger whole; that love and acceptance matter; that we're here to learn from our mistakes and give our gifts;* they will have completed an Initiatory journey of sorts... You don't have to be 'broken' to embark on this journey; any 'normal' human will do: - one who recognises and embraces thresholds, change, letting go, expansion, and mastery, as some of the correlates of authentic living. Just as there is an opportunity to 'ascend', with practices that enhance our 'energetic' and physical selves; so too is there a need for 'descent', to face what has been suppressed, denied, cut off, defended against. Crossing many thresholds leads eventually to the human being acquiring 'integrated webs of embodied knowing' that will serve the collective, yet inevitably also, to the decline of our days, and the final Initiation for all of us... ***Death.***

Oxytocin and Testosterone

Humans take the longest of all warm blooded mammals to mature and leave the 'nest'. The process of parenting requires a continuous re-generation of warmth, attunement and safety to enable connection and exploration, continuing into adolescence and beyond; and as a child matures through different stages, the type of support given has to evolve in order to remain relevant. How best might we provide the 'secure base' to young people in our modern day - not as a bunker that they hide inside - but a spring board they can run out from, and leap off? Those of us with an interest in the young might develop an 'Eldering technology' that seeks to design appropriate 'initiatory spring boards' - providing longed-for structured challenge and witnessing from a foundation of care.

Paradoxically perhaps, *both* the comfort derived from safety, and finding necessary courage when confronting danger, open us up to new ways of seeing, knowing and *feeling* our part in the grand scheme of things. A life well lived encompasses the full range on a dynamic spectrum, and both extremes - fear and trust - call us into being; there's a kind of sacred vertigo that wells up inside at any point when we're facing the unknown - digging deep and encountering new capacities in the process. Oxytocin and testosterone, at the hormonal level, orchestrate and inform aspects of the dance; the former bonding hormone being present in the body during breast feeding and sex, whilst the latter is used to accomplish acts of physical strength and courage.[28] 'Deep belonging' as a felt sense of safety still opens us up to Mystery because allowing ourselves to fully lean into another means welcoming an element of unpredictability, creating an 'open system' of relating.[29]

Sitting in a circle of breast-feeding mothers and babies, a few fathers, and natural health practitioners (I was one of them) at a parenting support day recently[30]; the air was thick with inflammation-reducing[31] oxytocin... This was a rare and precious opportunity to experience and study the 'energetic template' or 'emotional field' if you will, of tribal living, that inspires so much of the writing of this book. The field is invisible (and invaluable!) and we have to work with sensation and intuition here, because of the lack of available contexts to experience for

---

28. Sue C. Carter. "Sex, love and oxytocin: two metaphors and a molecule," Neuroscience & Biobehavioral Reviews (2022): 104948

29. Dan Siegel, "Emotion as Integration," in The Healing Power of Emotion: Affective Neuroscience, Development, and Clinical Practice, ed. Diana Fosha, Dan Siegel and Marion Solomon (W. W. Norton & Company, 2009), 172–204.

30. Organised by Olivia Seck. "Olivia Seck", last modified 2019, 15 March, https://oliviaseck.com

31. Sue C. Carter, et al. "Is oxytocin 'nature's medicine'?," Pharmacological reviews 72, no. 4 (2020): 829-861

real these phenomena in the West today. Lab experiments have been conducted to measure the effects of oxytocin, which is not the same as sitting in a circle of breast-feeding women, of course, but which I will bring to bear, nonetheless. Listening to the doctor hold forth on the oxytocin-informed lecture[32], I wanted to exhort him to take off his white lab coat and sit with the women described above - not in a sterile environment - but one with comfy coloured cushions: *'put down your clip board, and **feel!**'* Instead, the experiment he described involved being injected with the hormone in a separate room from the other volunteers, then deciding if you wanted to share the $10 given as part of the procedure with people you've never met. Turns out that: ***yes, you do***... Which kind of begs the question: - why don't we go back to sitting in circles amongst breast feeding mothers, and half the world's problems would be solved?

Unfortunately for us, the West has been on a different trajectory for several centuries, at least, and simple solutions are often 'overlooked', as they don't tend to make anyone any richer (financially)... Since the time of Galileo[33], we seem to be interested, obsessed even, with measuring things, rather than experiencing them directly in the body. In doing so, the 'scientific method', on which so much of 'Enlightenment' thought was built, has thrown the baby out with the bath water, if you'll excuse the pun, leading to a distrust of sensory reality - describing everything 'subjective' as 'unverifiable woo-woo'. As we'll see in the chapter on non-duality, subjectivity is much more likely to be 'all there is' - a line of thought pursued in modern day philosophy also.[34] This subjective reality, counter-intuitive though it might be to the modern mind, is one determined largely by neurotransmitters and hormones we manufacture in different social contexts; and so it actually makes more sense from a scientific perspective than might at first be imagined - positioning intra-subjectivity at the very heart of everyone's lived experience.

32. Paul Zak. "Trust, morality -- and oxytocin?", TED, 16:18, 2011, 14 July, https://ted.com/talks/paul_zak_trust_morality_and_oxytocin
33. Naydler, Living in the Shadow of the Machine
34. Robert Strozier, Saussure, Derrida, and the metaphysics of subjectivity (de Gruyter, 2012)

The 'Full spectrum' experience tentatively described here was controversially explored in the 1950s and 1960s, when Harry Harlow demonstrated in his experiments with primates[35] that the warmth of a mother's presence provided baby monkeys with the courage they needed to go and explore the scary toys and other features of their environment. Without the mother, or a surrogate mother, the infants cowered in a corner of their enclosure, unwilling to move towards potential threat, or equally, potential adventure.

Infants, both male and female, under normal circumstances, are born into a social context where oxytocin floods the immediate environment, creating blissful sensations and emotions that help with bonding, which in turn increases survival rates. Initiation (at least for boys) in effect cancels the 'free oxytocin' contract of childhood between progeny and a fully functional, loving mother (and her entourage); flagging the end of this phase of life, and the beginning of a new relationship to self and world. In this new relationship, bliss-inducing oxytocin has to be 'earned' or produced in a different way – via sex and other bonding experiences (such as mutual adornment and grooming). Initiation for boys marks a role reversal of sorts. The emotional and physical 'holding' of children performed by women, after male initiation, is replaced and reversed with a masculine capacity to 'hold' and contain the feminine polarity, and with it, many facets of a fully functional society... Women intuit, via chemical signals, social cues and 'masculine bearing' whether the man in question has developed sufficiently to enable him to 'hold' her; physically and emotionally. Of course there are age discrepancies here – we aren't talking about young men incestuously courting their mothers(!) but hopefully the principle's clear. As we'll explore in the next chapter 'Eros Betrayed', sexual polarity is an important part of attraction.

With initiation, we're describing a bio-psycho-social landscape of evolution and change, one where the overwhelming power of the mother, for a boy child, both in her oxytocin-induced bliss

35. These famous experiments, though cruel, offer fundamental insights into the importance of appropriate care in the developmental processes of infants.

and collective synchronised menstrual cycles with other clan women[36], creates a hormone-rich 'magnetic field' that needs to literally be 'broken out' of. Boys do this in order to create an opposing polarity to that of the feminine nurturing container so vital to successful maturation of the infant and child in the first decade or so of childhood... Not just in this scenario, but in fact in every social configuration, what we think we have choice over is often in fact been being controlled by bio-chemicals influencing mood and states of arousal, in concert with other people. Neurotransmitters have been, and still are, the hidden orchestral conductors of human behaviour, active since the dawn of time (and incidentally all warm-blooded mammals have similar chemical wiring, which is why stroking a pet feels so good to the pet as well as the owner).

The contention here is that the primary function of Initiation is to produce males of the species who have broken their childhood bonds with the mother, and as a direct consequence, are able to *create, maintain and uphold social order*, in *tandem* with women. Traditionally; and when we think 'traditionally' – we mean for 99.99% of the time Homo Sapiens have been on the planet – the biological roles of men and women have been *different, and complimentary*, with females being more focussed on nurture and creativity. Make no mistake, women were still pretty 'bad ass' at the dawn of time! In his book 'Sand Talk', native Aboriginal Tyson Yunkaporta discloses that mother-in-laws and aunts had the power of life and death over a husband who was considered to have stepped out of line in the way he treated his wife![37] Nonetheless, what I'm invoking here is a competent, initiated masculine presence, who, as well as providing and protecting, had the capacity to *restore order*; much more often by *demeanour* than by decree. The following piece implies daily training and practice over years, of course; reminding us that whilst Initiation represents *crossing a threshold*; skilfulness and powerful presence require regular cultivation... Shiny Cadillacs, Hollywood villas

---

36. Ping Wang. "Neural functions of hypothalamic oxytocin and its regulation," ASN neuro 14 (2022): 17590914221100706
37. Yunkaporta, Sand Talk

and Prada handbags are not what this man is offering! Likely *some* worldly wisdom and business nous still go a long way, and you could say that acquiring business savvy is a different type of Initiatory journey incumbent on women and men in our age, alongside the traditional Initiatory material discussed here.

"A Samurai Creed'
(*anonymous circa 1300*)

I have no parents; I make Heaven and Earth my mother and father,
I have no home; I make awareness my dwelling.
I have no life and death; I make the tides of breathing my life and death.
I have no divine power; I make honesty my divine power.
I have no means; I make understanding my means.
I have no magic secrets; I make character my magic secret.
I have no body; I make endurance my body.
I have no eyes: I make the flash of lightening my eyes.
I have no ears; I make sensibility my ears.
I have no limbs; I make promptness my limbs.
I have no strategy; I make 'unshadowed by thought' my strategy.
I have no designs; I make seizing opportunity by the forelock my design.
I have no miracles; I make right action my miracle.
I have no principles; I make adaptability to all circumstances my principles.
I have no tactics; I make emptiness and fullness my tactics.
I have no talents; I make ready wit my talent.
I have no friends; I make my mind my friend.
I have no enemy; I make carelessness my enemy.
I have no armour; I make benevolence and righteousness my armour.
I have no castle; I make immovable mind my castle.
I have no sword; I make absence of self my sword".[38]

38. *"A Samurai Creed". Chris Corrigan, https://chriscorrigan.com/parkinglot/a-samurai-creed*

I don't know about you, but in *my* mind when *this* man walks into the centre of the circle, the chatter and bickering ceases, and whoever helped themselves to the bones and herbs to season the soup from the spot you were pointing at *over there*, doesn't seem to matter anymore! (You're probably getting a bowl *anyway* if you're prepared to toddle off and do something else, meanwhile...)

Women respect this power; need this power; *long* for this power. *All of society needs this power!* When women feel men are 'in charge' by virtue of an inner authority, there is a 'swoon effect', making her want to share and make oxytocin with and for him all over again, in a different context to the mother-child bond. Women are suspicious of the immature masculine because she senses he wants to steal her oxytocin by tugging at her (raw hide) apron strings, rather than unlock it skilfully on a pile of animal skins around the fire at night when everyone else has gone to bed...! Before some 'feminists' want to shoot me down in flames – there are always caveats...

The female *only* swoons if she senses the *virtue* of the male, described so eloquently in the Samurai creed above. Masculine virtue includes deep respect, veneration, even, for the feminine principle. This man is *awed* by the nurturing and creative capacities of the feminine, just as *she* is awed by his strength and proficiency. Remembering for a moment the science that tells us oxytocin also delivers discernment; men are further awed by what has been called '*the X-Ray vision of the feminine.*' This is the intuitive, possibly oracular, capacity of women to be so in tune with their environment that when they speak they become founts of insight: – scrying smoke and mirrors in a bid to infiltrate the 'heart of the matter' and deliver an unparalleled level of 'reconnaissance information' to any gathered assembly, at any moment; when both time and respect are accorded her. A woman's intuitive discernment could be one of the reasons men came to fear women in the past; although in *this* day, where so often men are reduced to talking about cars and football (or else risk being branded 'gay'!) it can be an equally important reason why men seek women out!

The *evolved* masculine has similar capabilities - reading signs is second nature to a hunter, or Shaman, for example. Perhaps the gift of *his* sensitivity was used in targeted ways, whereas a woman's was and remains more diffuse. When men and women refine their capabilities, there are overlapping qualities that emerge, as well as differences, which is why gender has been described as a '***cloak***' in some spiritual traditions. Gender has us act in certain ways, often based on the internal neuro-biology of the individual, as well as some social conditioning undoubtedly, and yet there is another 'human' reality where similarities rather than differences define us, *cancelling the import of gender altogether,* so to speak, and recognising we're all in the same boat with similar fears, foibles and aspirations... We *all,* after all, pray to the same *Merciful God* for succour, at times, *do we not?!*

The First Fall

From around 5,000 to 3,000 BCE, Temples were erected to Gods and Goddesses in ancient Mesopotamia expressing wide ranging human emotional realities entwined with spiritual cosmologies. Their Pantheons comprised some of the most complex Mythology, and possibly one of the most sophisticated societies of the ancient world, centred on the city of Uruk, known in the modern day as part of Iraq. Interestingly, during this era, the worlds of Gods, Goddesses, men and women interpenetrated each other, for example with Inanna marrying the shepherd Dumuzi, strongly suggesting humans had supernatural power, strength and sovereignty allying them with the Gods! These powers were separated over time, until the realms of 'God' and 'Man' became entirely separate, reflected in modern day Christianity. Ancient Uruk celebrated Gilgamesh, Enki and Erishkegal; legends of descents, abductions, seductions and intrigue. During this era, women resided in Temples, themselves Initiates and Worshippers of the many Gods and Goddesses depicted in stone carvings and cuneiform clay tablets we still can learn from today.

Temple Priestesses throughout the near East once performed an especial task. When men had been bloodied and traumatised on the Battlefield, their first stop on the return journey was to these very Temples. There; wounds would be bathed, skin and garments cleansed, the sweat and dirt of days and months living on wit and will alone washed away. Temple offerings brought sustenance to the men who had given so much in defending their homelands from invaders... The Temple space was an opportunity for the men to rest; receive restorative balm, eventually allowing them to return revivified to fields and villages; wives, children, kith and kin anxiously awaiting news and signs of fathers, husbands, clansmen. In these special places, where every entrant crossing the threshold petitioned the favour and fervour of Gods and Goddesses to restore balance, harmony and abundance to the Land; its numberless creatures, crops and people; the Temple Priestesses shared oxytocin with the men. In these 'decompression chambers', boudoir magic was part of the repertoire and training of skilful female healers who may have spent decades both learning their arts and living and tending to these sacred sites. When men visited, their nervous systems returned to a healthy base-line, post traumatic stress disorder was held in abeyance: - their bodies and minds soothed and calmed with the help of women over many days, whilst the kaleidoscopic Mythos of the place oversaw the to and fro; the healing and praying; bringing gravitas and glistening grace to bear on the proceedings.[39], [40]

... Once upon a time, a woman's 'purity' described a capacity for reverence, and an ability to channel certain Sacred healing qualities unimpeded; a friendly, unencumbered demeanour; whilst the word 'Virgin' described her as a being 'whole unto herself'; one who had chosen a path of Initiation and Service instead of that of Wife and Mother (also a path of Service!).[41] As Abrahamic religions gradually usurped the Polytheistic impulse of the Old World, Temple Priestesses were dubbed 'Whores', and new buildings erected where the body was described as sinful and unclean[42]; women's healing arts came to be deemed a 'disgrace',

39. Sarah Dening, The Mythology of Sex (Macmillan General Reference, 1996)
40. Gerda Lerner. "The origin of prostitution in ancient Mesopotamia," Signs: Journal of Women in Culture and Society 11, no. 2 (1986): 236-254.
41. Richard Henshaw, Female and Male: The Cultic Personnel: The Bible and the Rest of the Ancient Near East (Wipf and Stock Publishers, 1994)
42. Lerner. "The origin of prostitution in ancient Mesopotamia"

and her connection to nature and proclivity for right-brained perspicacity became reasons to fear and condemn her; burn her on a witch's pyre even! The perpetrators of these 'crimes against humanity', and in time the onlookers - those who dared show up rather than hide their faces and block their ears against the screams - congratulated themselves for bringing Civilised Rule to bear on Heathen Peoples. I want to make a clear distinction here that I speak out against the Church as one-time oppressive Institution, and not against the Teachings of Jesus Christ.

The word 'tragedy' doesn't do it justice; whatever it was, it developed over time: long periods of time - where men began to exercise power without customary and requisite virtue and veneration; taking advantage of their privilege. When this happened, the heart and mind-opening elixir oxytocin diminished in quantity and effect - since it has a very low base line and endures but a short time span in the body.[43] Women were eventually cast out of the Temples of old, and began to compete for high status men; using strategies that helped buffer and leverage their own compromised status. The wonderful and much celebrated reciprocity between the sexes thus declined; although it might persist in pockets where veneration and gratitude still hold sway, and extended families and clans thrive still. In those places, women are honoured as healers, mothers, artists; bringers of wisdom and grace, and men are regarded as maintainers of order and peace, providers, warriors, fathers and more besides. An absence of competitiveness might characterise these peoples and places...

In recent times, there has been some attempt at radical redress, in a secular, and severely compromised context, if we're seduced by the mytho-poetic lens as viewing platform for the vanished worlds depicted above. Women's participation in modern work schedules and conditions might be regulating and enhancing in neuro-biological terms for the top percentile, but for many, it's about juggling too many balls whilst living up to perfectionist standards, leading to burn-out and dissatisfaction, and resulting often in what has been termed 'unplanned childlessness' for those women who got caught up in careers and accidentally left it

43. *Zak. "Trust, morality -- and oxytocin?"*

too late to start a family.[44] In these conditions, different hormones come in to play: adrenalin and cortisol which have quite a different effect on the organism – causing stress, anxiety and inflammatory reactions (We look at the ANS more fully in chapter 4). Not only that: what energy is left for a sacred encounter between man and woman, or in same sex relationships, after the demands of the typical day have been fulfilled for working parents?

The long hours imposed on both sexes by the need to service ever-increasing quantities of debt, and the concomitant dismantling of our social sphere has caused unprecedented emotional poverty and chaos hidden beneath a veneer of 'productivity'. Not until recent decades with the study of inter-personal neuro-biology[45] have we been able to count the bio-chemical cost of this development; whilst the decline in our physical health as a species is apparent all around. As we've seen, the hormone Oxytocin produced by a mother in close proximity to her offspring promotes generosity, good will, rest, peace, love, safety and discrimination[46]... The demeaning of motherhood over the last century has had disastrous consequences for society, where the mental health of the child doesn't even seem to feature in the equation – Meanwhile, the State benefits greatly, via the tax man, who can now tax both sexes instead of just the one. This is not a diatribe against women earning a living and having agency in the world; for the record: writing is my fourth career iteration! I am shocked though, when we look at social history, to note the extremely short time frame often invoked by researchers.[47] It's my contention we need to think 'deep time' and 'bio-psycho-social evolution' to appraise our current behaviours in a way that makes more sense – bringing meaningful context to our current mental health crisis, in the absence of which it almost always looks like the answer is more medication!

Two parent families can provide stability for children, yet it

---

44. Chris Williamson. "What A Feminist Has to Say About Masculinity - Christine Emba | Modern Wisdom 664", YouTube, 1:26:57, 2023, 7 August, https://youtube.com/watch?v=cWnEaU1TXDw

45. "Dr. Dan Seigel", 2021, https://drdansiegel.com

46. Zak. "Trust, morality -- and oxytocin?"

47. Williamson. "What A Feminist Has to Say About Masculinity"

should also be recognised that groups, teams, clans, tribes and villages were and still are capable of providing *even more* said stability in the form of play opportunities with other kids, social opportunities for adults, and an easing of the burden of care falling so often now exclusively on the shoulders of one, possibly two, adults, with the concomitant distress.

The gender identity movement of the last decade can be examined against the backdrop of the controlled demolition project of indigenous cultures (including our own) on a global scale in the last millennium and beyond, hollowing out meaningful identities, turning us instead into blank canvases for the latest social media 'influencers' of the modern day to doodle all over. So quick has been the change to detach traditional bonding and relationship rituals and practices in order to accommodate a culture of 'totalitarian' diversity, as to leave a collective gap in social memory, and a shattered mirror to glimpse into as we seek pleasure and connection.

Intimacy as Initiation

Anyone remember 'Romance'?! ... Who would argue new love isn't just as scary and preoccupying as planning to sky dive or abseil down a cliff?!... What has become evident in our new 'medicalised milieu' is that we can't suppress one type of emotion without suppressing the whole range - people on anti-depressants will tell you this. It's at times of facing the unknown, including in new intimate relationship, that we feel most alive and exhilarated, and get to harvest the bounty of emotional depth, aka 'resourcefulness' accruing from 'leaning into our edge'. These times are also when testosterone and oxytocin levels are likely to spike, and jump across barriers! All this seems so obvious to be barely worth mentioning - or could it be that in the space of just a couple of generations, something that seemed obvious to most might actually be being obscured by dating apps, the pornification of sex, health and safety edicts cancelling risk altogether, the invention of new gender identities and other forces of occlusion and confusion?

... Alarmingly, in our culture, we seem to have come to a point now where we avoid extremes of both danger and safety (as intimacy) most of the time - meaning many live in a kind of twilight zone where the deep reset, comfort and peace of feeling fully held, and the visceral heart thumping moments of genuine danger and challenge elude us altogether. Could it be that the engineering of modern life to avoid the need for close connection and courting danger, both, is actually the primary cause of depression in our time? There's a general malaise - a sense at the cellular level that there should be 'more to life' than this - yet whilst the intellect is not the best tool for distinguishing deficits, our hearts *feel* the lack, often keenly.[48]

Nefarious Ends

Is it possible in today's world that Harlow's insights are being co-opted by people in power who stand to gain from our discomfiture? They seem to be 'hell-bent' on 'keeping people safe' - the mix of metaphors seems quite apt - so much so that profiteers have realised there's a lot of money to be made and power to be had in alarming people - and then restricting their freedoms and selling them 'solutions' - as a promised return to 'normality', comfort and security. The glitch of course is that: 'alone at home, staring at screens all day' never quite hits the oxytocin button in a state-enhancing way, like the safe circle of breast-feeding mothers does, or the mother monkeys, or Temple Priestesses, for that matter: - Quite the reverse in fact, as we'll explore in the chapter 'Psychological Warfare'. The makers of mandates say: '*please* don't worry too much about this' - we have medications - strong opioids for example, to soothe anxiety and rectify the imbalance, causing legions of addicts, and an abundance of profit for Big Pharma and their stake holders.[49]

Terms have been coined for this manoeuvre: 'Predatory Philanthropy' and 'Disaster Capitalism' - tactics cynically based

---

48. 17% of the British adult population were prescribed anti-depressants in 2017-18. "Prescribed medicines review: summary," Public Health England, last modified 2020, 3 December, https://gov.uk/government/publications/prescribed-medicines-review-report/prescribed-medicines-review-summary

49. Katherine Rejer. "Fentanyl in the Global Market: Examining the New Opioid Epidemic at an International Level" (University of San Diego, 2022).

on the wiring of the human nervous system for secure attachment, as well as our natural proclivity for steering toward social inclusion – leading to 'virtue signalling' and other compliant behaviours that we'll explore more fully later on. Of course, deceptive **propaganda** campaigns are nothing new – Matthias Desmet[50] reminds us that they've been with us for around 200 years, along with increasing levels of **isolation**. Yet, modern technology allows for Propaganda to become ever more insidious and pervasive. It is these two factors, he believes, that enable *'mass formation' events* – a kind of collective hypnosis, such as took place in the Nazi Third Reich, and such as we witnessed and indeed participated in during the Covid-19 'pandemic'.

These days: – it's virtually all virtual: smoke and mirrors, including the wall to wall 'fear porn' that characterised the Covid years. We live so much of life now from the sofa constantly glued to at least one screen – meaning lessons to be gleaned from grappling with reality 'in the body' remain elusive, and with that our (oxytocin induced) 'discernment superpower', enabling the telling apart of truth from fiction, and *real* safety from *real* danger, is also compromised. In days of yore, *wrestling crocodiles and tackling rapids on a small raft* might have formed part of Initiation rites (Possibly extreme versions, but you get the drift!). Testosterone would have been healthily channelled during the dramatic bits, whilst oxytocin would have been a part of the chemical cocktail of the return, when safety, admiration and acknowledgement prevailed. A modern day 'epic drama equivalent' might entail summoning the energy to walk to the shop instead of ordering a takeaway, and the only river rapid shooting and crocodile wrestling taking place is endless rounds of gaming, on a screen, and no one to pat you on the back either. In this subduing, subjugating, taming process, we are cut off from our innate ability to court danger and develop the deep trust intimacy requires of us, and healthy boundaries simultaneously. Some might call it *'killing two or even three birds with one stone'...*

---

50. International Covid Summit. "ICS4 – Day 2 – 18. Mattias Desmet", YouTube, 7:47, 2023, 4 December, https://youtube.com/watch?v=vrHcdS4ma7U

Post Traumatic Growth

There's a relatively new concept in the therapy world known as 'post-traumatic growth', and some really good work has been done in this field. People who experience it tend to experience three types of change:

> "Realistically stronger feelings of vulnerability that are none the less accompanied by stronger feelings of personal resilience; closer and deeper relationships with others; and a stronger sense of spirituality".[51]

It's good to see clinicians recognising that wisdom, resource, and fortitude can be harvested from some of life's misfortunes, yet I believe we need to go one step further and deliberately design challenge - as Initiation - into the playbook of modern living. When we experience trials alone, the personal growth is haphazard - clearly not everyone benefits - whereas the presence of others - especially Elders - enables us to weave our initiatory experiences into a bigger picture; revealing how the *implicate order* might, in fact, be manifesting through us in the way we live our lives... This might seem like a bit of a stretch, yet many, myself included, have spoken of studying psychology, religion and philosophy in our early 20s, and the disappointment we felt. We were looking to have meaning and purpose inculcated via our studying efforts: relevance, embodied learning, and belonging; yet, more often than not, the intellectual version didn't cut the mustard (*How could it?*)

In so-called intact cultures, where Initiation is still practiced, life follows a pattern where Youth learn to flex, endure, overcome, invent, get to grips with, and *go after life,* in rites of passage. They learn these things alongside older members of their clan they respect and look up to, and the physical, moral, emotional, and spiritual aspects of the experience are all interwoven. Personal qualities, once acquired in rites of passage, are lodged in the neural circuits and memories of the individual, equipping him or her for life. The result is greater competence and capacity to overcome challenges, and thus appreciate rewards on the long, winding road of life we all must travel... Could it be that the

51. Lawrence G. Calhoun and Richard G. Tedeschi, Facilitating posttraumatic growth: A Clinician's Guide (Routledge, 1999)

prevalence of a 'trauma' diagnosis in the therapy field today is related to the absence of Elders who once helped metabolise challenge; weaving instead from difficulty: meaning, purpose and identity?

Crossing Thresholds

The late Buddhist psychotherapist John Welwood[52] used to say: *'The heart doesn't break; it breaks* ***open****'...* Our heartbreak makes us more human and helps us empathise with others - in feeling our own vulnerability - our narcissism is attenuated, and our empathic capacity increases. As difficult as embracing pain or unfamiliar situations might be at times, it is when we face unchartered territory that we learn to get a measure of our resources; something fierce or wild, tender or true, inside. We gain a capacity to think on our feet, find an ingenious solution, weather a storm, love and accept life, ourselves and others more fully. Rising up to meet new challenge catalyses growth, so that eventually the experience becomes integrated into the fabric of our being and we become 'Elders' ourselves, over time. The wheel comes full circle, and those who crafted Initiatory spaces for us in our youth - were really busy crafting the Elders of tomorrow. When Elders come to shuffle off this mortal coil, they leave with the satisfaction of having contributed to the continuity of their culture - The Ancestors are Honoured; and the wheel continues to turn.

Young men especially were Initiated in this way; marking the shift from boyhood to manhood. For girls and women, Menarche, Motherhood and Menopause were the transitional events; natural, biological initiations... As such, a woman's cyclical reality[53] was

52. John and his wife Jennifer used to run couples' workshops which I attended, teaching communication skills, meditation practice and more. He's the author of several books included 'Perfect love, Imperfect Relationships' and 'Journey of the Heart'.

53. A 'Visionary Educator in Feminine Power' co-authored a book about the 'magic of the menstrual cycle' and set up the Red School. It removes the patriarchal overlay of menstruation as 'unclean' and reconnects us with the various phases and emotional realities experienced by women at different points on the cycle. My attendance at a one-day workshop, and subsequently using her workbook 'the Women's Quest' were transformational. She is committed to bringing awareness of menstruality out of the shadows and into the workplace, and has also recently co-authored a book on Menopause. Sjanie Hugo Wurlitzer and Alexandra Pope, Wild Power: Discover the Magic of Your Menstrual Cycle and Awaken the Feminine Path to Power (Hay House, 2017)

the power of creation expressed within her own body... The 'Red Tent' of the bleed time, a place to rest with other women and enter menstruation as the seat of women's contemplative, sensual and sensate, interior power: a monthly initiation of sorts... The impact and import of these key differences in initiatory journeys between male and female should not be underestimated!

In these strange modern times of transhumanism and Cyborgs, we're told we can replicate these timeless realities and their attendant social contexts with surgery, artificial hormones and the right quantity of 'identity-affirming, empathic counselling'. It seems the ideologues and professionals employed (handsomely rewarded, needless to say!) in this new 'field of dreams' are seeking to become modern day Shamans – yet the institutionalised bleached white corridors and often convoluted, contradictory narratives suggest a pale simulacra of the initiatory journey – one that will leave many hapless victims scarred for life as a direct consequence...

Of course – there's crossover in the masculine and feminine polarity: giving birth as an endurance test is hard to beat – and many men love and care for their children, wives and communities too, and can demonstrate their exquisite sensitivity in playing music, for example. *This* alongside the man receiving, one hopes, the *transmission (physical and chemical)* of love in the arms of a woman, whilst she might receive his containment and focus as a different, complimentary gift during said exchange. These realities are encapsulated in the ancient yin yang symbol, where a dynamic 'S' shape separates (and joins) masculine and feminine principles, and a spot of black is found in the white and a spot of white in the black, meaning the masculine polarity contains elements of the feminine, and vice versa. We'll explore these realities and philosophies more fully in the next chapter.

In so-called intact cultures, Initiation events could involve weeks or months spent together in single sex groups – both inside and outdoors in nature. Historically, these challenges have involved feats of endurance, even ritualised wounding and pain. Perhaps traditional societies knew a thing or two about Narcissism, in an intuitive rather than a 'clinical' way, and these ceremonies were designed to nip it in the bud. There's nothing like anticipated or actual physical pain to make us feel small. For the sake of clarity – I'm not advocating the practice of FGM (female genital mutilation) or even male circumcision, which can probably best be understood as ritual abuse. There are shadows and extremes in this territory that need to be skilfully, soberly apprehended. Yet it seems that tests of courage and strength, accompanied often by nature immersion, are global phenomena that have been with indigenous cultures for millennia, documented by people like Joseph Campbell, Malidoma and Sobonfu Somé, Martin Prechtel, Gregory Bateson, Tyson Yunkaporta and many others.

Memoir: The Power of Ceremony

There's also cross over between initiation and ceremony, and I've been privileged to attend several Native Mexican ceremonies, including one involving a skin piercing practice. Events took place with the participation of both genders, in day light, and overnight... May this sharing help modern peoples better understanding the practices and wisdom of the Old Ways, and not contravene any sacred protocol – Aho Mitakuye Oyasin...

We were at base camp, while several individuals had gone onto the mountain to fast and pray for several days in a practice known as the 'vision quest'... They staked out circles for themselves with small bundles of tobacco strung together on a string – each bundle made in a conscious effort of prayer – entreating the Spirits to bring a Vision on the mountain that would help initiates live in a good way. On the mountain, they sought insight into the powerful, personal gifts to bring in service to their community in ways best suited to their temperament and calling... Those remaining at base camp were witnesses of a ritual, with all involved in petitions and prayer, calling the 'Spirit Realm' for Intercession. We watched the woman, in this case, process inside the sacred compass of the circle, held up by two Elders who gave gentle encouragement. She was almost fainting from the pain of having a thin stick pushed through the flesh of each upper arm, bound around with a thong of leather. Emotionally supported by two men, one on either side, who whispered encouragement in her ear, she walked, as we looked on, gathered in a Tribal circle.

Using an act of will, she had to break free from the sticks pushed through her flesh with the leather thongs attached to a stationary pole... Once again, for the sake of clarity, she'd volunteered for the ritual, no one forced her. It was a way to 'call in power' and receive 'Medicine' – in the traditional meaning of the word – as an inner state of being, bringing with it new courage and capability. In traditional cultures, contrary to the New Age movement, 'personal growth' was not attempted for its own sake, or for self-aggrandisement. Acquiring 'medicine power' was a reciprocal process, enabling the individual to contribute more to community and thus gain more respect; in the context of the woven web of the whole tribe.

... It's impossible to be at an event like that without entering into the process of the main protagonist. We lent her strength with our undivided attention, and by the strangely bonding experience of sharing her pain. Enduring pain sharpens the mind, bringing focus and vulnerability – reality takes on immediacy; our intentions count for more – maybe 'Spirits' bring their Full Attention; as we gave them ours through petitions and prayer. Neither Life nor Change is easy; the ceremonial circle giving us added strength to face doubts and fears. It also granted requisite self-esteem, as the initiate stepped out of her comfort zone to achieve what seemed impossible, being witnessed whilst doing so... This is something of the collective cathartic process that takes place in ceremonial rites of passage where the entire group enters the process of change. It's a place where chaos meets order – like the metamorphosing soup inside the chrysalis, at the stage between caterpillar and butterfly – and it takes an act of will – paradoxically entwined with surrender – to catalyse Transformation.

People assembled together like this are somehow more able to kindle the flame of courage than one person alone – a group field is generated. Ceremony, ritual and rites of passage enable us to metabolise and assimilate emotion individually and collectively, keeping our communities alive and vibrant, and 'up to date' – processing trauma as we go, rather than storing it up for years when it becomes re-labelled in modern times as Complex Post

Traumatic Stress Disorder (CPTSD). There are many ways to engage the parts of the brain involved in rites of passage – ritual pain is only one of many such ways. Fasting, art, poetry, dance and drama, meditation, prayer, sex, yoga, breath work, therapy, plant medicines, cacao ceremonies, even journaling with intent, all provide ways for us to dialogue with and participate in the mysterious, hidden processes that govern life.

'Getting Well'

My own experience in ceremony 28 years ago entailed ingesting certain plants, which gifted the circle the ability to meet life in new dimensions. In Central and South America, and all continents on Earth, these powerful ceremonies have been performed for several thousand years.[54], [55] *Some plants are 'emetic', meaning they induce vomiting. This is called 'getting well' and is an act of purging that helps connect body, heart and mind; ridding us of what 'no longer serves' in our lives. For me, it took a lot to overcome my resistance to the purge – all of this was part of the process of becoming 'aligned': – being willing to meet my demons, and in the end; let (at least some of them) go.*

The Circle of Initiates sat through the night, around a sacred fire, 'getting well' individually and collectively; the inner journey combined with the spoken word; as tobacco and herbs rolled inside a fat corn husk were burned and passed around the circle; inviting us to connect earth and spirit via the smoke, reaching out with prayers spoken aloud. We entered a collective, timeless journey that lasted countless hours, our voices calling out into the darkness; revealing ourselves; our visions and challenges, to one another; whilst entreating the collective energy of the group – a 'hive mind' of sorts – to be opened and informed by the 'Great Beyond' in an act that was at once humbling and strengthening. 'Grandfather Fire' sat in the centre symbolising continuity and change: on a particular hillside in South Eastern Spain – a flickering, dynamic hub – the ultimate witness and catalyst. The night was long, chaotic, intense; eventually dawn came.

---

54. Matteo Politi, et al. "Beyond the psychoactive effects of ayahuasca: Cultural and pharmacological relevance of its emetic and purging properties." Planta medica 88, no. 14 (2022): 1275-1286.

55. Sandeep Vishnu Binorkar and Dilip Khemji Jani. "Traditional Medicinal Usage of Tobacco – A Review," Spatula DD (2012): 127-134.

With the new day everything shifted; the morning light brought calm and healing somehow, the struggle of the night subsided and we emerged reconfigured... Time stood still, hours slipped by; the Shaman pouring forth boundless gratitude for the Abundance of Life in endless prayers over the food; and when we stood to walk and process around the circle, with the fire still at the centre, we knew ourselves as a People with a Heart and a Home centred around the Fire; no longer separate; entwined with one another and the Power of Life itself. The binding experience of this ritual is difficult to put into words – the sense of being part of 'a People'; the arrival of some kind of 'new world' with the dawn is something I've never experienced in quite the same way either before or since.

What Might Men Need?

Most males, it seems, need to pit themselves against their own inner limits, each other, and the great forces of Nature; overcome obstacles; channel their healthy drive for action, adventure, sex and success, in ways that enable them to deepen their appreciation of who they are and what they are capable of. We have to create modern day equivalents of traditional initiation rites to engage the young - energy channelled is energy released: - As long as we don't have ritual containers that help boys grow into men, the allure of the military and War will always draw them instead; paradoxically preying on the vulnerability of their need to be seen and admired as powerful and capable.

Initiation - with its choreography of rupture, challenge, and return[56] offers us all a chance to test ourselves in extreme situations, and then go back to where we came from enlarged, ennobled, vivified and most importantly witnessed. Elders, and everyone else in a tight-knit community, take on the hugely important role - vastly under-estimated in our modern culture - of witnessing change. Change un-witnessed is, in fact, not change. Re-orientation without support is not re-orientation, it is being cast adrift without a compass, or reference points, without a North Star; without that type of eye contact where everything

56. According to author, story teller, and Rites of Passage leader Dr Martin Shaw.

else falls away and only the present remains; breathing, pulsing, unfolding.

Many grown men have spoken to me of the fear they feel in relation to their anger. They don't know how or when it will spill out, and worry about hurting those who happen to be caught in the cross fire. One of the primary purposes of initiation is to channel testosterone - the aggression and sex- drive increasing hormone, which has been declining in men globally in recent decades.[57, 58] Well-held groups for young men provide 'yard sticks' for 'testing mettle'; precious containers where Boys get consciously fashioned into Men. We live in times where the pervasive 'health and safety' mentality, combined with women dominating the scene in schools[59], means boys and young men often miss out on opportunities to engage in this way together.

In an UnEldered culture, few have been encouraged to actively encounter, court and engage dimensions of 'Sacred Danger' and develop the skills and mental fortitude that come with it. Not only physical endurance is called for in modern day Initiations... From speaking to several men about their experience in contemporary rites of passage work, there is also a need to share vulnerability, tenderness and emotional pain.[60] Many feel lost and unseen in today's world, and in coming together and letting their guards down, are able to express long-buried emotions - disavowed aspects of self - issuing in no small part from our 'big boys don't cry' cultural conditioning. It's not a one stop shop, though! 'The Work' documentary shot in a US prison shows this kind of deeply therapeutic process in action.[61] In our 'culture of

---

57. Sofwatul Mokhtarah Maluin et al. "Effect of radiation emitted by wireless devices on male reproductive hormones: a systematic review". Frontiers in Physiology 12 (September 2021).

58. Possibly a related phenomenon: Birth rate is dropping in America (and Europe) whilst suicide in men is increasing. Peter M. Robertson and Nicholas Eberstadt. "The Depopulation bomb," The Hoover Institution, last modified 2022, 14 September, https://hoover.org/research/de-population-bomb

59. Rober Glover, No More Mr Nice Guy: A Proven Plan for Getting What You Want in Love, Sex, and Life (Running Press Adult, 2003)

60. The Unmasked Man offers nature retreat and Initiation opportunities for men in the UK. Based on the archetypes in: Robert Moore and Doug Gillette, King, Warrior, Magician, Lover: Rediscovering the Archetypes of the Mature Masculine (HarperCollins, 2013)

61. The Work, directed by Jairus McLeary (Blanketfort Media, 2017), 1:27:00

absence', including absent fathers; all too often, young men end up initiating each other – in criminal or self-harming ways – with drug over-doses, car chases, gang warfare and prison sentences often the bitter harvest of their endeavours. Not to mention the self-harm scars we see on the arms of so many of the Youth in our times – female and male.

The more virtualised danger and violence become, the less equipped people are to deal with the challenge of encountering it in everyday living. We need to know our capabilities in an embodied way, and to learn to meet our own shadow. This has been well documented in books like 'Waking the Tiger' by Peter Levine and 'The Body Keeps the Score' by Bessel Van der Kolk. These contemporary therapists and recognised trauma experts note that fight or flight impulses trapped in the body need to be 'completed' in a chain reaction that is hard wired into the Autonomic Nervous System (ANS). Without working through lived experiences of danger or anger even; our bodies can remain in a state of chronic activation for months, years, decades; lifetimes.

The energy of Initiation helps complete 'trauma reactions' stored in the body. Paradoxically perhaps, men's ritual experiences include elements of enchantment, whilst also being sobering – there is an intentional grittiness acting as 'great leveller', turning the healthy narcissism of the child inside out – letting its contents spill on the ground… Learning to live within limits is part of the lesson of pushing beyond them. The spillage is simultaneously humbling and strengthening; bringing depth, stability and belonging after the event, especially when a witnessing takes place that helps anchor the achievements in a person's psyche. The 'dancing with one's edges' encourages coming to peace, in time; being able to reach into consciousness as courage: a place of potential and potency that might divert the need to seek 'limitless attention, or limitless growth' in the outer world. Not to say there isn't friction and heat at one's edges, and a need for action as manifestation of the will; necessary aspects of forging a sense of self. Learning to *accept limits* though, for men, might translate into a greater ability to love and contain the feminine on the return; receiving her emotional sensitivity and flux without losing centre. In this way, a man finds the courage and capacity to lower himself down towards the dark nectar of her yin void[62]... More on this in the next chapter.

Without the mould offered by Initiatory journeys – it's possible men might never quite know who they are – failing to encounter their own physical limits in real-time challenging situations, or to learn etiquette, trust, complexity and subtlety... The containment and confidence Initiation brings, once it lands in the nervous system - widening the 'window of tolerance' - alters perception and modus operandi. UnInitiated men are liabilities: ships without a compass – attention seeking everywhere they go – Witness the current building of space rockets by billionaires in the vain hope of colonising barren planets far from our own, or tourist trips into space (!?!) at huge expense and resource consumption. At the opposite end of the spectrum, depression blights the lives of many men who've imploded in the belief there isn't a place for them any more in the modern world...

How much more beautiful could we make our lives and the lives of so many if the money, resource and expertise spent engineering 'look at me' exploits, were channelled towards life-affirming projects *here*, on our *only* planet of choice: reforesting deserts, for example. Never mind space ships – how about running water for everyone?! Then there's building food, energy and community resilience into people's lives in human-scale solutions, pre-empting the 'technocratic takeover' already knocking at our doors that we'll explore in depth in later chapters... The neutering of ordinary men makes top-down control so much easier to implement, and could well be part of the covert Agenda of the Global Elites we'll explore in detail. The Transition Town movement has been developing and implementing 'resilience strategies' for some time now.[63] One of the lessons of Initiations, new and old, seems

62. Jeannie Zandi. "Divine Feminine", Wisdom2Be, last modified 2021, 29 January, https://wisdom2be.com/essays-insights-wisdomwritings-spirituality/divine-feminine-by-jeannie-zandi

63. Rob Hopkins, The Transition Handbook (Green Books, 2014)

to me to be to *learn to live and love abundantly within limits*: finding quests in connection, communication and communion; 'engaging the wilds' within and without. 'Regenerative practices' - spot the new buzz word - weave together a world where everything is here for the taking: an abundance of recognition, creativity, intimate, nourishing sex, security, comfort, adventure, simplicity. In this vision of the future, our beautiful children are placed at the centre, lighting the way. In fact, our children *are* the way...

What Might Women Need?

Women tend to be more porous to emotion and more tolerant of, and interested in, what lies outside the province of logic and rationality than men. Emotion doesn't faze women - they treat it like the weather, with monthly cycles entailing transitions through a variety of moods, according to hormonal changes. Couple this with the growing and birthing of babies from our own flesh, followed by years of nurturing new lives to maturity, and we begin to understand women's deep capacity for connection, surrender, empathy and care, whilst giving us a ninja ability to surf chaos, as mutable, multi-tasking entities.

Women have an innate capacity to 'trust the process' when in ritual space; allowing themselves to enter sensation and emotion fully and freely - letting down their guard and fear of being judged. This might be achieved more easily within the compass of a single sex circle. Women's wombs offer a gravitational pull - a kind of inner compass, that keeps them focussed on a grounding presence inside their own bodies, and a monthly cycle that embodies the full yin-yang spectrum of experience. Alexandra Pope has written extensively on these topics - a one day workshop with her in my thirties was illuminating and life changing... She spoke of the 'via positiva' and 'via negativa' of the monthly menstrual cycle, using the metaphor of the tide coming in and out. The *via positiva* begins as the bleed ends and culminates in ovulation. This phase is characterised by creativity, stamina, focus and drive, including, but not limited by, an increase in libido, as the tide comes in...

After ovulation, if the egg remains unfertilized, the tide turns, and the *via negativa* reigns. In this phase we notice what gets left behind as the waters recede (those bits hidden from view at high tide) – the mood becomes reflective as the focus turns inward - culminating in the still point of the cycle which is the bleed. The shedding of the lining of the womb offers space for what dies, decays, rots away. As women, we *are* this dying away in the bleed time, requiring peace, rest, space, down time. PMT is the pre-emptive panic of knowing that in our culture, none of these things are likely to be accorded us as women during the bleed time - the Holy of Holies of our monthly cycle.

Other ways to understand the via negativa is to view it as a kind of descent or underworld experience. Where the 'via positiva' scaffolds and articulates; the 'via negativa' kicks out the ramparts of structure at ground level, causing an entire edifice to crumble. It jumbles certainties and syntax, messing with platitudes and definitions; turning language into fumbling and mumbling. It plays tunes and memories and films backwards, confusing beginnings, endings and linear time. It reverts to messiness in spite of Curby grips and conditioner. It appreciates the beauty of all that is dishevelled, embracing slowness and lacking an understanding of the meaning of, or need for, 'productivity'...

Jeannie Zandi calls this quality 'Yin' and describes it as her greatest initiator. Yin unravels us, as we cascade in unquiet riot - dipping into sleep's sumptuous silver – where fish kiss the curling quicksand and coral of dreams – Talismans our waking minds struggle to decode... Yin loses schedules, refuses to read instructions, insisting on breathing, being, witnessing, gestating, contemplating, becoming, emerging instead.

Yin is not necessarily 'irrational'; more likely immersed in a supra-rationality or pre-rationality that understands decay and disorder are necessary companions of control. Dissolution allows for change. Letting go permits deep relaxation which is the alpha and omega of the contemplative impulse, enabling the cultivation of qualities that make life worth living: connection, belonging, pleasure even. And the Dark allows all things to return home without the tiresome need to 'account for their movements'.

Yin appreciates that in the end, fixity leads to Wars, whilst decay creates fertile soils, feeding the multitudes of life forms passed over by those with 'important business' at hand; yielding up, in time, vitamin and mineral rich fruits to nourish bodies, hearts and minds. For the Yin insider, darkness is delicious; resting is when and where the healing happens, and a cocoon is a protection allowing soupy transformations to reveal undreamt of possibilities - iridescent beating wings - in time - for those able to tolerate disintegration, gestation, and the gifts of the Unknown.

Yet, women have been branded 'hysterical' for millennia: in ancient Greece, the womb was thought to move around in the abdominal cavity, leading to 'suffocation and death'.[64] Latterly, in the last century in fact, the medical profession resorted to the practice of 'hysterectomy' to cure a woman's 'hysteria'. It's entirely plausible, in fact, that 'hysteria' arises in women when their sensitivity and receptivity are unacknowledged; or pathologised as a kind of 'bizarre aberration' in today's logic and 'science' - focussed world. Also discussed in the 'Power Dynamics' chapter, Judith Herman in her book 'Trauma and Recovery' describes how Freud spent ten years in the Salpêtrière asylum in Paris studying 'crazy' women and children. When he realised the cause of this was mostly sexual and other forms of physical abuse perpetrated by men, he made a wise career move that swept these realities under the carpet. Instead, he focussed on a kind of psychological 'Edu-tainment' in lectures aimed at the Viennese middle-class clientele of his day (available on the Audible App) - avoiding the need for any 'inconvenient truths' to come to light. Witness the frivolity of a 'Freudian slip', or even 'penis envy' for that matter... Much more likely to be 'womb envy' - but *which male psychiatrist is likely to posit that?!*

Maybe women are naturally Temple dwelling creatures - or creatures who thrive in 'sisterhood settings' - at the very least. As we've already seen, oxytocin has a very low base line and doesn't last long in the body, suggesting it needs to be constantly

64. "The Wandering Womb: Women's Health Nursing Past and Present". Royal College of Nursing, last modified 2021, https://rcn.org.uk/library-exhibitions/Womens-health-wandering-womb

produced and constantly replenished... In effect meaning sensual, safe, soft, colourful (sometimes dark and still), playful, restful, non-competitive, non-rushed, right hemisphere, body based, clock-free environments suit us best. When our oxytocin levels rise, it feeds and sweetens us in ways that benefit all of society; young and old, men and women alike. I challenge any man, or woman, to tell me the description of women's space above, doesn't paint a picture of a lost world we *all* long for - at least *sometimes!...* Unfortunately for men though, when our oxytocin levels rise, alongside our delicious, bond-inducing sensual side; our capacity for discernment increases too - you could call it our BS detector: very useful in survival terms! Hence why we need male initiation alongside the female version to enable men to withstand and successfully navigate the 'bad ass' impact oxytocin can have on our psychology and emotions.

The poem below, by Jennifer Welwood - Buddhist psychotherapist and widow of the late John Welwood - expands the qualities of ruthless discernment characterising the spiritual feminine. The Dakini is a Mythic Tibetan entity - combining sexual and spiritual essences, as She dances through space - depicting the resultant freedom of Initiation, where high states of consciousness are achieved, embodied and integrated.

The Dakini Speaks[65]

My friends, let's grow up.
Let's stop pretending we don't know the deal here.
Or if we truly haven't noticed; let's wake up and notice.
Look: Everything that can be lost will be lost.
It's simple - how could we have missed it for so long?
Let's grieve our losses fully, like ripe human beings,
But please, let's not be so shocked by them.
Let's not act so betrayed,
As though life had broken her secret promise to us.

---

65. *"The Dakini Speaks", Jennifer Welwood, 2024, https://jenniferwelwood.com/poetry/the-dakini-speaks*

Impermanence is life's only promise to us,
And she keeps it with ruthless impeccability.
To a child she seems cruel, but she is only wild,
And her compassion exquisitely precise:
Brilliantly penetrating, luminous with truth,
She strips away the unreal to show us the real.
This is the true ride- let's give ourselves to it!
Let's stop making deals for a safe passage:
There isn't one anyway and the cost is too high.
We are not children anymore!
The true human adult gives everything for what cannot be lost.
Let's dance the wild dance of no hope!

The Power of the Circle

The power of the collective in traditional culture was able to take us to depths of trust mostly absent now. Groups bear interactive, fluid, flexible witness; navigating towards an evolving, sensitive expression of truth, meaning, and accurate perception; enabling all voices to be heard. We're not talking political debate here around fake news channels. We're talking *engaged and interactive* sharing that uses mind and body as tentacles and sensors, enabling us to perceive reality by *feeling and knowing* it...

We stay tuned, grounded, focussed and we make eye contact around the Circle and in this way come to a shared sense of reality. Circles and rituals are immersive, learning containers; especially when attended by well-seasoned, highly skilled Elders, who are gifted and trained to 'hold space' with a light, yet profound touch. Each circle an 'experiment in living'; an indispensable part of a life well-lived, that we carry in our hearts forever. Even 'botched' circles led by unskilled facilitators are teaching circles. If you are awake, resilient, and mindful enough to tolerate and observe the nuances of a clumsily held group, these teach as much about what *not* to do, as expertly choreographed situations might... And circles should be *interactive*, so we get the chance to course-correct by tapping into the wisdom of the collective. *Repair* is another function of group ritual, meaning that when we encounter challenge or conflict - bumps in the road - there is enough flex in the container to enable an unpacking of the problem - collective witness provides safety, containment and perspective - allowing for problems to be aired and rifts healed: - when that is the orientation and intent held by all present. *But don't take my word for it!* Why not create a ritual of your own?

ACTIVITY: Creating Your Own Ritual

Find three others – you want to be at least four, including yourself – maybe as many as 30, depending on the possibilities you have, and your level of confidence and courage, and the size of your network. You might ask people to bring objects from nature – pebbles, leaves, flowers, pine cones or berries. You should have gathered some of these things yourself to hand out, if needed.

Be aware of the ages of those present; and gender; and how place, time of day, season and mood might be having an influence on the gathering. Some variables you can control – for example you may choose a single gender group – and others not – maybe there's background noise – or someone decides to leave. As facilitator, notice how you are with 'what is'. Are you able to open to the possibilities of this constellation of people in this place and time? Can you press 'pause' on your story about what it means and how it will work out? Can you tune in to what wants to unfold in Beauty here and now? Maybe you've invited one or two trusted others to help co-facilitate the ritual, and you share steering and guiding between you.

Ask people to place their items in the centre of the circle. You may have a candle, or several night lights on the floor/earth, or even floating in a bowl of water. You may have lit incense or pungent herbs – to help 'clear the space', and 'connect earth with sky'. Ask people to make a prayer as they place their item in the centre – making patterns as you assemble each piece. Maybe there's a theme to the gathering – fatherhood, puberty, spring time, earth healing ... and the prayers will relate to that – and the collective piece of art in the centre will grow and gather depth and meaning as people place 'offerings', turning the collection into ritual art. This encourages people to drop mental chatter and enter 'deep listening' – crossing a threshold from day to day consciousness into a potent realm of connection and synchronicity. Use your own body/mind as antennae – sense what wants to unfold. Maybe after this initial piece people want to move, or sing or offer sensitive touch, or take part in meditation. Weave together working with the collective, and then working in pairs or smaller groups, invite people to connect using guided exercises to ask and answer specific questions. A wonderful depth exploration can take place in pairs with one person asking the other: 'How are you?' ... followed by simply: '**...and how is that for you...?**' repeated over and over for a space of five or ten minutes, even longer; whilst listening and waiting for the answer from the other. The pace should be slow, the person being questioned should have the time to unpack what is moving inside them at leisure and the questioner should listen in a non-judgemental, calm, curious way. This will be a test for both of you - since we have to learn to listen as much as we might need to learn to open up and share our inner life more fully.

As you add elements to the group, be aware of the energy and level of engagement. Encourage sharing and feedback. The ending of the ritual should encourage everyone to feel seen and heard, by coming back to the circle - to the centre. People could be encouraged to share - popcorn style - something about their experience or current state of being. One-off rituals are sometimes the best we can do in our culture, but repeating experiences and exchanges within a group over time can deepen what unfolds - although it's also likely to open up more 'bumps in the road' and depend on skilful facilitation to encourage depth and evolution. I've been part of many rituals and groups over the years, the most powerful have been week-long Zen meditation retreats. Having a tradition that goes back in an unbroken lineage hundreds of years adds power, yet it also depends on the calibre of the individual leading the retreat; I've been to wonderful and awful Zen retreats! Creativity and spontaneity via innovation infuse a different kind of energy to group gatherings. Structure and play are both needed to create successful rituals. Good luck!

Chapter Three

Eros Betrayed

We tend to have short memories when comparing ourselves to past iterations of humanity, yet much of the interpersonal neurobiology we'll examine in chapter four considers our evolution over millennia, describing the autonomic nervous system as evolving out of communal, co-regulatory living environments[66]. To talk about sexuality in the here and now is to talk about individual women and men relating to each other in the relatively newly conceived 'romantic' sphere. Yet, not so very long ago, we spent most of our time together in single sex groups performing specific tasks. Some might argue the autonomic nervous system - primarily responsible for intuiting danger and safety - hasn't caught up with modern lifestyles... Back then, when we lived in tribes, the expediency of single sex groups happened to provide emotional nurture in sustaining, varied and dependable relationships difficult to imagine today. Our social history is the story of the steady decline of community living, for better or worse... Over time, the tribe was supplanted by the village and extended family, which in turn got whittled down to the nuclear family, or single parent family, whilst today many live singly between four walls, and never experience raising children... Progress has declared collective cultures 'obsolete', often making the broad everyday currencies of companionship and mutual support, and the rich field of inter-generational living, rare commodities, at least in the modern western world...

Viewing humanity through the lens of dyadic romantic relationships therefore misses the one-time normalcy of a communal tribal social sphere - a context that has applied for well over 95% of the time span of our species' tenure here on Earth to date... Way back, it's likely individuals absconded to engage in the

66. Pioneering in this field. "Dr. Dan Seigel", 2021, https://drdansiegel.com

(often brief) adventure of sexual intimacy, returning a little flushed (!) to the round of daily activities and interactions... Collective social structures (inside of which long-term couple relationships might still exist) took pressure, expectation and intensity out of the one-to-one equation. The psychological ramifications of modern lifestyles, where we often 'only have each other' (or oneself) should not be over-looked or under-estimated... Of course, there's opportunity in modern relating to nurture depth and skilful communication; yet; it's only one, relatively recent, social arrangement, and one that might represent a re-purposing, or distortion of our finely wrought interpersonal neurobiology, at that.

In her Couples Therapy sessions, psychotherapist, author and relationship expert Esther Perel always asks what kind of support networks her client couple has in place – you can find recordings of these sessions on Audible. Reduced social circles and faltering long-term relationships seem to go together. No one person can be the be-all and end-all for another. The mythologizing of romance by Hollywood hasn't helped – it would be nice to find some middle ground and nuanced discourse between fairytale 'happily ever after' endings, and the disposable encounters depicted in porn-influenced hook-up culture... We can demand and expect too much of each other, with the tasks managed by a whole village falling to just two, or even one person now. Developing hobbies, group activities and friendships, and cultivating extended family ties might seem counter-intuitive in the short term, yet actually promote relationship resilience in the long term... It's easy to get embroiled in relationship dynamics – One thing a breadth of connections outside of a romantic partnership provides is perspective.

Emotional impoverishment is the result for many forced to cope with the rapidly diminishing face-to-face opportunities of the modern day... Couples and families always have and always will need the support of the wider community to flourish. In subsequent chapters we'll look at how engineering a climate of isolation can be used for social control... For now; I'm going to indulge a Mytho-Poetic lens to examine up close one particular spiritual tradition's account of the fabled Erotic encounter between man and woman ...

Archetypes

Modern day mystic Caroline Myss[67] has described Archetypes as the 'cookie cutters' that give our personalities discernible shape. Depth psychology, in a less facile definition, draws on the realm of the collective unconscious – a theory put forward by Carl Jung in his 1916 essay 'The Structure of the Unconscious'[68] to describe the web of meanings and associations found in the recesses of the human psyche. The Collective Unconscious 'encompasses the soul of humanity at large'. When we name a person king, queen, warrior, mother, lover, coward, geek – we are invoking Archetypes.

The related field of Etymology studies the origins of words, excavating the fecund soil of language in search of clues and pointers to 'primary meanings' as they were constructed over time... In this context, Archetypes are steeped in ancient history: – glyphs depicting larger-than-life Personae, enabling us to intuit definitions via our, often unconscious, heritage. They help bring into focus human and 'divine' characteristics that have informed, inspired, and terrified humanity for millennia... involving a cross-pollination of the Human Realm with the Abodes of the Old Gods, who once fed into our conception of reality. Our imagination reached into what was known in medieval times as the 'Upper Border'; crossing thresholds into contemplative territory rich in symbolism, portent and interconnection.[69]

Traditionally; aspects of the Initiatory journey would have guided individuals into the imaginative, larger-than-life Archetypal Realm; helping forge associative understandings and, in modern parlance, 'new neural pathways', between diverse aspects of Self in the process. Jung might have prescribed a recipe

67. Myss, Caroline, Advanced Energy Anatomy (Sounds True, 2006)

68. Source of term the 'collective unconscious'. "Collective unconscious", Wikimedia Foundation, last modified November 27, 2023, https://en.wikipedia.org/wiki/Collective_unconscious

69. Naydler, Living in the Shadow of the Machine

of struggle and resistance, love and security, discipline and drive, and encounters with the Mythic imagination and creative process as a pathway towards full 'Individuation'... The work draws together competing impulses of the psyche towards an internal 'evolutionary conversation' of sorts - weaving vibrancy and colour into the 'soul making' process...

Tantric Archetypes

Eros is old as the hills; animating the whole of the natural world in the Springtime of the year, when the mating rituals of creatures large and small take centre stage in woods, fields, rivers and valleys... At this time, the British Pagan calendar celebrates 'Beltane'; using intricate dances to weave coloured ribbons around the feted 'May pole' - a tradition that continues to this day in parts of Avalon (the Old English name for Britain, meaning 'Isle of Apples').

I'm going to travel farther afield, though, to flesh out, if you'll pardon the pun, a discussion of the sacred union of God and Goddess invoked in ancient Beltane rituals, to the Tantric traditions of India and Tibet where the meeting of Shiva and Shakti has been enshrined in religious texts[70] for centuries. Western Neo-Tantra has focussed on the sexual aspect of the tradition, whereas traditional Tantric texts explore a wide-ranging approach, with sexual union comprising only a small portion of the practices involved in 'spiritual realisation'.

In Tantric Buddhism, seen as the 'crowning cultural achievement of medieval India',[71] 'Shiva' denotes the masculine archetype, and 'Shakti' the feminine principle... This 'cosmic man' and 'cosmic woman' represent and engage the notion of 'polarity' - defined as the interaction of the separate, yet complimentary essences, of male and female. The more sharply and keenly the masculine and feminine experience their own embodied essence, the more

70. The 'Kaula Nath' written between the 10th and 15th century AD. Maya Devri. "The divine union of Shiva and Shakti in traditional Indian Tantrism", Yoga Alliance International Journal, April 20, 2018, https://yogaallianceinternationaljournal.com/blog/the-divine-union-of-shiva-and-shakti-in-traditional-indian-tantrism

71. Cultural and religious Historian breaks new ground exploring the role women played in Tantric Buddhism. Miranda Shaw, Passionate Enlightenment (Princetown University Press, 1994)

heightened is the Erotic attraction, and the greater the likelihood of sparks flying and energetic waves of bliss flowing between them. In this tradition, the harnessing of sexual energy was a type of Yoga; involving special practices, rituals and a kind of 'Courtoisie'[72] all its' own.

Shiva

Shiva is well known for hanging out on mountain tops meditating... He holds the polarity of unwavering, focussed consciousness; his primary quality is to 'stand his ground', un-distracted by the multitude of changing forms that parade before him with tantalising hooks and smiles, or the tittle-tattle of gossip and 'opinion'. The late Buddhist author and psychotherapist John Welwood has described the essence of the masculine as 'Detachment', whilst defining the feminine principle as 'Adornment'[73] – More on that shortly... The 'detachment' referred to entails a robust ability to 'find out for oneself' – 'not outsourcing one's due diligence' as someone in the business world said to me once... Shiva is sovereign, centred; self-reliant, un-dupable – he would never be caught out like the Silly Old Emperor with No Clothes depicted in Aesop's fables, for example! His presence of mind requires a powerful ability to muster and master consciousness and skilful action via self-discipline, study, solitude even; the flavour of the 'strong, silent type' rather than a 'cold or dysfunctional' version of detachment. Non-attachment might be a more appropriate, nuanced, descriptor; granting the practitioner the possibility of closeness, flexibility, humour even... Oh – and I'm not advocating constant silence as a quality of the sacred masculine, btw!

... Quality conversations are part of relational etiquette for women and men alike. To do communication skills justice would require a whole book – and many have been written. Maybe 'etiquette' sounds flippant, yet manners denote a level of skill,

72. From the French, meaning the etiquette of court, and encompassing the tradition of 'courtly love' – a romanticised expression of 'love as longing'... By contrast; 'Tantrikas' put the time and effort in to make of erotic love an energetic, psycho-physical exchange geared towards bliss and enlightenment.

73. John Welwood, Love and Awakening: Discovering the Sacred Path of Intimate Relationship (HarperCollins, 1997)

self-awareness and mutual respect – and as such, shouldn't be taken for granted. Learning to 'own our own stuff' rather than projecting blame onto each other is just one aspect of mature relating, so too is asking for what we want, and being able to say 'no' as a pre-requisite for saying 'yes'...

Ultimately, Shiva cultivates himself in service of the sacred Dance of Eros he enters into with Shakti, enabling her to surrender open to the depths of her own true nature via his all-pervasive focussed consciousness (symbolised as having the third eye, or brow centre, open). His self-mastery offers Shakti containment; her sensitivity benefitting from his grounding presence – ballast for their journey together across the scintillating sea of intimacy...!

Shakti

The feminine essence of 'adornment' can of course be taken literally; a woman's devotion to beauty signifies her cultured nature... In modern times beauty has been monetised and commodified; yet our sensibility to beauty offers us an altered state of awareness – a crack between the worlds – a passport into what was called the 'floating world' in the Geisha quarters of medieval Japan... A place where we slip unnoticed into the enchanted, unchartered realms of Eros – a charged non-dual world where *everything* has a ripple effect... The Universe of the Sacred Feminine is construed as a Feast for the senses; nourishing and elevating heart and mind in subtle ways difficult to articulate with the blunt tool of language...

Adornment extends to include the world of beliefs and ideas: – Shakti is not afraid of try them on for size – magpie style! Her eclecticism doesn't mean 'amateurish', in the way it might for a man; just a lover of variety and novelty! The Shakti iteration of woman does not feel the need to impress with intellect; she is more at home in the fluid realms of sensation and emotion... The feminine is often symbolised as chalice, in this instance filled with Shiva's focussed and activating attention – awakening her yielding, open-hearted essence. In communion with the Sacred Masculine – Shakti's receptivity, as consort, informs his skilful presence - bringing nuance and *resonance* to his prowess and proclivity for *impact* - with her finely tuned, embodied sensitivity.

Matter, Mother, Matrix; all share the same etymological root; Shakti weaves them together - fully and unapologetically inhabiting the body... Movement, sensation and emotion are her realms *par excellence*. *Motherhood* - Cradling infants and responding to their ever-present emotional and physical needs, hones feminine responsiveness; lending it a spider-like quality that picks up every vibration when Shakti is seated at the centre of the indivisible web of the world...

Modern day Wounding

Modern day woman might need some kind of initiatory experience - enabling her to inhabit the spacious, even luxuriant grace and ease of the quintessential feminine. Shakti needs encouragement to relax, granting access to surrender, where she opens to love, pleasure and beauty; and the healthy healing contexts that permit her to drink from the deep well of her femininity. The rushing and competitive culture we live in negates a woman's ability to discover her cyclical, open nature. Beauty today is a multi-billion dollar industry, sucking the joy out of the ritualised and communal aspects of adornment. A friend who lived with the nomadic Berber last winter in Morocco for two months told me eligible women carried no mirrors; instead beautifying *each another* in preparation to meet eligible men... He was moved by the harmony, lack of competitiveness and quality of sisterhood he experienced among them.

Through the lens of the wounded masculine, men might often both envy and fear the emotional universe of women; testosterone surges rendering the pull of the feminine overwhelming; especially considering the feminine archetype of the *Mother*: - once safety and ground for infant boys.

Single sex groups as described in the 'Initiation' chapter, when purposefully choreographed, can help men develop the confidence of Shiva's unshakeable, single-pointed Presence - so very attractive to Shakti! Initiatory journeys help men learn to detach from the Mother archetype; allowing for the sexes to meet as 'complementary equals'... Where once the wounded masculine judged women 'fluffy, chaotic, indulgent or weak', the initiated masculine offers a kind of containment the feminine can surrender into. In an uninitiated landscape, many women (and men) adopt distorted strategies in an attempt to get their emotional needs met...

The Psychology of Polarity

When she is able to access her fluid essence, Shakti is naturally empathic, yielding and alive, opening to her body as conduit for pleasure[74], [75]. We are looking here at 'archetypal qualities' - portals into the dynamics of the Tantric tradition[76] that might help inform today's gender conversations. An enlightened 'Shiva' has worked through judgements, distractions and resistances (the shadow aspects of detachment). Using initiation, he's cleansed the 'doors of perception', learnt to metabolise fear - enabling him to see and feel into the 'heart of a woman's heart' in a new way... His detachment (from personal history, agendas and schedules) provides a gravitas that invites Shakti to drop out of her head and into the body. For him the yielding quality of the feminine is a place to rest; dance; play - a Holy place of Welcome and Timelessness. He knows that yielding will only happen for a woman when she feels safe around him; and he knows her Safety is the product of him plumbing the depths of his inner and outer worlds via Initiation.

Thus, the paradox of finding one's own centre, only to allow it to dissolve into an expansive, numinous, ecstatic field of awareness, is realised. Rumi says:

> "... The clear bead at the centre changes everything. There are no edges to my loving now. I've heard it said - there's a window that opens from one mind to another. But if there is no wall, there is no window, and if there

74. Women and men learn to conduct sexual energy. Shashi Solluna, Tantra Made Easy: Discover the Path from Sex to Spirit (Hay House, 2018)

75. David Deida and Margo Anand are pioneers of the neo-Tantra movement

76. David Deida's many books and lectures wax lyrical about men and women in 'Tantric style' romantic relationships in a poetic, spiritual vein.

is no window, there is no need for a latch. There are no edges to my loving now. The clear bead at the centre changes everything".[77]

Mindfully noticing fear and distractions arising, and the possibility of being pulled off balance, Shiva returns to Presence; offering deep relief and release for Shakti. She no longer feels a requirement to 'hold things together' on his behalf; neither over-burdened nor overwhelmed; the union of Shiva-Shakti Dances in the liquid perfection of the moment, where polarities engage and ultimately disappear.[78] The sharpening of polarity is responsible for its ultimate dissolution, in a Cosmic exchange that prefigures, Mytho-poetically, the strange convolutions of some of the gender discourses of our day...

Do not confuse Shiva's ability to metabolise fear as invincibility - an expression of the immature shadow masculine. Everyone has a breaking point. Shiva is not interested in the insanity of pushing beyond all limits, *or of sending rockets to the moon!* He has practiced non-attachment long enough he's able to be with whatever arises, remaining un-fazed and open – to the unfolding of each new moment: *intimacy as great adventure!*

... Initiation teaches us all how to widen our 'windows of tolerance', thus *meeting the fear erotic encounter naturally generates*. This is a world apart, and a healthy alternative, to *dissociation or re-enactment!...*[79] Shiva holds a woman (and himself for that matter) through challenges, and out the other side, expressing love as energetic activation; waves of bliss: – he teaches Shakti the art of letting go, cultivating these qualities in the service of the sacred feminine, and not for personal gain. A student of Tantra once told me: 'Shakti yields to Shiva, but *Shiva yielded to her first*'.

77. Translation: Robert Bly and Coleman Barks, "A poem by Rumi: The Clear Bead at the Center", Wild Moon Bhaktas. October 16, 2015, https://wildmoonbhaktas.com/a-poem-by-rumi-the-clear-bead-at-the-center

78. Alex Grey's spiritual and medically precise art blurs boundaries between science and mysticism, bringing cosmic realities to life, by showing meridians, chakras and circulatory systems in the same painting. The difficulty in categorising his oeuvre has perhaps contributed to his remaining a 'niche' artist to this day.

79. Harmony Place Monterey with Dr. Mark Schwartz. "Lovemaps as Trauma Reenactments with Dr. Mark Schwartz and Lori Galperin, LCSW", YouTube, 2:00:09, 2019, 3 May, https://youtube.com/watch?v=8g5fcjOp39M

All very Cosmic - *no doubt!* - yet the interplay of power and submission keeps gender roles supple in day-to-day life. In 'The Art of Sexual Ecstasy', a landmark book of its time, author Margo Anand elaborates the 'Yin-Yang Game', where couples explore the power dynamics of polarity in master-servant role play... The game can last an hour or a day; the importance being to swap roles eventually. As caveat, the vulnerable 'yin' servant is accorded the power, the choice, of 'no' to be respected by the 'yang' master in control...The freedom of exercising 'no' lends extra power to the ***'yes'*** - the gateway into the delicious, deep-dive of the game!... Power dynamics are hugely important aspects of life we'll explore in a subsequent chapter, and power as polarity is a vital ingredient of Erotic attraction. Exploring power dynamics helps us become unstuck from traditional masculine/feminine stereotypes, avoiding the grievance and sense of oppression that comes with being locked in a particular role. It takes a certain level of evolution to play as adults; an ability to let go and 'make believe' once more, teaching vital communication skills to negotiate wants, needs and boundaries - useful skills, surely, for any life situation.

Shakti Sighs!

Shakti's yielding requires *surrender.* Sex without a fully-felt surrender equals porn - something ultimately boring and banal, without soul or sentiment. Porn involves a kind of crass submission; but surrendering *open* has a different, intimate quality, where depth and skill in communication are contexts for connection. In Tantra, the invitation is to empty ourselves in order to conduct energy; allowing us to experience qualities and sensations that take us beyond the 'stuck record' of the limited self - and stereotypical definitions of male and female. In spiritual reality, identification *with* anything whatsoever is limitation:- being bound to the over-simplified glyphs of egoic consciousness, whereas non-identification is seen as the royal road to liberation, peace and flexibility.

Today's arena of sexual politics tells us identification *with* a chosen gender is cool; whilst spiritual traditions of the past focus on dis-identification (non-attachment) as route to discovering and recovering more of ourselves... To produce consistent results, 'Erotic Tantra' might involve as much self-awareness, openness, discipline, and care in the bed chamber, as the spiritual renunciate's 'meeting himself' might take sitting alone under a tree, or retreating to a mountain cave... That's the possibility when we engage these qualities as ritual practices in our long-term relationships, rather than relating to them as just one-off 'freak', or 'peak' events.

'Kink' was well understood in the ancient art of Shibari (partnered rope tying) and precursor of BDSM, where the people I've spoken with tell me the practices are often to do with emotional healing as much as they are to do with sex. We can learn to trust one another in intimate power plays in ways that are difficult to imagine or replicate in any other sphere. It's understood that we show up in role to play a game. At the end of the game the role is relinquished, something is harvested, tasted, some neural connections forged that might help us navigate the power struggles of the world more readily, or resolve past pain... There's a light, playful touch here, with whole spectrums and worlds explored and expanded, without the need to take a scalpel to the physical body, or ingest hormone altering substances!

The entire initiatory journey, in fact, is there for the claiming: – severance (from the 'normal' day-to-day world), adventure (in the world of imaginative role play) as experiment, and return (to 'normality') via discussion and loving acceptance afterwards; with two people learning together the art of holding one another through a 'depth experience' and out the other side...

I'm not trying to debase 'normal' romance here – this illustration is intended to disrupt habitual perceptions - opening us to all forms of sensual love as a kind of 'play'. Secure attachment (more on that in the next chapter) is paradoxical in that it offers a spring board where we feel safe enough to risk diving into the unknown together - revitalising the bonds of love and discovering more about ourselves and one another in the process...

Whilst it's important to sever the infantile connection with the mother and father archetypes for functional adult relationships to succeed; we nonetheless need to have *had* a healthy bond with our primary care givers to enable authentic exchange. This allows integration of healthy nurturing aspects of mother and father energies, merging with a broader palette of loving play. No one is suggesting a cold or impersonal approach here.

Sex allied to Eros has the potential to be intimate, exploratory, joyous, revelatory and expansive. In autonomic nervous system terms, feeling safe and comfortable with the person we are with brings deep relaxation, which in turn allows the body more sensation and excitement - expanding our hearts and 'windows of tolerance'... Safety and excitement go hand in hand - this is the real 'edge' of Tantra and exploratory sex - undertaking a journey without destination, increasing levels of sensitivity and surrender; entering a world where giving and receiving blur and become a dance of mutual acceptance and empowerment... In letting go of control; offering something up; experiencing a nameless exchange - a physical and emotional communion - we are touched in unforgettable ways. In letting go we receive something from the 'beyond' that in normal waking hours our ego defends against... *Or at least so it seems to me when lost in love play...!*

Befriending the Self

With a sudden jolt, we emerge into today's reality, where the atomisation of the 'scientific approach' has taken precedence over liminal, archetypal realms; of Eros frolicking with the power of imagination in embodied loving... Screens provide an external locus for our attention so much of the time, compromising our ability to engage, even minimally, with rich inner worlds...

Psychotherapist Dr Matt Licata recently defined the task of our times as 'dis-fragmenting the psyche', which he described as the 'Art of Befriending the Self'... The 'dis-fragmenting' glyph is a slightly awkward double negative; yet one that resonates when we consider the dissociative results of trauma (explored in the next chapter) and the relatively recent adoption of 'scientific rationalism' as primary paradigm - one that engages world by focusing on 'the measurable'. Using this approach; feelings, energies and qualities: the nebulous, numinous, archetypal, messy, blissful, chaotic - *all* are discounted in an attempt to 'further' 'progress' - a purely utilitarian approach to life where Data Sets trump The Mystery every time. Perhaps the psychic fragmentation described by Dr Licata makes more sense when we realise our dominant mindset has required us to sweep so much under the carpet for so long...

As we'll see in the 'Non-Duality' chapter, logic and rationality rely on the left hemisphere of the brain which loves to compartmentalise and simplify - to offer 'representations' as ways to stream-line the thinking process. Whilst logic offers a 'method' - a way to think - it is stripped of content- of knowing *what it is* we are supposed to be thinking *about.*[80] So often now, the virtual world takes up all the room inside our heads; robbing us of the discovery of the creative depths and power of conscious awareness; connected to and embedded in the real world of nature, the realms of imagination and intimate encounter with self and other. Forging internal maps of meaning where *thinking* is allied to *feeling, connecting and exploring,* in the *physical* realm over time, is surely the way to weave an embodied, and thus *real,* kind of *knowing.*

> "The... virtual world... can seem more appealing than the world of nature to which we really belong, and we witness today a mass migration of people's desires, affections, and loyalties from the natural world to the virtual. But the virtual world is **parasitic** upon the real world, and because it presents to us a simulation of reality, there is a danger that we embrace an illusion while turning our backs on reality. Our peril today is that we become spellbound by a relationship that gives us a false sense of power, comfort and reassurance, but does

80. Daniel Schmachtenberger explores this: Rebel Wisdom. "Resilience and Sensemaking". March 28, 2020. YouTube, 14:19. https://youtube.com/watch?v=GACFCnXTs9M

not truly nourish the soul. The danger is that the soul is hollowed out, our relationship to nature devitalised, and our physical wellbeing undermined. And all the while we far too readily fall back on a merely utilitarian attitude, naively thinking that because the technology is so useful to us it is entirely benevolent, despite innumerable studies pointing to the contrary".[81]

In Archetypal parlance, and in today's world; the connective tissue of Eros has been severed by the double-edged sword (Twin-headed God?) of Science and Technology... We poke and prod the dismembered, unrelated objects littered at our feet, in the forlorn hope of turning a profit... Under Capitalism, these 'discrete objects' become 'tokenised' 'icons', manipulated according to human whim and will. Thus, we bestow upon ourselves some kind of 'God Illusion' in an impossible-to-quantify mash-up that threatens to drag us all into a Hell realm of Epic proportions... Some would say we're there already... In the New World Order chapter, we explore in depth the multiple forces at work hastening in the new 'Technocracy', or 'Gamification of Humanity' (and Nature) as Alison McDowell[82] prefers to call it...

Breaking Away or Breaking Down?

Creating new 'gender identities' seems to me to conform to the dystopian nightmare described above, as part and parcel of the misguided notion of 'playing God'. I understand young people need to forge their own 'brave new world' as a way to break away from parents, and I don't wish to deny them that... I also believe in the reality of a tiny minority of people perceiving they were born into the 'wrong body', before it became a way to stand out from the crowd on social media...

Could it be, though, that the current appetite for 'identity politics', running parallel with the over-reach of science, the pharmaceutical industry, and global governance by unelected elites, is more than mere coincidence? The complex intelligence inherent in Evolutionary Biology and Language in the past decade or so, have been co-opted, rearranged, re-defined and

81. Naydler, In the shadow of the Machine
82. Alison McDowell deftly explains the real 'Fourth Industrial Revolution'

re-purposed. This post-modern mash-up of sorts rubbishes the body: that finely-tuned, delicate product of countless millions of years of evolution; not to mention the thousands of years of received wisdom encoded in language, culture and mytho-poetic traditions worldwide... In the socio-political developments of the modern era, gender has become un-tethered from genetics, physiology and etymology to become something we invent and create ourselves instead. ' The non-binary gender identity iteration seems to make perfect sense in an age where the hearts, bodies and minds of men and women have been somehow devalued and homogenised.

Once upon a time, the breaking away from parents, and forging of adult 'identities' was taken care of in highly orchestrated fashion by Elders, myth makers and storytellers, master craftsmen and women who apprenticed youth formally and informally, 'midwifing' them for a second time; helping them bravely jump the gap between childhood and adulthood. Elders forged their minds, bodies, hearts and souls into vessels ready to receive the strong liquor of adult responsibility and opportunity. There was a direct relationship between how well the young were trained, their 'performance metrics', and the welfare of the whole (there is still – it's just more diffuse in large populations)... A poorly skilled, uninitiated young adult represented a threat for all; jeopardising the group's security and even survival.

... We now have a generation of molly-coddled (yet hollowed out) adolescents desperate to 'define themselves' hijacked by a plethora of professionals (including political theorists, 'therapists' and cultural 'influencers') who all stand to profit from their confusion: – An unholy alliance undermining the potency of Eros and power of Polarity, via the insidious proliferation of ideology; encouraging instead the hacking about of body parts and imbibing of hormone blockers...

Isn't this Vandalism of the most reprehensible kind? Is not the tinkering with the physical body and endocrine system a betrayal of our Youth by science, technology and the 'helping professions'? Even 'psychotherapy professionals' today are forced into supporting 'solutions' to the confusion and pain of young people via gender reassignment. We are no longer at liberty to call into question the 'identity politics' movement – to do so is (apparently) to align ourselves with the 'conversion therapy' of the past, where homosexuality was considered a 'curable disease'... Yet any fool can see 'transgender' is a totally different thing, by orders of magnitude, undermining the legitimacy of homosexuality, in fact, and *more* not *less* likely to cause life-long physical and emotional damage than offer plausible long-term solutions to emotional distress.

Experimentation in our Jeans

Rather than focussing solely on the transgender 'movement', let's consider the inter-sex phenomenon, examining statistics defining current rates and causes of 'intersex' births. An 'intersex' person is born with both male and female sexual characteristics, and according to The National LGBTQIA+ Health Education Center, up to 1.7% of the population may exhibit some form of intersex characteristic at birth, 'depending on how intersex is defined'.[83] 'The frequency of specific intersex traits varies widely; some traits are more common in certain areas of the world', according to their website.

The piece about 'in different parts of the world' is interesting, because a glance at the internet shows a connection between Endocrine-Disrupting Chemicals (EDCs) and the number of intersex babies being born. Reports document that workers exposed to EDCs are at greater risk of giving birth to intersex children.[84] Roach in English rivers are also becoming feminized due to 'gender-bending' oestrogen hormones found in the water as a result of the contraceptive pill[85], and EMFs (electro-magnetic frequencies) are responsible for lowering testosterone levels in men.[86]

---

83. "Affirming Primary Care for Intersex People 2020", National LGBTQIA+ Health Education Center, last modified August 6, 2020, https://lgbtqiahealtheducation.org/publication/affirming-primary-care-for-intersex-people-2020

84. Alisa L. Rich et al. "The Increasing Prevalence in Intersex Variation from Toxicological Dysregulation in Fetal Reproductive Tissue Differentiation and Development by Endocrine-Disrupting Chemicals". Environmental Health Insights 10 (September 2016): 163–171.

85. Charles R. Tyler and Susan Jobling. "Roach, sex, and gender-bending chemicals: The feminization of wild fish in English rivers". Bioscience 58, no. 11 (December 2008): 1051–1059.

86. Maluin et al., "Effect of radiation emitted by wireless devices on males"

Interesting research, beyond the scope of this book, is being carried out to determine whether the Y chromosome (giving male traits) is in fact less stable than the X chromosome. (XX = female and XY = male). Some predictions even suggest the Y chromosome may become extinct in the next few million years. I would have thought if the Y chromosome becomes extinct, we're all extinct – but maybe we'll all be test tube clones by then?!

It feels important to offer a bite-sized chunk of historical context here; validating gender experimentation, and indeed intersex individuals with their own stories and journeys; whilst acknowledging past iterations of androgyny and cross-dressing. The intersection of sexual expression, gender, identity, culture and environment is complex, rich and fascinating. Cross-dressing as 'dress code' was first introduced out of necessity in Europe in the 1800s when female spies called Vivandieres wore a uniform with a dress over trousers. Women's rights activists in Britain followed suit (no pun intended!) and eventually high fashion French stylist Coco Chanel began donning trousers in 1928.[87]

In indigenous cultures, such as the Sioux Indians, a Heyoka, or Sacred Clown personage, was allowed to break all the rules of the tribe – including cross-dressing, to entertain Clan members and shake up cultural mores: – social historians have concluded that culturally encoded transgression, even for a short moment, seems to actually help with observance of rules the rest of the time.[88]

Fools in Renaissance Europe performed this function – showing bare buttocks in court, telling inappropriate jokes and wearing silly hats! – providing a kind of safety valve to let off steam, whilst preventing Kings and Queens from taking themselves too seriously... The traditional Mardi Gras Festival in France was an excessive flamboyant party held just before Lenten penances and privations, intended, amongst other things, to use up all the fat in the house prior to Lent. Modern day Drag Artistes in the West may be vestiges of this much older tradition. Historical references

87. "History of cross-dressing", Wikimedia Foundation, last modified July 27, 2023, https://en.wikipedia.org/wiki/History_of_cross-dressing
88. Benjamin G. Purzycki, "Conceptions of Humor: Lakota (Sioux), Koestlerian, and Computational". Nebraska Anthropologist 21 (2006): 168–188.

nuance the sexual identity conversation; one that, over the last decade or more, has become heavily polarised and politicised-hijacked even, by woke ideology and neo-Marxists. Where today can we find the return to the rules after the frivolous display of the Fool, or to the Lenten penances after the excess of the Mardi Gras?

Convenient Distraction?

In today's socio-political landscape, we are witnessing the hubris of 'scientific rationalism' taken to extremes: - exploited by modern medicine and associated professionals, who assume the human body is theirs to modify, tinker with and 'reinvent' as a solid career path and income generator... Every gender reassignment, according to Matt Walsh, in the documentary 'What is a Woman?' is worth $1.7million. This is before we even consider the resulting ethical and sexual quagmire we might find ourselves enmeshed in; where 'Queerness' taken to extremes could include paedophilia, and children in some primary schools are being read fairy tales by drag queens. A closer inspection reveals it's often not even the interest group itself, but agitators and ideologues with covert political agendas making most of the noise to incite confusion and polarisation AKA 'divide and rule' - a distracting smokescreen behind which the rich and powerful operate with impunity.

The confusing; for some, *strangely absorbing,* world of identity politics happens to coincide with the very real spectre of the emergence of Global Tyranny - explored in later chapters: - It might seem strange, but sex and politics have a long history of being joined at the hip! In communist Russia promiscuity was initially encouraged, because the family was seen as being resilient to the imposition of the New World Order of the Day, and thus the destruction of the family and its values was concomitant with the implementation of Marxism - until state nurseries became prohibitively cumbersome.[89]

89. Natalia Chernyaeva, "Childcare manuals and construction of motherhood in Russia, 1890-1990", PhD diss., (University of Iowa, 2009).

The same was true in Weimar Germany, according to Will Zoll in his Substack series 'Prussia Gate'.[90] Today, a partnership between the WEF and UN spearheads the implementation of a New Global Government, under the aegis of the 'Fourth Industrial Revolution', using a diktat called 'Agenda 2030'. What is unfolding now in the West is a form of neo-Marxism with far-reaching consequences, unless we become fully aware of the implications, and question both the foundations and results of these pernicious ideologies...

Schools and the work place are enforcing this new ideology... YouTube is littered with 'helpful' videos explaining 'gender stereo-types' as pink and blue ribbons; football and cars, ballet and make-up, whilst 60 year old men in suits sign off emails declaring their gender pronouns, having been briefed on 'gender inclusivity'. We are told how damaging stereotypes are for young people (often by they themselves). Yet, what if these are *trifles* in the face of the multiple inalienable human rights robbed from us during the 'pandemic' - a potential 'dry run' for testing the efficacy of the infrastructure for Global Governance?

During the 'covid years', Freedoms of movement and bodily autonomy; the dignity of work and freedom to transact; learning opportunities at school, college and university were curtailed; so was our right to breathe freely, and access unbiased, transparent information; the prohibition of social gatherings, including for religious purposes, entertainment, or in celebration or mourning... These were just a few of the civil liberties taken from us. I'd rather keep those, *thanks all the same*, even wrapped up with a 'gender normative' pink ribbon or blue bow!

In giving us the illusion of 'choice', and getting us tied up in rainbow-ribbon knots of newly confabulated 'gender ideologies', we are shaped into opinionated enemies... All the while, our *real choices* are taken away from under our noses; as law suits are filed for 'incorrect pronoun usage'. This madness has to be called out, and a timely *review of our priorities* might be in order.

---

90. Will Zoll. "Not Since 1917 – Part III", Prussia Gate, last modified November 5, 2021, https://prussiagate.substack.com/p/not-since-1917-part-iii

The Language of Parts

Another flawed argument of the identity politics movement is that any of us possesses a 'singular' persona... Observing our own thinking process, we notice it's composed of conversations in our head. *How does that work then?* Because consciousness is, by nature, split into *parts* – the adventurous part, the shy part, the bit that takes after mum, and dad, and other important role models; the rebel, or class clown; the fussy eater, or sports fanatic, the addict, the super star, the sensitive type, the intellectual, the entrepreneur, the obedient pleaser, etc...[91] Aren't we all they/them?

It's important to name these distinctions and distortions, because some would have us believe that LGBTQi+ is some kind of 'community' of mutually supportive people touting a singular, coherent ideology under the beautiful rainbow banner... Many, both under and outside that banner, have reservations and don't dare speak out. Tensions within the 'movement' include sex changes possibly destroying the legitimacy of being 'gay', male to female sex changes giving men an unfair advantage in sports; and children being sexualised from a young age when they should be being protected from such concerns. A complete exploration of the philosophic basis of the current situation is beyond the scope of this writing... Max Reynolds's book discusses in great detail the origins and development of the philosophy behind today's identity politics movement.[92]

False Binaries as Self-Evident Wisdom!

In Zen, another offshoot of Buddhism, not too dissimilar to Tantra, the principle of non-duality, conceptualised as 'the Void', allows all things to return to themselves – morphing and changing; birthing; flourishing; withering and dying... *All* phenomena, experience and perception are understood as co-arising[93], due to

91. Richard Schwartz follows a long line of other therapeutic modalities with 'Internal Family Systems' theory that encourages clients to 'speak the language of parts

92. Max O. Reynolds, The Revolutionary Renaissance: A study on the dialectical evolution of totalitarian thought (Amazon Kindle Direct Publishing, 2022)

93. Termed 'quantum entanglement' in contemporary scientific parlance. Karen Barad, Meeting the Universe Halfway: Quantum Physics and the Entanglement of Matter and Meaning (Duke University Press, 2007)

the enmeshment of causes and conditions: 'as ye sow; so shall ye reap'. Thus, 'context' is the interwoven 'ground of being' and foundation of reality, with all inner experience in constant flux with outer reality: – Inner and outer worlds 'false binaries' separated by a flimsy semi-permeable membrane. A later chapter is devoted to 'non-duality'. Quantum mechanics[94] aligns with ancient wisdom when it professes: 'the observer changes the observed'.

The radical view of inter-connectedness intuited by Zen and other spiritual traditions is confirmed by the most basic study of synergistic elements in natural ecosystems; whilst numerous studies have demonstrated the significant positive impact of love and nurture on social development[95],[96]. Ancient wisdom traditions, ecology, observable behaviour and Quantum mechanics all point to interconnection at the heart of reality – meaning young people are sensitive to the effects of bonding and proselytising experiences with teachers, parents, media and peers. This *cancels* the idea that 'gender identity' is something most of us are 'born with'. The 'gender orientation' that children as young as four, five, and six are being asked to provide in some schools in the UK is undoubtedly shaped by the messaging in their environment.[97]

The Impact of Porn

This is just the latest onslaught concerning young people and sexuality. In a 2012 TED talk, late author and researcher Gary Wilson described the proliferation of online pornography

---

94. Science editor's pick: Ethan Siegal. "Observing the universe really does change the outcome and this experiment shows how". Forbes, May 26, 2020, https://forbes.com/sites/startswithabang/2020/05/26/observing-the-universe-really-does-change-the-outcome-and-this-experiment-shows-how

95. Marga Vicendo. "The evolution of Harry Harlow: from the nature to the nurture of love", History of Psychiatry 21, no. 2 (2010):190–205.

96. Jiawen Jin. "The Impact of Parenting Styles on Children's Social Adjustment and Development." Journal of Education, Humanities and Social Sciences 22 (2023): 867–872.

97. Planned Parenthood helps 'inform parents' about 'talking to preschoolers about identity. They assert that most kids begin to identify with a gender around age 3. That includes transgender and gender nonconforming also having a sense of their gender identity at this stage. "How do I talk with my preschooler about identity?", Planned Parenthood, 2023, https://plannedparenthood.org/learn/parents/preschool/how-do-i-talk-with-my-preschooler-about-identity

as 'the biggest uncontrolled social experiment of our time' (pre-pandemic!), asserting that boys are looking online for pornography by age ten.[98] Mark W from After Skool (3M + subscribers) has created a more recent animated depiction of the predicament after interviewing Bret Weinstein who calls porn an 'apocalyptic catastrophe' that's 'messed up all the incentives for partnering romantically', 'replacing three and a half billion years of evolution' with 'nothing meaningful' - available on YouTube. Normalising porn risks accepting violence and crime, especially against women and vulnerable children. Highlighting these issues, Fight the New Drug – a not-for-profit fund-raising organisation with a YouTube channel – interviews women trafficked into pornography. The 2023 documentary 'Sound of Freedom', which strangely took several years to be released, provides a harrowing testament to the reality of child sex trafficking, fuelled by the spiralling demand for child pornography, presented by Jim Caviezel and Tim Ballard.[99]

How might persistent exposure to porn affect the sexual experiences and mental and emotional health of young people and adults? In a 2019 series called 'Porn Laid Bare', women admit to porn desensitising them and to not knowing how to distinguish 'real' or 'natural' desire from desires created by watching porn.[100] One woman speaks of seeking out older men because she saw this dynamic a lot online, and she described wanting and expecting to be treated roughly because that's also what she witnessed online. The article speaks of compulsive porn watching as being more about escapism than sex: another symptom of a society where people distract themselves with a kind of fakery that makes 'reality' worse not better, and where the distinction between fact and fiction becomes blurred, perhaps irreparably.

Whilst it's easier to access porn and dating sites than ever before, the documentary the Social Dilemma[101] tells us dating

---

98. *After Skool. "How Pornography Distorts Intimate Relationships - Bret Weinstein", YouTube, 13:33, 2024, 10 January, https://youtube.com/watch?v=eTAfCxExiFg*
99. *Sound of Freedom, directed by Alejandro Monteverde (Angel Studios, 2023), 2:11:00*
100. *Porn Laid Bare. Series 1, episode 2, "Porn on the Brain". Aired March 14, 2019, on BBC Three. https://bbc.co.uk/programmes/p072n1xn*
101. *The Social Dilemma, directed by Jeff Orlowski (Exposure Labs, 2020)*

amongst young people is on the decline. Is there a hidden cost; a loss of spontaneity, 'magic and mystery' even, that is rarely acknowledged or explored, in normalising porn, 'sex services' and easy hook-ups? Young people learn about sex as a stripped down, mechanical, empty act; and one they don't know how to evaluate as such - because they haven't anything to compare it with. And instead of signalling liberation; isn't the pervasive silence of porn (other than animal noises and 'dirty' talk) a kind of anti-intimacy; a legacy of oppressive servitude difficult to name?

If you're a young person reading this, I'm here to tell you that porn is not 'normal'! - porn is sex devoid of intimacy, and intimacy is the true spark that makes sex vibrant, nurturing and alive! Intimacy involves a deep kind of relaxation, sharing and intuitive listening, where responsiveness and sensitivity are key. Talking, holding, eye gazing, whispering, breathing together, kissing, and, believe it or not: - ***feeling at peace*****, can all be part of intimate sex. Instinctive, wild and raw sex can exist too - as part of a 'natural spectrum'. It's important to remember that in intimacy-based sex; no one - perhaps especially the female - should simply be 'putting up and shutting up'.**

In Nicole Arbour's interview with Jordan Peterson[102], she broaches the subject of sex in your 20s and 30s in a good way - a light hearted exchange about some deadly serious subject matter. You need to be patient, or fast forward to about 15 minutes from the end of this characteristically long interview, to get the gold! The whole thing is worth a watch though, IMO...

Peterson (age 60) says the first time he saw a naked woman was on Monty Python when he was about 13 and it made quite an impression on him. Nicole noted how Instagram has changed. There are a lot more women showing bare flesh... She talks about men and boys (girls too) being able to access sex online at the touch of a button and being able to 'get off' looking at a screen, without any of the risk of rejection brought about by face-to-face encounters, whilst, conveniently, it takes less time! When people *do* meet, one-off sexual encounters make sense in the intimacy-

102. Jordan B. Peterson. "Provocations: Nicole Arbour interviews Jordan Peterson". May 12, 2021. YouTube, 1:16:55. https://youtube.com/watch?v=qGgEF-SlSEU

averse world that seems to be springing up around and within us – side-stepping the challenging business of getting to know someone deeply over time.

Mixed Messages

... It's more convenient to label a woman a 'slut' than it is to look at her world, where there may be a lack of empathic connection or opportunity, driving her to look for love in the wrong places. Adolescents today are often sexualised too young, and cynically programmed to be fixated on appearance as a way to commercialise their emotional needs in increasingly barren social landscapes. Women's covert 'body as bargaining chip' mentality persists, yet it's a difficult subject to broach in a 'culture wars' environment where identity politics, porn and even feminism sometimes cloud rather than clarify narratives. Emphasising consent is a good start, but it doesn't join up the dots between sex, conditioning and historical socio-economic realities that were part of the deal for women for a long time. Understanding our history helps us better understand our behaviour. Conditioning in the collective unconscious persists even after causes and conditions in the environment change – according to the emerging field of epigenetics: – trauma is lodged in the DNA.[103]

---

103. Brian G. Dias and Kerry J. Ressler. "Parental olfactory experience influences behaviour and neural structure in subsequent generations." Nature neuroscience 17, no. 1 (2014): 89–96.

INTIMACY VS PORN BASED SEX: THE DIFFERENCES

Characteristics	Intimacy based sex	Porn based sex
Eyes	Sustained eye contact occurs, sometimes known as 'eye gazing'	Very little (or no) eye contact
Tactility	The whole body can be experienced as an erogenous zone, time is taken for holding, stroking and exploring	Almost exclusive focus on the genitals. Actions are repetitive, rather than naturally unfolding
Foreplay	Women especially need time to feel open and ready for penetration... Gentle tactile and verbal exchanges build rapport and readiness	Foreplay is not acknowledged as helpful or necessary
Communication	Variation in communication: including pausing, sharing, humour, vulnerability. Partners are curious and engaged... Two-way sharing is common; perhaps the woman in particular learns to ask for what she wants	No talking, sharing, or listening of any consequence. Vulnerability is not tolerated. Partners are silent or confined to making noises... Likes and dislikes are never discussed. Partners show no interest in the experience of the other
Emotion	Emotional closeness, understanding, and mutuality, as well as discussing and accepting difference, is valued	The enactment of specific fantasies is prioritized over emotional connection
Consent	Mutual consent is clearly given, with both partners having equal say and influence over the encounter. Checking-in is part of ongoing unison. 'Stop' is welcome, heard and respected.	Re-enactment of power dynamics and scripts common in pornography, but not necessarily consensual or enjoyable in real life. Stopping is rarely an option!
Expectations	The varied nature of bodies, desires, and responses are recognized and accepted. Sex feels fluid and fun...	Fixed enactments; often unrealistic expectations of responses, physical appearance and performance
Attunement	Partners are attuned to each other's needs and individual experience	Sexual scenarios are replicated without attunement to real-time reactions and feelings.

The Bigger Picture	Part of a continuum, that might include dinner, reading, chatting, films, walks, sleeping, cuddling without sex	Regarded as a job – fixation on penetration, often including anal, and orgasm
Effects	Results in deeper emotional bonds and trust between partners, and their extended family and social networks	Feelings of disconnection, shame, inadequacy and discomfort. Often part of anonymous hook-up culture
Spirituality	The heart expands, love is felt, and there can be an experience of peace, silence, joy and fulfilment	A sense of dissatisfaction, low self-esteem, numbness, shame; inability to express authentic feelings
Pace	Slowness enables greater capacity for sensitivity, sensation, connection in real-time and expansive awareness	Rushing can compress and compromise capacity to feel and connect with self / other
The Breath	The breath can be focused on and used to amplify sensation, emotion and awareness	The breath is not regarded as an important component in any given sexual repertoire
Essential Qualities	Innocence, Purity, Curiosity, Playfulness, Authenticity	Power struggles, Egoic defences, Trauma re-enactments

Even though sexuality might be an awkward subject many squirm at the thought of discussing; Elders, parents, mentors and teachers could serve today's youth by taking the time and trouble to explore and explain the importance of forging secure attachment bonds. Sex education has to be about more than STIs, how to put on a condom, consent, and the de-coding of the recently confabulated 'rainbow flags' of the identity politics movement... (There are dozens).

Writers like Bessel Van Der Kolk, Peter Levine, Dan Siegel and Deb Dana do a great job of explaining the neuro-biology of secure attachment, and how we've been programmed to live optimally inside a safe environment where we can co-regulate and relax; more on this in the next chapter... Elders can indirectly support the unfolding of a more beautiful, tender, sensitive sexuality that develops over time, along with the indivisibility of other aspects of life. By modelling positive sex, communication and social skills, we can help young adults brave face-to-face encounters with real people, as a way to foster authentic relating, and reap the rewards of co-regulation.

In our modern-day climate, with increasing levels of top-down control and isolation: - to connect; to foster deep conversations; to have meaningful, soulful sex; to refuse to treat ourselves and each other as 'disposable'; to share our lives and our resources, beyond the couple, as small communities that create resilience to the geo-political changes afoot; all these become radical, political acts...

Sex in a Virtual World

The 'New World Order' wants us tracked, traced, atomised and hooked up to AI, harvesting 'data'; issuing punishments and rewards every step of the way. If this is *not* the world we want for ourselves; perhaps it's time to step up, step out, and take a stand? If we don't shape the future we want, others will shape it for us – they're doing it already. Whilst online porn may not be directly linked to the technocratic take-over (and it just *might* be – since it keeps us pseudo-sated and docile!) it definitely *is* connected insofar as it virtualises reality; turning us into addicts, removing the face-to-face, relational dimension - an essential element of our bio-psycho-social well-being.

One of the primary tasks for Elders in *this* society is to 'keep things real', by modelling how to navigate our social landscape in the threatened, and potentially threate*ning*, face to face realm. How might we reclaim Eros from the pornographers and Big Tech? Much will depend on the wholesomeness and skill of mentors and facilitators, and whether sexuality is integrated into a much wider conversation, as this chapter attempts to do. Boundaries and consent are an integral part of any and every conversation and perhaps offer a good entry point for much broader discussions on our sexual expression.

Back to Nicole and Jordan[104] - she answered some of his questions about today's online culture. Young men - the hot ones at any rate - expect sex at the drop of a hat. They both ruefully comment: 'It takes the game away'... The old-fashioned word for the game is *courtship*. They refer to it instead as 'the chase'. I prefer the word *courtship* because it relates to give-and-take, an unfolding process, a paced game of back-and-forth, gradually uncovering more of each other, and oneself. Restraint and reserve are part of the 'game' of 'courtship', since they allow for sexual charge to develop in the spaces between bodies, hearts and minds seeking to know each other, and thus themselves, better. What unfolds in an intimate exchange where love is involved, is a mirroring of primal beauty, innocence, and natural curiosity, reflected back from the eyes and heart of the Other. How and where might Masculine ardour meet Feminine delicacy? Circling and flowing around each other - rising and falling, receding and returning, their dance might owe more to mountains, clouds and rivers than porn re-enactments...

Letting Go of the Goal

'The chase' sounds frantic; always with an end goal in mind. To 'court' a person, or even an idea, is quite possibly goal-less,

104. Peterson, "Provocations"

containing a lesson I learned early on in life from my Zen teacher Reb Anderson: – *'Stay close, and do nothing'...* He was pointing to the art of letting the other reveal themselves to you, as you carefully engage without treading on toes. Social skills are often conspicuous, not exactly by their absence, but certainly by their unobtrusive and seamless qualities. They may be difficult to acquire, especially if there's a lack of opportunity to see them effectively modelled... Some of what's needed is an ability to read cues and facial expressions, whilst also noticing feelings and reactions without necessarily acting them out immediately – something therapists call 'impulse control'. Good impulse control creates space, and consequently more freedom to choose and *explore* – which is what makes life *exciting* – rather than getting sucked into repetitive behaviour loops. We could be forgiven for thinking 'impulse control' is boring – but what if it actually opens up an arena and time to discover *more* about ourselves and each other in safety? Psychotherapist Matt Licata quoted Winnicott in a recent Zoom meeting, saying a 'holding environment' is one where contact and space are *both* present. He was talking about the therapeutic space, but these conditions apply to any intimate environment.

... Nicole came to the realisation with Jordan's help that she didn't need to copy the bad ass boys that she actually didn't admire, just because it's the norm. She didn't need to think that because so much flesh is out there, she somehow needs to bring herself down to the lowest common denominator. Jordan seemed to be giving her permission to say 'no' – *recommending* she say 'no' most of the time, in fact – because instant gratification, though it might provide a dopamine hit in the short term – is never good in the long term. This has been proven with rats. When a female rat sidles past a male rat in a cage his dopamine spikes and he copulates. This works eight times – but the ninth time she sidles past he's like: 'yeah, what*ever*', and instead of copulating, he carries on chewing straw and chatting with his mates. It's called **habituation**, and this experiment is detailed in the book 'Cupid's Poisoned Arrow'.[105] Let this ratty experiment be a cautionary tale! The book explores the 'Carezza' style of love-making - recommended for a take on sex that is all about deepening intimacy and opening the heart, rather than focussing on the orgasm as some kind of jackpot experience, which can keep us stuck in limiting cycles...

We might consider ourselves Dinosaurs, those of us who grew up before dating apps (although I've used a couple of the dinosaur versions myself.) - But what if we hold an important piece for young people?... The knowledge of a different world, a world that - weirdly, may have all but disappeared... We represent a reality where encounter took place first and foremost face-to-face, and sex was uncontaminated by online porn. I'm not saying we knew what we were doing; yet there wasn't the elephant in the room at least, of boys expecting girls, and girls expecting themselves, to perform in ways they'd watched: - coming on her face, anal sex, sex without kissing, no talking, or resting even, fellatio after anal sex... I could go on, but maybe that's enough, and it is somehow painful to list these things. I feel my heart contract, and wonder whether it's 'right' for me to call all this out - or what the kick-back might be? I sit at my computer, and there's a kind of silence in the room, and sadness.

---

105. Marnia Robinson and Douglas Wile, Cupid's Poisoned Arrow: From Habit to Harmony in Sexual Relationships (North Atlantic Books, 2009)

Memoir: Blurred Words

... I feel tears come, I'm mourning something... and I don't know if I'm crying for my own unheld teenager, or for all the emotionally UnEldered teenagers of today... I imagine tears falling onto fresh ink on a white page, and in the blurriness, it's the same teenager, even the gender doesn't matter anymore. I say this as a girl who was once cajoled to give something precious and unnameable to boys who didn't value it, and who was then literally spat on and labelled 'slut' and 'whore'. I feel the ignorance and stupidity of the boys as a wound too – as an expression of their UnEldered Insensitivity. I'm so grateful the internet wasn't around then and I didn't have to worry about images or videos of me posted online – stuff that could never be deleted. I don't know how I could have coped with that. Some young people these days jump off bridges.

I'm painting a black and white picture here – projecting my own history into the scenario. Not all young people have boundary issues – some grow up 'well adjusted' and enjoy good sex and nourishing intimacy – and not all Elders can be saviours in the graphic, grimy, compulsive world we're discussing! It takes a special kind of calling to work in this Arena... young people are also taking matters into their own hands with sites like Nofap.com – 'a secular community-centred sexual health platform designed to help you overcome porn addiction, porn overuse, and compulsive sexual behaviour'.[106]

Sweeping it all under the carpet is not an option for those who profess to care about Youth. Elders are concerned about the emotional lives of future generations – they feel a duty and responsibility to them. We all *know* the internet is riddled with porn and that young kids find ways to access it, and that this is how most of them learn about sex nowadays, and that it's impossible to 'put the genie back in the bottle'. I'm saying: – just because it's *'impossible'*, doesn't make *turning a blind eye an adequate response*. The mental, emotional and spiritual well-being of the young is incumbent on Elders. End of.

106. "NoFap", 2023, https://nofap.com

Jordan and Nicole[107] go on to discuss that it's 'up to us' how others treat us, and speak about getting clear with what we really want – creating a wish list of sorts – which I think is important – although we need to consider what it is we ourselves are *offering* as well as what it is we hope to receive. And I don't mean using your body as a bargaining chip either! – I mean what nurturing, creative qualities do you have, and what practical skills? I have to admit, I've done wish lists myself in the past, sometimes riddled with a sense of futility; unable to recognise my own self-worth, so deep was my sense of shame. The kind of wounding I experienced created cynicism and reserve when it came to engaging with the world, and I feel it still. *So;* having owned that: Let's do Take #2 on wish lists, with more enthusiasm; beginning by acknowledging all our acts and intentions have far-reaching consequences! Every drop in the ocean causes all other drops to displace themselves slightly. It might be unquantifiable, but cumulatively drops make a difference: a dripping tap will fill a bucket.

107. Peterson, "Provocations"

ACTIVITY: Making a Wish List

Every wish list is a *ritual* - an opportunity to clear your mind and connect with your heart. So let's take a moment to settle and deepen our connection to what's going on inside. All those cynical voices that might be arising in *you* now; thank them for their opinion, and remember what they have to say is only that - *opinion.* Tell them to go and take a break right now... Focus on your breathing and on softening your belly. See if you can allow the breath to slow down and come into the lower abdomen. Allow your shoulders to drop. Put your tongue on the roof of your mouth; let your forehead be smooth. Rest in that. Allow the 'tentacles' in your brain that seek to forge new neural pathways to tingle and come alive - we're wired for curiosity and to constantly revise and update our 'maps of understanding' (according to neuroscience and the work of Peter Levine). Staying connected with that tingly feeling in your brain; ask yourself:

'What do I most deeply desire to experience in relationship?' (It could be an intimate relationship, or any way of relating to anyone - It could be ways to upgrade an existing relationship). Allow yourself to taste and feel the question in your body. Don't look for solutions or answers in the mind. Keep your focus, your belly and your breath soft. Imagine yourself living the kind of life you long for - imagine eye contact, smiles, forgiveness, open-heartedness, mutual support. Imagine resting with another, feeling totally at ease; being able to experience safety and adventure within the same relationship. Imagine being able to be assertive and set clear boundaries, imagine being held and touched exactly the way you would like to be touched and held. Imagine letting go and trusting and what that might allow in the realms of sensation and emotion. Take your time with this exercise. Let your imagination take over. Write as much as you like, or draw a picture or a symbol, or even dance, gesture or sound the way you'd like to feel in relationship with another, or even touch yourself the way you'd like to be touched by another...

Take some time when you feel you've completed the imaginative part of the exercise to write down what you felt. It can take the form of a wish list: (think of what you have to offer as well as what you wish to receive)... or maybe just some free-flowing writing about what you need to change in yourself, or what actions you need to take in order to have more of what you want in your life. Be kind to yourself. Make a cup of tea and put a hand of your belly and heart to soothe those parts of the body that you've been tuning into and asking to reveal themselves more deeply to you. Be curious about what sensations arise in the body when you place your hands on these intimate, vulnerable parts of yourself that have many secrets to reveal about your current emotional state. You can return to this exercise anytime you wish. Thank yourself for being open to participate. May we all practice in nourishing and useful ways that yield fruits over time... Maybe you have a friend, coach, mentor or counsellor you could share this exercise with, and chew over your experiences together, helping them to become more integrated.

Can elders, mentors, therapists, teachers, parents, couples, and friends, at least hold a space in their hearts - and circles - where we can access, and possibly process, the grief, longing and confusion of our history and current predicament? Can we *hold the line* and say: some things are beyond the reach of the 'post-modern mash-up', and simply 'Not for Sale'? If we're able to do this, we might somehow harness the 'righteous rage' needed to power a return to Eros as connective tissue in a world where 'nothing works'[108] any more. In this way, the neural networks and social impetus needed to meet our visceral longings and perennial emotional needs might just re-emerge and re-assert themselves once more...

108. Giannina Braschi, "Lorca, Duende, and Art", Art of Individuation (Lecture series, Center of Applied Jungian Studies, November 7, 2022)

Chapter Four

Nurture, Neurobiology, and Narcissism

In the last chapter we looked at sexuality from an archetypal perspective, including some of the cultural developments responsible for eroding the healthy, potent current of Eros running through our lives. In this chapter, we take a look at interpersonal neurobiology and psychology, and how they shape our capacity to connect. Eldering as a project of restructuring society at a more intimate, human scale requires us to understand how nature has designed us for connection, and what results when circumstances throw spanners in the works, dis-regulating our systems and making it harder to develop a sense of belonging. In this chapter, we will gain a basic understanding of the autonomic nervous system (ANS) and its connection to our emotional state, bringing us up to date with the latest neurobiology and 'trauma-informed' understanding... Attachment styles are implicated in how good a job we make of all our relationships, and, when combined with an understanding of the ANS, offer a detailed road map of our often perplexing behaviours. Concurrently, we will take a closer look at one specific diagnosis, its origins and the way it plays out in relationship. I felt moved to share my own personal story here, confessing my naivety about 'healing' Narcissism, and demonstrating how pernicious and intractable the effects of neglect and isolation can be for all of us. It may be the Narcissistic developmental wound urgently needs to be understood and addressed.

Co-Regulation

Co-regulation means growing up with responsive care givers who meet our emotional needs – it's a 'to and fro' social engagement style that teaches trust, communication skills and ultimately self-regulation. Without attuned care, the neural pathways of the brain and other interactive bodily systems don't develop properly.

The best illustration I know of this is the 'Still Face Experiment' (available on YouTube[109]) conducted by Ed Tronick in the 1970s. The essence of his work on co-regulation is captured in this short, impactful clip of a mother and baby. The change in behaviour in the infant when the mother stops interacting in an attuned way, remaining expressionless for a couple of minutes, demonstrates the importance of sensitive engagement from day one. For those of us who didn't grow up with the soothing, confidence-building gifts of a co-regulated existence, but instead regularly faced absence, anger, abuse or unpredictability – 'what then?' Hyper-vigilance becomes the norm because we're expecting the worst; impacting our ability to respond to caring cues: we misconstrue or miss them altogether – unconsciously sabotaging others' attempts at reaching out to us.[110]

... Safety was never learned in a vacuum – it was first experienced interactively. With isolation at epic proportions in the west, it may be that many of us living alone have only the self-soothing routines of a solitary mug of tea, bath, or walk in nature to promote relaxation; alongside the sedating, addictive effects of screens... But humans first learned safety in the arms of caring others when life was interwoven with gaggles of kids, and the intergenerational warmth of a communicative clan. Safety and play are closely connected, and the more opportunities we have to take pleasure in each other's company, as children and adults, the more we learn to co-regulate our nervous systems, with the possibility of experiencing relaxation as expansive and joyous.

On a week-long course entitled 'healing the wounded child', a few years ago, I recoiled when the group facilitator treated me in a heavy-handed manner; becoming defended and circumspect around him. The day after our fall-out; a 'dressing-up party' was planned, and he wanted to wear make-up and paint his nails! I was the one who attended to his request, and as we engaged

109. Mindyour class. "Still Face Experiment Dr Edward Tronick". March 15, 2016. YouTube, 2:49. https://youtube.com/watch?v=YTTSXc6sARg

110. Experiments prove sensory impairment. Dysregulation of the ANS can lead to an inability to recognise or read a smiling face, or inability to identify an object pressed into the palm. Bessel Van Der Kolk, The Body Keeps the Score: Brain, Mind, and Body in the Healing of Trauma (Viking Press, 2014)

with body adornment in close physical proximity; our defensive dynamic was healed, with no words spoken. (For the record - I dressed up as a Pirate!) It's slightly ironic that modern education seems to separate out learning from play. We learn best, quite possibly, when we are at play - and not just facts and figures - but more importantly, perhaps, the subtle, almost magical arts of co-regulation and reconciliation. Trying stuff out without fear of judgement; injecting humour, having a twinkle in our eye; these are all signs of feeling safe and secure. It depends on the type of humour, of course - barbed humour and sarcasm are defence mechanisms, and belong to the 'activated response' category.

Polyvagal Theory in a Nutshell

In his groundbreaking book examining Polyvagal Theory,[111] Stephen Porges describes the three settings of the nervous system: one corresponding to a felt sense of safety; and two belonging to feeling unsafe - which we all experience in similar, but not identical, ways. The 'safe' setting is part of the parasympathetic system; experienced as calm, socially engaged, and well-attuned. This state is experienced when the ventral vagus nerve, reaching from the head and neck and connecting with all the major organs of the body, is dominant. Most - 80% - of the messages travelling along this nerve are from the organs to the brain (afferent); showing to what extent safety is being measured by our bodily senses, rather than our thought processes. We call this 'bottom-up awareness': - a jargon-free way to say the same thing would be to quote Bessel van Der Kolk's best-selling book: 'The Body Keeps the Score'... Whilst the mind likes to think it is in control, in effect, it is responding to stimuli from other biological systems, often below the threshold of consciousness.

When we experience threat in the environment, in the first instance, our system shifts into 'fight or flight' mode - a mobilised response involving the amygdala in the brain and activation of the sympathetic nervous system. The attack and defence mode might reveal itself in a clipped communication style and subtle

111. Steven Porges, The Polyvagal Theory: Neurophysiological Foundations of Emotions, Attachment, Communication, and Self-Regulation (W. W. Norton & Company Ltd., 2011)

clenching of the musculature; our heart beats faster, sending blood to the limbs, the face becomes flushed, the voice gets louder or quieter, we sweat more, and the frontal cortex (the reasoning part of the brain) shuts down, because it is too slow. If the threat continues, we might have to resort to drastic action. Even though most of us live with far fewer physical threats than our ancestors, these ancient systems in the body are 'wired in' and continue to operate - for example, an accusatory tone in someone's voice can be enough to awaken the fight or flight response.

Concurrently, isolation can trigger a threat response below conscious awareness, because we equate safety with being part of a group – the 'safety in numbers' feeling... Many, especially the elderly, but also increasingly the young too, live in isolation and experience a constant state of sympathetic system arousal, which is felt as anxiety. In Stephen Porges' account of the ANS, if it proves impossible to fight or flee, for example in children, who often don't have this luxury when forced to live with abusive care givers, then the body has another very ancient technique available to help us endure the unendurable: the freeze or collapse response.[112] This response is part of the parasympathetic system regulated by the dorsal vagus nerve, so called because it runs along the back of the body - a branch of the vagus nerve found in the fossil records of fish many millions of years old. Deb Dana[113] describes how the Dorsal vagal system is the oldest part of the nervous system at 500 million years old, followed by the sympathetic (fight or flight) system which is 400 million years old, with the ventral vagal system being the newest adaptation in tandem with the frontal cortex of the brain (both around 200 million years old).[114]

Unlike the ventral vagus, the dorsal portion of the nerve is unmyelinated. Myelin is a kind of sheath made of protein and fatty substances surrounding nervous tissue that allows faster transmission of electrical currents between nerve endings.

112. Porges, The Polyvagal Theory

113. Deb Dana, The Polyvagal Theory in Therapy – Engaging the Rhythm of Regulation (W. W. Norton & Company Ltd., 2018)

114. David Robson. "A brief History of the Brain." NewScientist, September 2011, https://newscientist.com/article/mg21128311-800-a-brief-history-of-the-brain

Without myelin, the process is much slower, which shows up in the effects dorsal vagus activation have on other systems in the body... The dorsal vagus nerve offers a way to escape hyper-arousal, when feeling safe is not an option. Think of it as a kind of safety valve which reacts to an activated state in a situation where the impulses of fight or flight are not able to play out. It slows everything down drastically, bringing the system into hypo-arousal; a state of torpor; provisioning an 'off switch'. This is because being constantly triggered or 'activated' is untenable over a long period – if you are unable to take action – it becomes a crazy-making torture. Deb Dana describes the emotional effects of Dorsal vagus activation thus: 'Alone, lost and unreachable'... (Which is a partial way to describe Narcissism discussed below.)

However, it's important to realise that during homeostasis all aspects of the ANS have interactive, positive, regulatory functions. The dorsal vagus branch of the nerve supports digestion, whilst the sympathetic system supports the heart rate and breathing. In fact, without the inhibitory effect of the ventral vagus nerve, the heart would beat dangerously fast. This is known as vagal tone and vagal break – where the vagus nerve inhibits the heartbeat, enabling it to beat slowly.[115]

The signs of being in a dorsal vagal state range on a spectrum from complete dissociation, to disinterest and lethargy. Depressive states, even falling asleep unexpectedly, can be a sign of dorsal vagal activation. Other symptoms include a sense of paralysis, an inability to speak, and feelings of numbness or collapse. An example from personal history: in the initial stages of getting to know an already formed group at university (they had been together for a year when I joined the class), I fell asleep several times. I feared rejection, which was experienced below my conscious awareness, causing me to literally cut out – the manifest behaviour was the clue to the buried emotion! I named this in the encounter group during my counselling training a few years ago, and once I took the plunge to describe what was going on for me, naming it as 'fear of rejection', and the body's shut-down system

115. Dana, The Polyvagal Theory in Therapy

activating to protect me from emotional pain, it stopped; allowing me to fully engage with the group... The power of confession is something we'll unpack in the non-duality chapter.

We should remember these are adaptive responses that can help us survive danger, and go easy on self-recrimination... In psychological terms, the dorsal vagus can be chronically activated in people with trauma histories, manifesting as dissociative, splitting tendencies in the organisation of the self. Not only does it become harder to form lasting relationships when we have protective amnesiac barriers in place, there is an absence of the full spectrum of emotions in those who grew up without a predictable sense of safety and connection. In an 'unplugged state', awareness of body, heart and mind are diminished; hollowing out the relational field... Sedatives artificially induce this state. Late authors and rites of passage leaders Sobonfu and Malidoma Some, from the Dagara tribe in Africa, say that if we are unable to 'emote' as a culture – for example through practicing grieving, then we sedate.[116] The dorsal vagus could be seen as nature's way of providing sedation.

Learning to Distinguish the three States

We can think of the nervous system as generating a 'cascade' of physiological responses[117], bringing order and hierarchy to the body's naturally programmed way of interacting with relational cues. Peter Levine speaks of envisaging the three nervous states as dials being turned and tuned constantly: – *all* are functioning, *all* the time.

*We are helped to increase **ventral vagus dominance** when we are greeted by a warm, friendly face – the belly softens, the heart opens, we are able to enjoy eye contact, the shoulders relax, there is a musical tone (prosody) and mellowness to our voice, as well as innumerable signs of our facial muscles relaxing and softening. Open relating, playfulness, tenderness and empathy are all behaviours associated with ventral vagus dominance.

116. I heard this in a grief ritual led by Briony Greenhill, based on Dagara.
117. Stephen Porges' theory is translated into practical exercises for the therapy room. Dana, The Polyvagal Theory in Therapy

*__Sympathetic activation__ occurs as a response to a predatory, angry or aggressive presence: – our heart rate increases, our face might flush, we get louder or quieter, the body tightens, and the rational, decision-making brain (frontal cortex) closes down, meaning we lose the ability to think clearly, because logical thinking takes too long in survival situations. The reflexes associated with this are fighting or fleeing. Isolation is also interpreted by the body as a type of threat... We also have trigger points (fear of abandonment, for example) that might elicit an anger response in us. Anger is mobilised in this instance as an attempt to prevent loss of some kind.

*The **dorsal vagus dominates** when we are unable to complete the fight or flight response, instead, we go 'offline'. At times, invisibility is clearly advantageous in survival situations, which is not in itself a problem. It's only when we start to believe that hiding or shut down are the only ways to experience safety that we become stuck and might need help. The reflexes and reactions associated with dorsal vagus dominance are: giving up, hiding, freezing, collapse, numbness, falling asleep, depression and dissociation.

When we find ourselves at the bottom of the hierarchy, in order to restore our nervous system to optimal, we must *complete* the dorsal-vagus induced '*aborted* trauma reaction'. We do this by somehow dragging ourselves out of a state of torpor and asserting ourselves; either with the person who caused the shock in the first place; or by re-enacting the fight or flight response, perhaps with a professional acting as an ally... Finding ways to bargain with life that give us back at least some semblance of empowerment and dignity are at the root of moving back up the ANS hierarchy.[118]

Case study: A recent client came to see me who was constantly weepy, which I recognised as a collapsed response. She had experienced a very difficult birth of her second child when medical professionals unexpectedly took over and performed a Caesarean section where she was heavily sedated. Her husband

118. A system called 'Emotional Logic' created by Devon based Dr Trevor Griffiths to help understand and act on the bargaining process. "Relatedness", 2023, https://relatedness.net

passed out at the sight of blood. The clinical de-brief that was supposed to happen between her and the doctors never took place in the hospital. She was stuck with a sense of helplessness, was often depressed and at times even felt suicidal because she saw herself as 'useless' in being the rock she wanted to be for her family. We worked together in role play to confront the medical professionals who had behaved in a high-handed manner and then refused her the opportunity to process the experience in a meeting afterwards. After only two or three sessions, her collapse abated and she was able to reengage with her own sense of agency, and thus with her family. The work was relatively simple, and we carried on looking at other material for several more sessions; yet she had been stuck in a weepy, powerless state for a year and a half before accessing the help she needed to effect a return to the optimal ventral-vagus dominant state[119] by completing a trauma reaction.

Learning to Self-Regulate

Let's review, for a moment, some of the approaches on offer helping us better understand and come to terms with our own histories, the traumas we have endured - to a greater or lesser degree - and the post-traumatic growth available from leaning into the challenges and obstacles we face with the help of one, or a number, of therapeutic modalities. Choosing a trauma-informed therapist who understands the power and pervasiveness of the ANS in our lives can help us, over time, to access our full emotional range, including joy and trust. We can learn to channel the fight or flight response appropriately, for example - through becoming assertive - rather than simply 'unplugging' or 'zoning out' via the dorsal vagus. All of these responses are our birthrights, and when we learn to monitor, interpret and engage our nervous system consciously, we 'enlarge our window of tolerance', and our sense of agency, meaning we get to stay longer in a ventral vagus state. In this way, we gradually learn to assert ourselves when necessary, and thus self-regulate; pre-empting our own reactions by tracking ourselves moment to moment and

119. *Peter Levine, Waking the Tiger: Healing Trauma (North Atlantic Books, 1997)*

introducing practices like soothing self-talk, or learning how to communicate more effectively with others in situations beyond the therapy room. Sometimes having stronger boundaries might be the answer. Even just a simple breathing exercise where we clench and release the fist once per breath cycle helps us to attune to our tightness, and capacity to release, over and over, so we become familiar with the ever shifting patterns of our emotional responses, and use the fist as a representation of our conscious capacity to regulate.

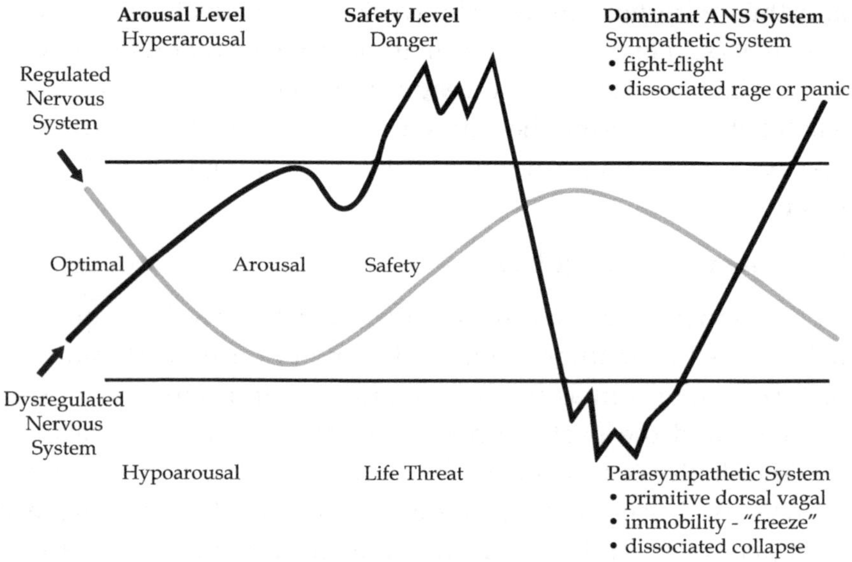

Figure 1: Window of Tolerance[120]

All states experienced by us are symptoms of the condition of our ANS, and are healthy and normal, evolving as they did in tandem with our environment. It should be good news to us, in a certain sense, that emotions like anger and withdrawal all make perfect sense in the survival realm. The only problem is when we get 'stuck' in any one place and don't know how to dial up or dial down into a different response. Judging ourselves adds insult to injury and is a sure way to make things worse... Humans are possibly the only species who can bring conscious control to the nervous system, yet by the same token, we're also the only

120. 'The Healing Power of Emotion' Siegel, Focha, Solomon et al. J. Wheatley-Crosbie, based on Porges 1997.

animal who gets lost in fruitless cycles of unhelpful behaviour; reinforcing it with repetitive thinking and neurotic behaviours. Caged animals exhibit neuroses too, but wild animals literally shake off any trauma stuck in the body, regulating themselves naturally. We're not seeking to eradicate any of our responses, but to understand more fully the physiology that happens 'under the radar' of our conscious perception, enabling us to better manage our emotional and inter-relational reality.

The Role of Elders

Once upon a time, in group settings, Elders were tasked with 'enlarging the windows of tolerance' of initiates in their care. Circles where many used to gather, and in some places, where they gather still, are ways to choreograph opening to Self and Other, gaining courage and visibility in the process. In traditional cultures, this would also entail attuning to Nature and the power of the Great Beyond... These are ways for us to flex our nervous systems still, changing the prevailing hidden beliefs that so often end up running the show, with the possibility of building a sense of Belonging – beyond protective insularity – that's eluded many of us thus far. Despite our modern-day, remote-controlled, private lives secretly clouded with free-floating anxiety; we are born hard-wired to connect with the depths of our inner worlds, one another, and the potent power of Life.

In the relational field, safety is experienced as being able to stay with what is unfolding moment to moment – whilst experiencing a sense of 'standing our ground' – it's ok to bring our uniqueness to the table, relaxing into the felt sensations of the body. Sharing more of our authentic selves is a risk that becomes easier as we build rapport and learn to trust... We might find ourselves softening and relaxing one moment, then fear of overwhelm might cause our muscles to tighten. Can we learn to enjoy the rise and fall, the sway and swoop; can we dance and be danced by life in ways we only partially control? Can we touch the place inside where we don't seek to know the outcome, but where meeting the other is an unfolding, precious adventure without destination or goal?

Therapeutic Considerations

If you know you have trauma to work through (termed 'undigested experience' in Psychophonetics)[121] - group work might feel too intense or prove difficult to access; in which case, a skilled therapist might be the best option... Sometimes one-to-one therapy is the optimal choice if quiet, focussed attention are needed to help connect with deeply buried pain. The therapist becomes the ally in the room, enabling a detailed, patient exploration of your inner world...

In the person-centred approach, the exchange centres on empathy, enabling the client to set the pace in exploring whatever he or she wishes, in a non-judgemental atmosphere. We might engage the many facets of the self, known as 'configurations', treating them as individual characters in the theatre of our inner world – noticing how they interact and perhaps who they represent from the outside world that we have come to internalise. Dick Schwartz, the creator of Internal Family Systems (IFS) specialises in this method. There are so many therapeutic approaches that finding the right one might be a challenge in itself. CBT (Cognitive Behavioural Therapy) is often short-term and solution-focussed. An article in the BACP journal[122] from 2021 states that 70% of clients are looking for more than empathy from a therapist – they are seeking challenge to enable evolution – demanding both 'yin' and 'yang' qualities from the practitioner. A good therapist, like any well-integrated person, will have developed a spectrum of responses that can be soft, subtle and deeply empathic, or gently challenging, unapologetic and laser-sharp.

Therapeutic capability enables clients to contact 'core wounds'; finding ways to process deeply buried pain and move towards integration, displayed in real-time as flexibility and competence. Cultivating 'integration' in a therapeutic container is based on

---

121. A therapeutic modality where parts work, the inherent qualities of sound, and the work of Rudolf Steiner combine. Yehuda Tagar, Philophonetics love of Sounds: Language for inner life (Persephone Publications, 1996)

122. Matthew Wotton and Graham Johnston. "Embracing challenge in therapy." British Association of Counselling and Psychotherapy, November, 2021. https://bacp.co.uk/bacp-journals/therapy-today/2021/november-2021/articles/embracing-challenge-in-therapy

the idea that we have 'disavowed' aspects of ourselves, that, once brought into awareness, and given permission to express themselves, form a fluid, yet coherent, 'self-actualised' whole. In the person-centred approach, our exile from the authentic, 'organismic' self within, is deemed to have taken place in childhood, when the introjected values of our parents - known as 'conditions of worth' - became obstacles we had to mould ourselves around to win love and approval. Whilst there is undoubtedly truth in this approach; some sort of acculturation process, in the form of rules and acceptable behaviour, exists in all societies. We often call someone with robust mental health 'well-adjusted'. There is a balancing act of compliance and self-expression taking place, both in childhood and adulthood... Setting a limit, perhaps, to the notion of what an 'integrated' or 'self-actualised' person might actually look like...

The Illusion of 'Enlightenment for Sale'

'Self-Actualisation' as a tenet of the person-centred ('humanistic') approach founded in 1950s America, by Carl Rogers and others, has been seized upon by Gurus of the 'New Age' personal growth and enlightenment movement that took off in the 1980s and '90s with programmes like EST which then morphed into Landmark Education. The latter used to describe their teachings as 'applied philosophy', which I actually found to be very useful in my late 30s and early 40s... Notwithstanding; the commercialisation of psychology and 'spirituality' known as 'growth work' would have us believe in an 'end goal' with price tag attached. Advertising campaigns focus on stock images of elated individuals jumping in the air and waving their arms in the middle of a sunny field of wheat - totally de-contextualised.

But what if 'self-actualisation' is all about the right conditions - social conditions - that might enable us to flourish?... What if it's down to all of us to work to provide the right climate for 'actualisation' to embed itself in individual lives...? The institution of Elders in traditional cultures understood this well; 'personal growth' is first and foremost a collective endeavour, which has also been a tenet of the liberal-leaning left, before the

Woke polarisation of recent years. The 'Enlightenment' taught in Buddhism is based on the notion of liberation as a profoundly *social package*, at least in the Mahayana/Soto Zen tradition I've been exposed to. This is in sharp contra-distinction to the idea of *individual* 'Spiritual Awakening' bought 'off the peg' and marketed as such... The idea it has to be woven collectively, and cultivated incrementally has less commercial appeal, *no doubt!*

In the Zen Buddhist 'field of inter-dependent co-arising' we're all in it together; *I am* because *you are*, and I can't save my own ass without saving yours and vice versa. Incidentally, Christians have something to say about 'coveting your neighbour's ass', which might or might not be related! The admonition (in both camps, it seems to me) helps nip competitiveness in the bud, recognising cooperation as a much better way to live. It implies we're all interconnected; there's nowhere to get to, except here & now – with whatever is arising... It means that 'inside' and 'outside', 'self' and 'other', are false constructs employed to enable us to pick up and put down concepts, objects and opinions in a world dominated by defensive egos that never learned to co-regulate with attuned others. In Buddhist Enlightenment, the world of discrete objects crumbles along with the ego's ramparts; everything becomes fluid and inter-related, impermanent and contingent on everything else. Which is why the art of 'letting go' – or 'non-attachment' as they like to say – is so important, and why 'self-actualisation' is *not* for sale: – simply put – it's *not* a *thing* that can be grasped or bottled, and so – how could it ever be *traded*?!... More on that in the chapter on non-duality.

One-to-One or Group Work?

It seems we're getting ahead of ourselves right now – meanwhile, back in the relative realm of duality, we can envisage limits to the reach of one-to-one therapy. Therapists are not Gods, nor, *alas,* are they the loving parents some of us never had, although they might act as suitable stand-ins for absent attachment figures, enabling us to forge new neural pathways; developing trust and relational depth in the process... Therapists are individuals holding space for exploration as best they can, within the confines of their own conditioning, some of which we hope they have worked through in their own therapy. As therapists, we are trained to work with and alchemise our own reactions, and to continue engaging openly and empathically with our clients. Therapy is not a magic wand though, nor a perfect formula.

'The group' supplies a quality of interaction one-to-one work never can; a dilated lens through which to experience our own aliveness - only in community settings can we develop the wide array of responses that define 'social intelligence'; an immersive great adventure forming a key part of our humanity.[123] In group work, we find that building resilience, empathy and listening skills is part of the group dynamic, also (not to be ignored!) offering a more affordable approach to therapy... New cultures are created and witnessed in groups. What might emerge when we start from scratch, interacting and engaging with each other, with awareness and candour, in a confidential, safe container? The wisdom of the collective emerges thus. We briefly explored the original 'power of the circle' in the 'Initiation' chapter; in modern times, the 'encounter group' emerged out of the person-centred approach of Carl Rogers. More recently, the 'World Work' of Amy and Arnold Mindell engages 'the circle' on this basis; harnessing conflict in group settings, unpacking layers of grievance, hostility and preconceived ideas, in search of common ground and healing. Not for the faint hearted, perhaps, and yet essential work for our troubled times...

'Meta Cognition' and Therapy

One of the skills developed in social interactions of all kinds is 'mentalising' - a term coined by Peter Fonagy, eminent psychoanalyst and clinical psychologist, to describe the process of conceptualisation and socialisation. The term implies a level of 'meta-cognition' - being able to 'run the story' of what's going on in any given interaction - taking into account social and environmental cues and more. 'Mentalisation' is an extra-

123. Irvin Yalom has perhaps written the most authoritative guide currently available on the subject: Irvin D. Yalom and Molyn Leszcz. The theory and practice of group psychotherapy (Basic books, 2020)

ordinary feat of human computation that involves our whole self: - mental, physical, emotional and intuitive - and one that also weaves together past, present and future time, no less. We 'guess' at meanings in the present, and derive from the imputed meaning a sense of appropriate behaviour... This, because we have intended outcomes for the future (and if we're well attuned, a sense of 'how we come across' to others, including the likely outcomes of our behaviours) whilst also holding in mind wider contexts informed by the past and the world around us. We seem to have to pick apart the process to realise just how complex it is, and how accomplished we often already are (assuming developmental and social cadres have allowed us to develop some skilfulness).

Therapists are trained to 'upgrade conversations' using meta-cognition, meaning we take the risk of noticing and drawing attention to the import of twists and turns of any given exchange during client sessions. We may remark on repeating patterns, and wonder what might be behind them, asking whether the client would like to explore them, or even try on 'alternative possibilities' within the frame of the 'mentalising' process. In mirroring back to a client what we perceive in their behaviour, we are enabling them to see themselves more clearly. Ongoing professional supervision offers the same kind of mirroring process to the therapist.

We are *all* navigating exchanges with others all the time with greater or lesser degrees of success. If success is defined as harmonious relationships; it's more likely achieved in those with well-regulated nervous systems, than those 'well versed' on the theoretical models (Hopefully one enhances the other…) Meta-cognition is an advanced practice, building on previously completed developmental stages, starting from birth, and emerging as balance between the left and right hemispheres of the brain. Rapport-building is primarily an activity of the right hemisphere that reassembles the world after the left hemisphere has pulled it apart for 'analysis' - more on this in the non-duality chapter.

When healthy to-and-fro exists, both internally and externally, the emergent-self intuits 'all is well' - the world feels safe, comfortable; somewhat predictable, and to some extent, we have a sense of *mattering* to the outside world. This brings with it a palpable sense of self, originating in the embodied experience of the responsive other. Thus: because I matter, I must *exist* (it's *that* fundamental!), and hence my feelings will prevail upon others who will seek to meet my needs...

The Personal is Political

Imagine an opposite scenario for a moment, if you will; one where I am ignored or side-lined, or possibly even actively abused. The co-regulatory functions provided by face-to-face attunement are now denied the individual. This can happen at any age or stage of childhood development, but is perhaps most impactful in the infant, and because we're born 'hard wired to connect', the failure to do so is catastrophic. The result is we begin to *doubt our very existence,* and certainly our inherent significance, since the people in our life failed to validate it in a powerful enough way for us to feel soothed and satisfied. Attention is then perceived as a rare and precious, unpredictable commodity that needs to be fought for and fought over, engendering the fight or flight (mobilised) response. The identity forged in this unfolding drama can be labelled 'attention-seeking' - one of the defining traits of the Narcissist, a condition we'll examine in more depth later in the chapter...

Notice how much easier it is to pathologise a person, than it is to name, for example, the struggle of families to meet the needs of curious, lively children, due to economic pressure necessitating long working hours. To reform the latter would require some kind of revolution: the restructuring of society from the ground up, in order to give infants and children the attuned care they need. The alternative; preserving the status quo; then diagnosing and labelling people with a multitude of 'disorders', continues to propel big business across many verticals, including Big Pharma and even the helping professions; generating revenue for CEOs, shareholders, and the individual. Of course, it's complex and nuanced, yet it is hoped broad brush-strokes help us perceive a note-worthy pattern, nonetheless. Clearly, a pill will never be invented to cure the Narcissistic wound, although if it were possible I'm sure they'd be working on it! The *only* cure for Narcissism is better family and community care which requires stronger social cohesion. Yet parents and other helpers can't do their job properly in a vacuum... To jump back on my soapbox, one of the wealthiest families in the world, the Rockefeller dynasty, are largely responsible for the founding of modern medicine.[124], [125], [126], [127], [128]

Attachment Theory

Attachment theory, first developed in the 1950s, by Bowlby and Ainsworth, and later Main and Solomon, was one of the first attempts of 'science' via experimental psychology, to understand the importance of strong bonds between mothers and infants (and other attachment figures). The 'truths' discovered, described and endorsed by these researchers were instinctively known and enacted by our forebears, especially mothers who have always understood the importance of tender rapport and attuned care for the young. This makes *them, extended family, and indeed the*

124. Anne-Emanuelle Birn and Elizabeth Fee. "The Rockefeller Foundation and the international health agenda." The Lancet 381, no. 9878 (2013): 1618-1619.

125. Eric Schmidt. "How Rockefeller Created the Business of Western Medicine", Meridian Health Clinic, last modified December 27, 2019, https://meridianhealthclinic.com/how-rockefeller-created-the-business-of-western-medicine

126. Compare the Lancet article with Eric Schmidt. The Lancet lays bare the thinly veiled playbook of the RF. One of the greatest achievements cited in the Lancet article is tackling Yellow Fever, but only in cargo shipments that carried the mosquito to distant shores, since locals seemed already resistant! Before getting his tentacles into medicine, Rockefeller owned around 90% of oil refineries at the turn of the 20th century. He saw the potential to synthesise medicines using petro-chemicals.

127. Only 3% of the oil industry is used for pharmaceuticals, but 99% of pharmaceuticals contain petro-chemicals. Agnes Zalewski. "Petroleum in Real Life: Pills", Context – Energy Examined, last modified November 23, 2019, https://context.capp.ca/articles/2019/feature-petroleum-in-real-life-pills

128. The Rockefeller Empire, in tandem with JP Morgan Chase, owns over half of US pharmaceuticals. In 1939, a 'drug trust' alliance was formed between the Rockefeller Empire and IG Farben (now Bayer). Auschwitz, was a 100% subsidiary of IG Farben. Rockefeller funded institutions that preached the new model of medicine based on synthesised drugs. The importance of herbal medicine and diet were disregarded, ridiculed and de-funded. Doctors who resisted were sometimes imprisoned. "Pharmaceutical industry", Sourcewatch, last modified July 17, 2017, https://sourcewatch.org/index.php/Pharmaceutical_industry

clan, village or tribe (including, of course, the Elders) the *original 'experts'* in the field of creating co-regulatory environments to meet a child's emotional needs...

The Four Attachment Styles

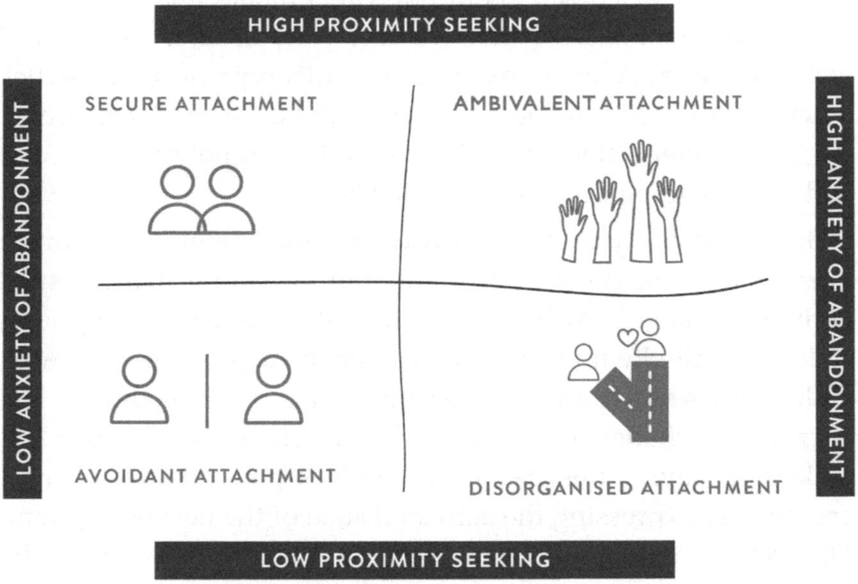

Figure 2: *The Four Attachment Styles (Source: Motivating Marriages)*

Nonetheless, Mary Ainsworth and colleagues[129] 'discovered' **three distinct behavioural responses** in infants up to the age of two by noting their behaviour in the 'strange situation' experiment. This experiment consisted of researchers observing the reactions of young children using two-way mirrors, when the primary care giver left the room for a short time. From repeated observation, the enactment of this brief 'rupture and repair' ritual are detailed below... We are all likely to have a default attachment setting that persists into adulthood; yet, the truth is more likely that our systems are adaptive and intelligent enough to use different attachment styles in different settings as we mature and engage with different individuals, notwithstanding that secure attachment may remain elusive for those who never experienced

129. *Samantha Reisz, Robbie Duschinsky and Daniel J. Siegel. "Disorganized attachment and defense: exploring John Bowlby's unpublished reflections." Attachment & Human Development 20, no. 2 (2018): 107-134.*

it in childhood.[130] We will also include the fourth attachment style in our discussion, which was discovered in subsequent research, and is basically a 'ramped up' version of one of the others.

The first style is termed '**Secure** attachment', and equates to what we have discussed about polyvagal theory and the ventral vagal dominant state when we feel safe, secure, loved, and welcome. In attachment experiments, this type of infant settles quickly after experiencing a rupture with her primary care giver. We have covered this above in the section on polyvagal theory, and nothing more needs to be added here.

The second style is '**Ambivalent** attachment', sometimes referred to as 'anxious ambivalent'; but for simplicity, let's stick with 'ambivalent'. With this attachment style, when the young child is reunited with her mother, he or she acts out angrily, with flailing limbs and loud protestations, refusing to be soothed. The energy is of challenge – 'where are you when I need you?' 'I'll make you pay!'... this behaviour evolves pre-verbally – sound and gesture expressing the activated state of the nervous system. The style is called 'ambivalent' because this type of infant can be very clingy in between tantrums – since trust in the caregiver's reliability and safe, soothing presence has been compromised. Whether the cause is work or study commitments, volatile behaviour and mood swings (the possible re-enactment of historical trauma in the adults' lives), addiction, distraction, or prioritising a partner or sibling over the infant in question – the care giver is not consistently available. The message the ambivalent infant internalises is: 'I'm unlovable'. This belief sets in motion '*giving to get*' behaviours, where he or she comes to believe love has to be earned. Notice again how easy it is to pathologise the infant by putting him or her into an attachment 'category', or if not the infant, then we can pass the buck to the care giver; when in fact the mother often has to do the work of a whole village – if we're to trust the African saying that: '*it takes a whole village to raise a child.*'

---

130. This is the way attachment theory was taught to me by Philip Jones at: "Philip Jones Couples, Relationship Counsellor in Devon", 2019, https://howloveworks.co.uk/therapy

Films like 'Sorry We Missed You' by Ken Loach in 2019 and 'Nest' in 2021 featuring Jude Law and Carrie Coon mirror to us just how fragile the nuclear family structure is, and how much children suffer in the precarious circumstances resulting from, amongst other things, the burden of debt heaped upon individual families in today's world – the essence of the former film, whereas in the latter, it's the protagonist's delusions of grandeur or 'Narcissism' that are his family's downfall.

The third style is observed in the **'avoidant'** child who uses a different way to communicate distress, becoming loose-limbed, whilst looking away and pouting with down-cast eyes. However, when a heart monitor is applied to these infants in the experiment, it reveals an elevated heart rate. What is happening here? The infant exhibits physiological stress and yet at the same time 'dumbs down' or 'masks' his or her reaction. In survival terms, proximity of the care giver is key, and it could be that a 'controlled response', buys the infant the desired closeness. These individuals suppress needs and desires in an attempt to please; to be a 'good girl' or 'boy' – someone exemplary at complying and adapting – enabling the care giver to continue doing 'a bad job', which is better than doing 'no job' at all (abandonment). Sometimes the child intuits that this is the 'safest way' to play the game, and perhaps the best way to keep mummy or daddy close; proximity being equated with survival in the instinctual reality of the infant.

The response is complex because it could denote having 'given up' in the dorsal vagal sense, and yet the elevated heart rate suggests the infant is still engaged and activated... Withdrawal might be the best chance the nervous system has to create a kind of 'truce', and yet, it's an uneasy truce, indicated by the conflicting signals of the rapid heartbeat, whilst looking away. In fact, the infant has come to know that adopting a passive stance is the best way to ensure the presence of the care giver. Passivity, after all, is much easier to tolerate, from the parent's point of view, and even the infant's, than rage. In this way, when needs go unmet, the young child is able to distance him or herself from unbearable feelings, in a trajectory that leads, over time, from 'distress, to despair, to detachment', according to the book 'Attachment in Psychotherapy'.[131] This is very much in line with dorsal vagus activation.

Mature Self-Regulation

'Avoidant' traits in an adult should not be confused with emotional self-sufficiency. The latter is an evolved, self-directed state of balance which comes about in maturity when the younger self has had their attachment needs met - making the transition to the relative independence of adulthood much easier. It reveals itself as a sense of stability, integration and creative independence, in someone who can tolerate solitude, and yet also enjoys company, and can switch relatively easily between the two: termed 'self-regulation' in developmental psychology. Conversely, 'avoidant' traits in the adult have a brittle quality, and these individuals are unlikely to take joy from their 'state of independence', but rather experience solitude as fear-based capitulation and withdrawal. Insecure attachment leaves a kind of hollowness in its wake, whereas securely attached individuals are calmer, and find social engagement and empathy easy. We should also consider the myth of competitive independence fostered by capitalist culture; idealising individual success, even at the expense of others. Stephen Covey[132] in his widely acclaimed book reveals that independence is simply a developmental step between the dependence of childhood and the more natural and highly evolved state of 'inter-dependence'.

Looking at power dynamics in the next chapter through the lens of the Karpman triangle, we'll see how our finely-tuned autonomic nervous system might work 'for and against'[133] us, depending on circumstance, often 'below the radar,' *and on automatic pilot.*

---

131. David J. Wallin, Attachment in Psychotherapy (Guilford Press, 2007)

132. First published in 1989, and has sold over 15 million copies in 38 languages. Stephen Covey. The Seven Habits of Highly Effective People (Simon arid Schuster, 1989)

133. This is not meant to sound judgemental. We've already seen how all ANS responses are adaptive to circumstance. However, the shaping of the neural architecture of the brain in childhood means we may have encoded deficiencies or repetitive loops that don't serve us as adults in our interactions with others.

There can also be a level of conscious engagement, even used manipulatively to trigger one another. For example, withdrawal can be used strategically, AKA 'the silent treatment' - a kind of punishment attempting to regain power in any given situation... When used on an 'anxious ambivalent' attachment type; a 'fear of abandonment' reaction is *sure* to follow - allowing the silent party to wrap the 'needy' one around their little finger... Securely attached people will also find protracted distancing difficult; as they won't understand its meaning - in an abundant, attuned universe - why not just talk about it? Sue Johnson and Diane Poole Heller explore the playing out of attachment styles in adulthood in more depth, especially in one-to-one committed relationships. As we will see later in this chapter, the Narcissist uses distancing and approach (devaluing and idealising) behaviours cyclically as a substitute for the intimacy that he or she finds impossible to navigate or tolerate.

Ramped-Up Ambivalent Attachment

Chaotic, Disorganised attachment[134] was classified later on from extensive research, and occurs when the conflicting neural messages described in the two insecure attachment styles above, reach their apotheosis. This pattern of insecure attachment occurs when opposing messages of 'run towards' (since we're hard-wired to connect) and 'run away' (since we're feeling unsafe in the presence of our care-givers) combine and collide in the nervous system simultaneously. The result is an inability to focus, a sensation of spinning on the spot, of being unable to rest or 'take up space' in a way that allows us to engage or participate in the world - meaning we are caught in a no man's land of contradictory neuro-biological and emotional impulses.

The results are a kind of hyper-vigilance and restlessness that correspond with many of the features of the ADHD brain: - easily overwhelmed, not knowing where to start in performing executive functions, poor impulse control - that jittery feeling causing us to 'blurt' rather than 'calmly consider'; difficulty in

134. This, the fourth attachment style was 'introduced' by Main and Solomon in 1990. Reisz, Duschinsky and Siegel, "Disorganized attachment and defense"

being on time, leaving things 'til the last minute; getting easily distracted and being poorly organised. It's not just a lack of suitable attachment figures, but the structure of modern life with its attendant multiple tabs and screens competing for our attention simultaneously, continuously; leading us increasingly towards the dizzying sensation of spinning on the spot, not achieving anything, and not being able to relate meaningfully and in depth with those around us. These are the hallmarks of chaotic, disorganised attachment – the most challenging kind of attachment style to live with – holding up the spectre of a possible 'new normal' in society at large if lack of attuned care, countless distractions, economic pressure and increasing top-down control continue apace. We'll look at the ramifications of this in the 'Psychological Warfare' chapter.

The Roots of a New Narcissistic Normal

All insecure attachment styles make us, to some extent, predictable puppets pulled by the strings of inescapable interpersonal neuro-biological deficits. When attention is scarce, children grow into adults with unmet needs, longing for the gifts of co-regulation to help with daily living, enabling engagement with the full range of highly-evolved social skills that might engender meaningful lives of our choosing. It's possible, as a culture, we emphasise left-brain intellectual achievement *at the expense* of social intelligence and empathy – those right-brain attributes that provide the cohesion and impetus for human bonding- oiling the wheels of wellness and stability throughout our lives.[135]

...When the attentions offered by primary care givers were insufficient to generate a robust kind of reciprocity, Narcissism is one possible result. Excesses of attention-seeking behaviour are all around, if we're prepared to look through that lens, pointing to a possible collective 'love deficit' in society at large. Buying flash cars, and consumerism in general, being obsessed with

---

135. ZeitgeistHungary. "Dr. Gabor Maté on ADHD, Bullying and the Destruction of American Childhood". October 1, 2012. YouTube, 33:40. https://youtube.com/watch?v=UrZL2CnUSRg

appearance and success, seeing other people as pawns in our own game, rather than as separate beings with their unique realities and needs, are some of the foremost, but not definitive, traits of Narcissism so common as to be unremarkable, in today's world. Furthermore, Capitalism feeds into our insecurities by providing us more and more opportunities to act-out; setting the bar ever higher, encouraging us to *'buy things we don't need, with money we don't have, to impress people we don't know,'* according to Dave Ramsey.

Narcissism and Mythology

The term Narcissism derives from the Greek myth of Narcissus who fell in love with his own reflection, demonstrating that self-obsession is nothing new... In our current 'age of malaise', we can look to many archetypes for reference; even the 'damsel in distress' could reveal Narcissistic tendencies... In the original version she appears an innocent victim trapped in a tower; yet today we can imagine her as 'lost maiden' (who never received enough love or attention) forlornly waving a hanky out of the 'tower' in which she's trapped (her limited childhood bonding experiences). Only the co-regulatory effects of the relational other can set her free... Along comes the unsuspecting knight full of good intentions... After a suitable number of battles with thorns, spinning wheels etc. (take note - play hard to get!) the knight's connecting kiss finally succeeds in unfreezing the realm. The kingdom comes back to life, birds sing in the trees, the rivers flow with milk and honey...

However, what happened to the missing chapters they skip in the original tale in the rush to arrive at the 'happily ever after' conclusion? The compulsion for validation might mean the 'rescue operation' becomes increasingly intense, as the princess keeps adding conditions and items to her Wish List. The partner meanwhile, becomes increasingly distraught and exhausted in a bid to satisfy her desires. There are many permutations on this theme which can happen across genders, and indeed in same sex relationships, and many different life scenarios. Equally, it could be the man making more and more demands on his partner

– needing her to demonstrate supposed 'loyalty' by giving up healthy platonic friendships, and interaction with family members, even: – a toxic trait that should be questioned and resisted at every opportunity. For the Narcissist, life feels deeply unsafe and very lonely, necessitating a need to control others at every opportunity.

The Narcissistic Wound

YouTube is full of videos explaining the perils of being hooked up with a Narcissist, offering tips and advice on how to spot one, and tales of hapless victims eventually recognising and extricating themselves from the situation. I'm not denying the reality of Narcissism – it's all too real – but in scapegoating Narcissists, we avoid the inconvenient truth that they are Grown and Made by Us, in the West, cultured and primed by the inimical conditions we are often forced to live under.

No one consciously plans to grow up to be labelled a 'Narcissist', yet children are naturally narcissistic. They think the world revolves around them, and in a sense it does, so long as they are not able to meet their own needs and care for themselves. Children's appetites and bodily functions demand adult attention, whilst acquiring communication skills, with nuanced tone, emotion, gesture and expression requires regular daily input, fuelled in part by children's endless 'Why...?' questions. Exchanges of all sorts help develop a context for the individual in space and time, whilst developing a multi-faceted, complex persona – a process we often take for granted, though psychologists have been examining the minutiae for some time...

Memoir: The Lonely World of the Narcissist

My ex-partner suffered from the solipsism of Narcissism, and our dynamic had a quality I recognised from previously observing certain traits in myself, previous relationships, and members of my family of origin. Rich (not his real name) has read this memoir and commented that he thought it was quite a compassionate rendition, which is part of why I feel ok about publishing it here. Most importantly, I hope to help people understand the origins, and recognise the signs, of this most intractable psychological condition. In our relationship, I wasn't very familiar with the symptoms from a clinical perspective; and when I stumbled across an ebook online, I was blown away by how much of it made complete sense and accurately described my relationship with him. I ended up screenshotting almost every page! Here's a sample:

> The narcissist... is still the hurt child. His attitude serves a paramount need: not to be hurt again. The narcissist anticipates his abandonment, and, by trying to avoid it, he precipitates it... To be in control - this unconquerable drive - is a direct reaction to having been abandoned, ignored, neglected, avoided, smothered, or abused at an early stage in life. "Never again" - vows the narcissist - "If anyone will do the leaving, it will be me".[136]

It's important to look deeply into the narcissistic condition because as Vaknin goes on to say:

> "it is a pernicious condition, the root of many mental health disorders, and very poorly understood, diagnosed, reported and studied. It was recognised as a mental health category only in 1980 (DSM III)".[137]

Whilst awareness and education are gaining traction, on my three counselling trainings, the topic was only covered once on a CPD day

---

136. Sam Vaknin. "Chapter 2, The Soul of a Narcissist, The State of the Art", HealthyPlace, last modified July 15, 2018, https://healthyplace.com/personality-disorders/malignant-self-love/chapter-2-the-soul-of-a-narcissist-the-state-of-the-art

137. Sam Vaknin. "About Sam Vaknin, Author of Narcissism Book", HealthyPlace, last modified May 13, 2019, https://healthyplace.com/personality-disorders/malignant-self-love/my-story

organised by an independent counselling forum. To go back to our relationship – we discovered a year in to our two and a half years as a couple that my partner's mother haemorrhaged at birth. She was taken away to receive emergency care, and spent four and a half weeks recuperating. During this time, Rich was placed in a cot in the hospital, where he spent his time looking up at the ceiling, swaddled tight in a blanket that prevented him from scratching his face. Occasionally a dummy with funny tasting stuff was pushed in his mouth – a sedative no doubt. He related all this to me after several hypnotherapy regression sessions that allowed him to recover memories... The only time he was picked up was for feeding or nappy changing. Hunger, wakefulness, confusion, disorientation, terror and isolation were the daily 'routine' for this tiny, new, intelligent, vulnerable, sentient being, on entering the world...

The Origins of the False Self

As a new-born baby in a cot, Rich remembers finding out he had a body by being able to flex his neck enough to look down and see it there. Warm blooded mammals normally become aware of their body first in contact with the mother's, and possibly siblings' skin, locating themselves in time and space via connection, warmth and belonging. Not so in this instance. The unbearable terror and confusion are hard to imagine: interminable days as a pre-verbal infant, without the benefits of language, logic, or a single friend who could explain the situation and offer some relief. In such scenarios, the human mind is capable of an amazing feat of inventiveness to fend off the excruciating sense of abandonment, and this is how Rich survived – by creating a 'false self'. The splitting of the self allowed for a saviour, soul-mate, and protector to materialise, providing Rich salve and sanity in a universe where his nervous system was constantly on red alert. The incomprehensible, endless loneliness and panic eased, and the world appeared at least somewhat safe. The dissociative splitting of Rich's psyche is what allowed him to survive the intolerable; enabling his nervous system to come to rest as he entered into relationship with an imaginary 'other'; even though this 'other' was an invention of his own imagination, and inside his own psyche. The adaptive capacity of human embodied consciousness is nothing short of extraordinary!

... Yet the split self becomes a permanent feature that can't instantly mend of its own accord when circumstances change for the better. This 'split self' makes a pact internally, that states the world is mad, bad and dangerous; safety exists only in facing inward, inside the Narcissist's self-created, delusional bubble. He or she creates a 'blood brother or sister' internal bond where the 'Oath of Fealty' extends only to parts of the split self; who promise never to leave, not even for a moment. This means for anyone getting involved with the Narcissist, that they are incapable of receiving your care. Love, for them, is deeply unsafe and also unreal. It's a difficult thing to compute: - while they surreptitiously try to claim all your attention; they will be incapable of the versatile, vulnerable, intimate exchange of true love shared...

As the Narcissist 'grows up', the split self is able to don a number of disguises that 'help' (in his or her view) with the need to 'stay safe' in a dangerous, hostile environment. The amnesiac barriers and dissociation that we discussed as part of dorsal vagus activation become permanent fixtures in the defensive ego structure. The notion of maturity for Narcissists is no more than that, since arrested emotional development is part and parcel of this kind of wounding, including the failure of certain synaptic connections to form in the individual's neurobiology, compromising the optimal architecture of the brain. The traditional association of Narcissism with a flaunting, exhibitionist demeanour describes a reinventing of the 'original false self', who first emerged to protect the abandoned infant from vulnerability and terror. This false self was given to understand that love and attention were scarce commodities, and thus the compulsion to 'amass' as much as possible governs his or her every move.

A person with Narcissistic tendencies feels totally unwelcome in the world. They evolve numerous personae to help navigate the stigma of 'Outsider status' they carry with them in all places and at all times. Covert as well as overt, often passive-aggressive, always intimacy-averse, the finger prints of Narcissism cloud the translucence of intimate relationships in ways that are difficult to imagine until you've been there... Ross Rosenberg[138] describes how the partner of the Narcissist is often intent on 'rescuing' or 'healing' the other. This was what I brought to the party, as an expression of my own lack of self-worth and general discomfort with intimacy.

Rosenberg states that 'co-dependents', who he repackages as suffering from 'self-love deficit disorder', are naturally drawn to Narcissists because they match the lack of attuned care experienced in childhood. Remember the 'giving to get' impulse described as part of the ambivalent attachment schema, equating lack of care giver attention with being somehow 'unlovable'? That pattern is at the root of co-dependency, meaning love is always one step away, and always has to be earned... Rosenberg states categorically that if you're a Co-dependent you can't be a Narcissist. My sense is it's more nuanced than that... consider that the root of both disorders is lack of proper childhood care, and that all children are born 'healthy Narcissists'. I can discern both Co-dependent and Narcissistic traits in myself.

It's only attuned care that helps us shed the cloak of Narcissism, which is why those of us who never received it can be blind-sided by our own Narcissism. It's not a strategy we acquire, but one we fail to relinquish; turning it instead into an exo-skeleton that keeps the world out as we gradually acquire an adult body with an immature child trapped inside. I continue to set a lot of store by Rosenburg's book; he's 'removed the scales from my eyes' when it comes to believing I have the ability to Rescue a Narcissist. I will say now, from my last relationship: **it can't be done**!... This is because pathological Narcissism is woven into the neuro-biology and psychic structure of the individual, who is not at liberty to choose to put it down. The terror, recorded in the nervous system, of historical abandonment trauma, allied to the split self, are too powerful to allow for that.

Roles, Split Selves and Authenticity!

We can link the Narcissist to the Tyrant (originally 'Persecutor') archetype; and the Co-dependent to the Rescuer in the Karpman

138. Ross A. Rosenberg. The human magnet syndrome: Why we love people who hurt us (PESI Publishing & Media, 2013)

triangle model[139] we'll be looking at in more depth in the next chapter. According to Karpman, we are able to adopt different roles in various threatening situations - and they are just that - **roles**, rather than the embodied, emergent exchanges that are the fruit of well-attuned interactions. When we're caught in drama triangle re-enactment, for example, it would be easy to attach conditions to our Rescuing, which means we are then veering towards the domain of the Tyrant; thus, the roles can dissolve and switch before our eyes!

Authenticity always includes an element of uncertainty, since it embraces the unknown, unpredictable qualities that attend spontaneous relating. The 'emergent' quality of securely attached exchanges means we can't pigeon hole what is happening as role play; mutual attunement means relationship dynamics happen very much 'in the here and now'. I'm not trying to make 'secure attachment' sound super-easy. Many (most?) exchanges - even those that appear calm, pleasant and attuned - remain so because those involved might be studiously avoiding bringing contentious material into the conversation! Deb Dana also notes in the book cited previously in this chapter that 'rupture and repair' are still common features of securely attached relationships. What characterises secure attachment is individuals choosing to focus on the repair job, and **not** the rupture!

We have to qualify and quantify roles somewhat. There are the Karpman triangle variety: Tyrant, Victim, Rescuer and, latterly, Bystander; and then healthy role models like Elders, Mothers, Fathers, Aunts, Grandfathers... Healthy role models are fluid and responsive, whereas the unhealthy roles we sometimes adopt are rigid and uncompromising, underscored by fear. You know how it is, for example, when someone is stuck in the Victim archetype - it doesn't matter how many helpful suggestions you make; in the end you realise they're simply not listening, and so you silence, via attunement, that aspect of yourself, to save yourself from getting sucked into the repeat loop of the person you're engaging with.

139. Ana Del Castillo. "The Drama Triangle", Medium, last modified April 29, 2023, https://medium.com/@Ana_DelCastillo/the-drama-triangle-19236425a4db

Memoir: Our Story; His Wound

... When working with my ex-partner to reveal the dynamics in our relationship, it felt imperative to acknowledge his 'split self' for doing an '11 out of 10 job' in protecting him from an insanely abusive situation. Having gradually woken up to the challenges we faced, we became increasingly aware of the extent of the damage done. The lack of intimate rapport suddenly made complete sense to me. I don't just mean sex, although that was part of it. I mean noticing that he was uncomfortable with flowing, warm, open exchanges of any sort, and would work to undermine them. I had become 'avoidant' too, as a way to keep my own nervous system regulated, not expecting there to be intimacy, avoiding eye contact, sometimes talking at him, rather than sharing with him. We adopted a kind of cringe-worthy Benny Hill humour around sex to help cope with or deflect the extreme challenge that trusting and opening to physical intimacy represented to one with a Narcissistic wound.

Acknowledging, even thanking the 'protector part'; 'un-blending' the two, to use Internal Family Systems terminology, allowed the 'protective' persona to emerge as separate from other facets of self. Whilst he prevented Rich from having a loving relationship; in the 'Protector's' world, he was doing a super-important job: – saving Rich from facing the world alone. I thought that if we could bring the Protector to the light of day we would allow other aspects of Rich to surface – parts that longed for a loving relationship, for example...If I'm honest, it was difficult to notice him longing to connect, and I'm looking forward to understanding more about the schizoid condition, which is beyond the scope of this book, but which may have been a co-morbidity. It's quite possible Rich felt bewildered at his own inability to make meaningful connections with others, without fully understanding why. I see now how I was living in hope, care-taking and doing too much work on his behalf, not wanting to give up, or wake up, even, to the perniciousness of this most intractable wound...

My Own Wound

I carried out an exploration of my own Narcissistic wounding over 12 years ago now during Psychophonetics training with Yehuda Tagar, when I discovered an aspect of myself I named 'Grey Dingbat'. This inner persona I described as 'Nailing himself to his own Cross', meaning he was stuck in the Victim stance to such an extent that he believed his only option was further sabotage. I would say this is what bullying and shaming did to me as a teenager. It was a kind of self-hate and world-hate and utter cynicism – probably a type of defence trying to protect me from pain –not too dissimilar to the Protector in Rich.

On my training course 12 years ago, I elaborated the 'Rules for Life' according to Grey Dingbat. They must have come to me unconsciously decades ago as adaptations to an (at times) cruel, hostile, unloving universe. Here they are (from my notes):

> "Trust no one (of course!)... People fall into three categories: 1. Weak, 2. Stupid, 3. Weak and Stupid. Life is a lonely struggle. It's dog eat dog. No excuses, no exceptions. Compassion is for time wasters. Scarcity prevails. Every ounce of everything has to be fought for".

When I sought to describe this internal character (whom I gendered masculine) on the training course, this is what I wrote: 'his demeanour is arrogant, rushed, hard, presumptuous, cutting, insensitive, disrespectful, competitive, disconnected.' I go on to say in my notes that it is my pushing (his pushing) that is the reason I end up with 'nothing' in life; no emotional connection with others, (which, admittedly, is difficult to disentangle from modern day atomised 'culture'). He generated a force field within and around me that kept people away. After all, for the Outsider, being sociable is constant effort, with no reward in sight for the 'chore' of following 'pleasant codes of conduct'... Grey Dingbat had already confabulated meanings to explain why he ended up 'on the Outside' in the first place, and most of those meanings hinged around his historical shame and unworthiness. Outsider status appeared as a 'done deal', and the effort involved in being 'sociable' seemed like a futile waste of energy, so we didn't make the effort – Grey Dingbat and me – but instead threw little darts of resentment over the wall that kept 'us' separate from the 'insiders'; reinforcing the status quo, and maintaining our beliefs, which cycled into self-fulfilling prophesies.

The Bigger Picture

The Outsider concept is not necessarily a new phenomenon - Rumi writing in the 1200s in Persia says:

'I'm knocking madly on a door, it opens
- I've been knocking from the inside!'

Outsider/Insider identities must be as old as humanity - for as long as we've had foraging bands, tribes, clans and villages - distinct ethnicities - to belong *to.* Once upon a time, ejection from Clan would have meant certain death, which is why Outsider status is felt so viscerally and persistently in our nervous systems and 'emotional body'.

Rumi was predominantly a Spiritual poet, as well as a social and psychological one, so his 'mad knocking' may describe his attempt to connect with God or Spirit, rather than point to him feeling like a social outcast. Like all good poetry, this poem can be interpreted in a number of ways. In the intervening centuries, Globalisation has swept across economic, political, social and geographical divides, diluting cultural identity; offering us the 'opportunity' to 'belong' to a 'brand' instead of a village. Once upon a time, we wove our own logos, but now they are designed and made for us - a flimsy swoosh with no substance - and no ability to reach into our interpersonal neurobiology where *real* change can be sensed, felt and *received.*

Disinheritance

We all need to feel we come from somewhere in order to belong. The wound I describe as my own form of Narcissism originated in a deep sense of disinheritance and dispossession - that's what I wrote in my notebook as being at the root of my own predicament all those years ago. I spent a whole week on a meditation retreat shortly after my initial discovery engaging with this part of myself; using active imagination, I described Grey Dingbat as a character from a film or a book, but make no mistake! –I'm describing an aspect of myself, from my notes:

"... I first noticed him during an exercise I was taking part in on therapy training. I seemed to literally catch him with his trousers down, in the shadows, out of the corner of my eye. He

had stringy grey hair and yellow teeth, and lived in a shabby apartment block with stained bare floor boards. I gave him a name – 'Grey Dingbat' – there's a touch of affection in the name even though it's disparaging, and that's because I recognise his behaviour as coming from a wound, and therefore I feel some compassion".

I went on to put him in a high security prison (in my imagination) with search lights and watch towers; then I put him on trial with judge, jury and public gallery, and eventually I had him come on board as an Ally. I contained the Narcissist in me so he wasn't omnipresent and (in his own delusional reality) omnipotent. We only seek omnipotence because of fear, and the pain of feeling invisible. In my studies of Rudolf Steiner undertaken on the Psychophonetics training where Grey Dingbat first revealed himself to me; one thing I read stuck with me. Steiner asserts that: 'Our inner world is more real than the outer world'.[140] *This startled me at first, and yet, I couldn't put the notion down, and the more I thought about it, the truer it seemed; which is why I relate this story here, and believe that this process – one of many – may have been helpful in healing my own Narcissistic tendencies.*

The 'false selves' we evolve make our isolation and Outsider status bearable. The false self might be the only Ally of the abandoned infant who was otherwise alone and defenceless in an incomprehensible and hostile, barren universe. This was the torture meted out in our hospitals around 50 years ago, and sometimes at home. Apparently, it was not even an unusual occurrence. Isolation breeds fear and mistrust, causing the mind to live in a delusional reality just simply to cope with the unbearable chaos of being alive: – when we are speaking of adult Narcissists in today's world, we are speaking of these abused and terrorised infants. My own father who is 80 this year had his hands tied to the cot as an infant in hospital to stop him sucking his thumbs. In Rich's and countless others' cases, we have to ask ourselves: –

'what kind of society, what kind of medical institution, what kind of mindset?...

would create a neon-lit room, containing rows of cots, full of wriggling

140. *Rudolf Steiner, Knowledge of The Higher Worlds and Its Attainment (CreateSpace, 2014)*

and shrieking abandoned infants?' Can we imagine doing this to newly born puppies or kittens, or any progeny of warm blooded mammals? The RSPCA would be called in an instant! The description sounds like an experimental medical lab from a sci-fi film, and perhaps that's the most accurate way to understand exactly what went on, and goes on still...

More About Us

In my relationship with Rich, I had a sense early on that something wasn't right (why did I persist...?) When we went for a weekend away to Dorset in our first year together, he made a point of misinterpreting me when I mentioned I'd 'rested really well', after a great night's sleep in our beautiful B&B. He took my comment to mean that I was there to rest – ergo there for myself – ergo dis-interested in him, and inferred from it that I didn't want to engage in sexual intimacy! This played out in a difficult and distanced dynamic for the rest of the three day holiday, even though I had been looking forward to both rest and intimacy, as 'normal' facets of a new, loving relationship... The rest of the 'holiday' was spent in exhausting mind games that led nowhere.

... When we came home, we were due to go away again for a once-in-a-lifetime experience. He'd arranged to fly us in his small plane to the Scilly Isles, and had booked us into a very posh hotel for three or four nights (there were 'special offers' on in between lockdowns). I just couldn't face the thought of going away again in the pall of suspicion and tension that still hung over us from the experience in the Dorset B&B. I said I wasn't coming. I felt I needed to make a stand. I surprised myself at calling off this holiday that I was looking forward to so much, and that had the potential to be such a special experience for us both – something I'd never experienced before, and may never get the opportunity to experience again...

...Boundaries become super-important in relationships with Narcissists. He accepted my decision silently, and never spoke about it again, although I brought it up a few times to illustrate what I felt I'd been driven to, and to remind him of what he's like to live with – it wasn't the only ruined holiday either...

I imagine we all want to be seen as flexible and friendly on the whole; perhaps women especially; rather than 'stern' upholders of rules. Yet sometimes we have to learn to unapologetically enact strong, self-protective behaviour. My feeling is that, at best, I have a playful, adaptable and open heart; and yet just like a good father does all he can to protect the innocent heart of his children, I have needed to find a part of myself that will 'kick ass', that will say 'no more', to protect my own inner sanctum; my sanity, in fact. Narcissism attacks that sanctuary, that sanity, even; not deliberately, but because the Narcissist has already made up his or her mind that no one can be trusted. Living alongside someone who has that kind of mindset wounds the Innocent Heart, day after day after day. It is corrosive; it destroys joy.

Because the Narcissist is a victim underneath, he or she has no room to consider the needs, wounds and realities of the other. They only have room for their own emotional needs, which trigger them on a constant basis. At the Dorset B&B Rich said that it was perhaps the first time in his life he felt he had 'room' to let another into his world... Yet, as John and Jennifer Welwood remarked on a relationship workshop many moons ago: ***'Our Realisation is always ahead of our Transformation'****, meaning: We perceive new truths ahead of being able to mend our undesirable attributes. Realisation is the spark that fires the motor of our inner reflection and subsequent process, which, in time, brings about change, or transformation –* ***maybe.*** *So Rich, maybe one day, you will have room for me in your inner world. In the meantime, I have needs too, and the 'room' you say you have for me is too tiny a space for me to thrive in.*

I hope this chapter cuts Narcissists some slack, reducing the flack and the need to attack. Let's write poems instead; about how we all have these tendencies. Maybe you can even look at some of your own behaviours and hold up your hand?! Yes: Narcissists are impossible, yes they need therapy, and to learn to tolerate their own pain, and to self-parent and self-soothe – to rewire the nervous system basically, for 'secure attachment', or 'ventral vagus dominance'. But it's not their fault they ended up that way. And guess what – it's a spectrum – and we were all Narcissists once, Narcissists who've grown up to be fully functioning adults, if we're very lucky, or failing that, Narcissists who've evolved elaborate rituals for concealing the fact, or, failing that, Narcissists who blend in all too well, amid the gilded shapes, colours, textures and enactments of the Narcissistic culture we all inhabit.

Surely the opposite of Narcissism is... Altruism?... If none of us are willing to accept the taint of Narcissism in defining ourselves, then we must all be perfect paragons of Altruistic human behaviour, ***no****?... Yet, wouldn't it be fair to say that there is a part in all of us that wants to, and probably does, pull away from the homeless beggar in the street, crossing the road a few parked cars away, hoping no one links the two events. It takes something to move towards – we mostly like to associate with people who enhance our status –* ***do we not****? (Unless, of course, it's part of our paid job remit; which also, conveniently, delineates our superiority.)*

Then there's the revulsion we might have, should we stay on the same side of the road, at the state of their clothes, hair, skin, teeth, tattoos. The process becomes convoluted further by the kudos of flaunting ourselves as the Good Samaritan, which mixes with the genuine compassion and concern we will be feeling in at least some corner of the psyche, and our legitimate desire to keep ourselves safe from danger.

Our responses are complex, and we are editing and navigating the push-pull of human interactions all day, every day – all of us! The reductionism of the 'goody versus baddy' that is the current popular discourse around Narcissism is frankly, not very grown up! It's great to get a compassionate and joined up understanding of Narcissistic dynamics out into the open; and I hope this chapter helps a teeny bit! I'm not denying there is a lot of suffering involved; I know this first hand, for many, many people who find themselves ensnared.

It might be illuminating also to ask ourselves how often we have colluded with a Narcissist, letting them get their own way for the sake of a bit of 'peace', even when we knew it would be our undoing? I wish I could say I'd 'conquered or healed or transformed a Narcissist' – but that would just be Narcissistic. The truth is I haven't. Or if I have, it's only Myself; and then: – only partially!

I used to think people talking about Narcissists ruining their lives were exaggerating, being too black and white, or not taking responsibility... My relationship with Rich has been a steep learning curve where I've learned so much more about my own patterns and limitations... Then there's possibly a devil's advocate Self saying: 'we're not just our diagnoses – we're humans with soft spots, humour, insight, hope, resilience, memories, perseverance, ideals and more'... There was something dogged in both of us that made us keep trying, like we imagined the summit was in sight... and on good days, we fitted well together. You've got to admire the Rescuer from a certain angle – some of the time – as well as recognising that the behaviour is compulsive and that relationships shouldn't be this much hard work.

... Maybe Rich is in worse shape now than he was during our relationship. I told him it wouldn't be an easy path – the path of self-awareness. I think the drowning child in him thought I was throwing him a rubber ring – but I wasn't – I was saying: here are some maps – you're going to have to take a lot of lessons in hieroglyphs to be able to decode them, and once you begin that journey, you'll uncover stuff that will hurt – ***a lot.*** *Hieroglyphs are not exotic memes, really, you see; they are the amnesiac barriers we've put in place to make the* ***unbearable bearable****... and then, if I'd had the presence of mind, I would have said: 'Baby steps are fine, but just try to ensure you don't back track and sabotage our progress, or even just our peace, too often...' I have to say, I failed at being able to cope with the lack of peace and stability. I've saved my own ass – for* ***now*** *– that's all...*

Chapter Five

Power Dynamics

Memoir: Writer's Winter Retreat

'Focus' I tell myself – whatever that means: writing; cultivating discipline; following through on stated aims. Honing this existence; ridding myself of the extraneous; heeding the call – keeping on keeping on, remembering that 'doubt is the virus' as Yehuda Tagar once said. I'm looking straight ahead, not to left and right, although what 'straight ahead' means when writing a book like this is anyone's guess! Living in my son's flat in Aberdeen, no car (just a bicycle) no Wi-Fi, I ran out of my 12Gig data allowance; so no internet, morning sun pouring in the window, memory foam mattress, good sleeps, some kind of reset and retreat, starting out again; in the here and now.

... Memories of this place from before, when my son was single, and I lived here with him for nearly a year; Gift of Gifts, opportunity to heal the unhealed from his teenage years. Me much calmer; and able to serve him more fully as a Mother can and should; in simple, stable ways, in between my one day a week university counselling course. Drinking rosé wine out of small engraved goblets he salvaged from my aunt's house when she died: 'He's done very well for himself', she'd said... I have a photo of us chinking mugs – his said 'Dream, Believe, Achieve'; my son getting on the property ladder aged 26, him scrabbling around to get the deposit together, emptying his accounts, a leg up from the Scottish government, second hand furniture – the family chipping in to cover fees.

Us together here when his dad died – Time Out of Time – sharing memories with him; grieving together – his boss gave him time off, saying – 'it's harder to grieve when you didn't know them'... Me woken up in the middle of the night from what felt like a punch in the chest – his father's spirit crashing through me. The father he never had and never knew whose inheritance paid for him to upgrade and leave this place so soon, within two years of him buying his first flat, and move closer to the sea with his new partner – marram grass dunes, and a garden front and back, and extended mono block drive for both their cars – just like the Neighbours.

... We planted a thousand bulbs this autumn: – snakeshead fritillary, tulips, crocus, daffodils, grape hyacinth, colchicums, camassia, and the utility room came in handy for muddy boots and all. My son aged 29 and possibly the only one in the family with a 'utility room'. I tried to pray in the garden with him in the dusk, on the last day of planting – trees and shrubs too – but he swore and said we didn't have time. I'm not the world's best time keeper, and we were supposed to be getting cleaned up and ready to go out for a meal. I feel the prayer inside me still that links it all up; connecting his father's ancestors, their blood, sweat and tears, with the bulbs in the newly planted garden, the unborn children, the colours, textures and warmth of their new home, built on the inheritance of the ones that once tilled the fields of south Wales; a full circle of sorts. His father with his birds of prey, horses and dogs, his 'tentacles' that helped him get deeper and closer to the natural world – those acres of land in a National Park that pushed up the value of his Estate. Perhaps we'll never make the prayer together. Perhaps he'll always be 'too busy', and maybe it's his prerogative; after all, he is the heir too, of the deep well of grief and rage that lives in the heart of every son abandoned by his father...

A couple of times I walked a razor's edge here, when I felt my son's absence, and those days in this flat together, gone for good. He has a fiancée now, and they seem very well suited, and I like her a lot, and we get on, and he's gone ... from here ... for good. Life shifting and lilting onwards, lifting strange weights and then depositing them again like jetsam and flotsam in the dark, deft, warm, receptive recesses of my heart.

Time and Space: – Gifts for the Living – I bring order to the potential chaos of my days, make my bed, cook properly just for me, fill the fridge, clean, feed the birds using the rusty feeders still hanging on the cherry plum tree from over two years ago. Small rituals, big tasks, dark red leaves almost all gone, gift of sun lighting them from behind – last stalwarts – short days getting shorter still, I cultivate a good routine.

Attempting waking at first light to get my vitamin D quota; walking along the River Don with its post-apocalyptic dead and fallen elms for an hour every day, joined after winter storms by hundred-year old beech trees toppled like dominoes... Seeing Pete almost every other day keeps me sane and safe from the burden of too much solitude.

Dysfunctional Archetypes

We have established a basic understanding of the importance of attachment and safety in the developmental psychology of the child; helping us glimpse what health and well-being might have looked and felt like in times when Eldering was still a 'thing', and organic child-rearing based on optimal neuro-biological conditions was pervasive. Now we turn our attention to examining adult power dynamics, in personal, social and civic spheres, via the Karpman Triangle. This model shows us how things can go badly wrong when adults who didn't receive the right kind of care in childhood interact - enacting the effects of fear-based dysfunction in interpersonal and even political spheres.

In traditional cultures, Elders were arbiters and mediators of self-governing groups, operating in the intimacy of the small collective... Thousands of years of history have impacted our societies, in Britain alone the Roman, Viking, and Norman invasions; the rise of Christianity, Feudalism, the Nation State and Capitalism, all played a part in dismantling close–knit communities: inter-generational 'micro-processes' were systematically destroyed and replaced by 'macro-versions', both impersonal and corruptible in ways not possible or even conceivable in the past. I name the shadow-lands of this evolution, so often blithely referred to as 'progress', to help calibrate loss – and to define and describe how Dysfunctional Archetypes have replaced counterparts once based on trust. Perhaps we can dare to imagine social systems where the equations of intimacy, patience, proximity and scale might again produce robust, cooperative individuals and societies... Perhaps examining the distorted versions will prompt a yearning to create something 'more beautiful', as Charles Eisenstein might say.[141]

141. Charles Eisenstein, The More Beautiful World Our Hearts Know Is Possible (North Atlantic Books, 2013)

It's my contention that our mental health is actually the poorer for modernity. Of course, there are personal and political dimensions we need to consider in this ultimately inconclusive, yet compelling, comparison between then and now, 'zooming in and out', looking up close at details, and the bigger picture to help evaluate the state we're in... Expect to feel uncomfortable as we pull back the curtain on behaviours that prefer to remain hidden. As well as exploring distorted archetypes, this chapter begins to question historic and present-day political power imbalances; an enquiry we will expand in the New World Order chapter later in the book...

The Power Dynamics 'Quadrangle'

As an eminent professor of Psychology and Transactional Analysis[142], Stephen Karpman won the Eric Berne Memorial Scientific Award in 1972 for his work elaborating the 'Karpman Triangle'. This construct describes three 'templates' or 'archetypes' present during human dramas as they unfold: the Persecutor (sometimes referred to as 'Tyrant'), Victim, and Rescuer. In 1968, following research into the murder of Kitty Genovese in 1964, John Darley and Bibb Latane drew attention to another important archetype – the Bystander. I've taken the liberty of adding this latter 'schema' to Karpman's original Triangle, turning it instead into a Quandrangle of sorts.

The Karpman triangle or quadrangle details the different positions we adopt in the face of challenging situations. Each role is actually a 'bid for power' in a climate of scarcity; or 'bargaining strategy', used by individuals and groups even, to attempt to stay safe, come out on top and get our emotional needs met. The less historical trauma you carry, and the more securely attached you felt to primary care givers, the less often you're likely to need to have recourse to this dubious toolkit. We have to acknowledge though, that life has a habit of throwing us curved balls outside our control, and so even those with well-regulated nervous systems might find themselves caught up in some of these dramas.

142. The basic contention with TA is that we always act from one of three positions: parent/adult/child. This lens helps us to examine our levels of maturity, vulnerability and tendency to control. Thomas A. Harris, I'm OK, you're OK (Random House, 2012)

By the end of the book, we'll have a better understanding of how corruption, via the capture of our institutions, came about and how it's being maintained... In this chapter we root business and political leaders' behaviours in developmental trauma and subsequent pathology, leading us to question their mental health...[143] Notwithstanding: '*Power Corrupts, and Absolute Power Corrupts Absolutely*'... This could be where Catherine Austin Fitts[144] is coming from when she says: 'they get away with it because they can'; whilst Iain McGilchrist claims our problems are due to the over-dominant left hemisphere of the brain in modern times: '[The Industrial Revolution] was obviously, colossally, man's most brazen bid for power over the natural world, the grasping left hemisphere's long-term agenda'.[145]

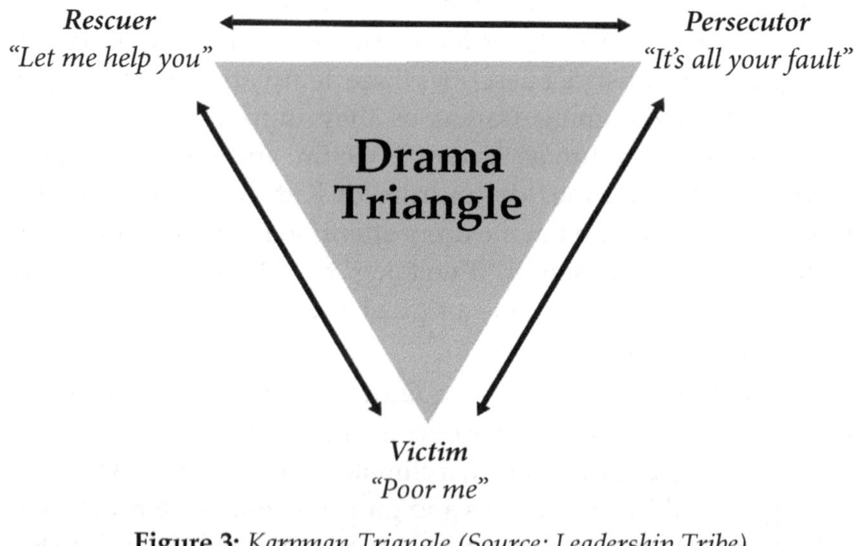

Figure 3: *Karpman Triangle (Source: Leadership Tribe)*

If it's dysfunctional at the top, that has an impact on everything downstream; creating demoralisation and fragmentation in

143. Eminent cardiologist Dr Aseem Malhotra explains that pathology is systemic in the modern-day corporation, including the pharmaceutical industry. He points to the work of forensic Psychologist Dr Robert Hare, and books by Joel Bakan 'The Corporation' and 'New Corporation'. "IA - The High Wire - EPISODE 296 - ON THE RUN - Del Bigtree", Odysee, 2:12:19. https://odysee.com/@lancewdetrick:b/IA---The-HighWire---EPISODE-296---ON-THE-RUN---Del-Bigtree:c

144. Catherine Austin Fitts was part of Bush administration, turned activist and whistle blower.

145. McGilchrist, The Master and his Emissary: 386

employees struggling to make sense of the cognitive dissonance bound up in systemic corruption. Institutions like the NHS in the UK were undoubtedly set up with the best of intentions, nonetheless, 20% of *fully qualified GPs under 30 left the profession* in the UK in the 12 months up to December 2022.[146]

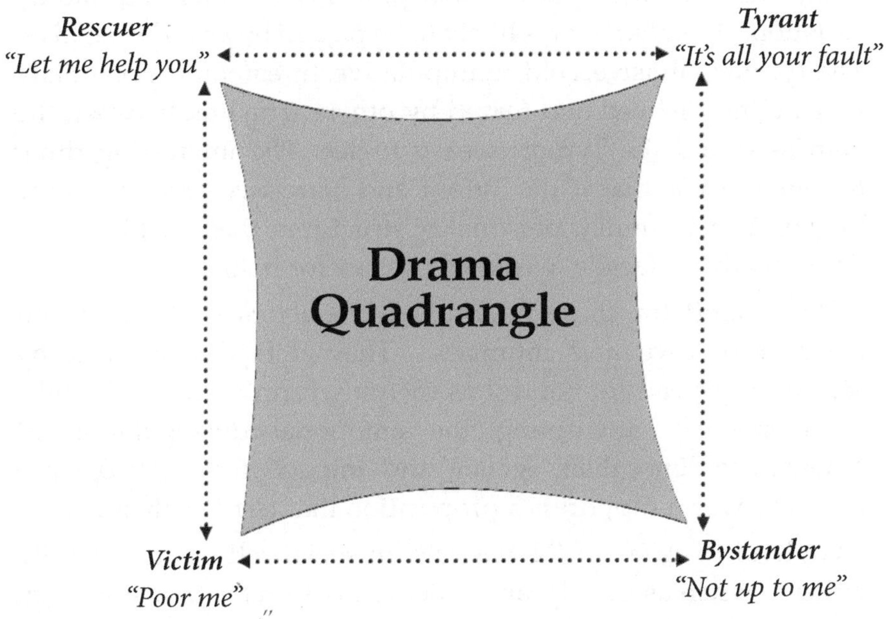

Figure 4: *Enhancement: The Drama 'Quadrangle'*

That's an unusual quantity of money, time and effort; AKA blood, sweat and tears, to suddenly pour down the drain... These people must be really up against it in ways hard for outsiders to comprehend, and possibly difficult to divulge if you're on the inside - subject to all manner of stress, peer pressure and even gagging orders![147] - explored further in the New World Order chapter. For now, let's look at each archetype in turn, gleaning

---

146. 21.6% of qualified GPs under 30 left the profession in 12 months to December 2022. "One in five GPs under 30 quit the profession last year", National Association of Sessional GPs, last modified March 3, 2023, http://nasgp.org.uk/career/one-in-five-gps-under-30-quit-the-profession-last-year

147. Why did it take so long? For the first time since the start of the 'pandemic' British MP Andrew Bridgen convened 2 hours of testimony about Covid deceptions for the Houses of Parliament from medical experts – Doctors, microbiologists and cardiologists, to name a few... Andrew Bridgen @ABridgen. "A Message from Andrew Bridgen, MP", X, December 8, 2023, 6:56 pm, https://twitter.com/ABridgen/status/1733198864725704996

clues about how the personal and political are intricately bound together.

The Tyrant

The Tyrant, or Persecutor, as often described in the literature, is the one who attempts to wield power over others. In family situations, this character is likely to be played by an older relative. The Tyrant is abusive, cold, manipulative, threatening, potentially violent and disliked and feared by others. The link between the Narcissist and the Tyrant is easy to see. The interesting thing to remember is that if the Tyrant and Narcissist archetypes are linked, sharing similar personality structures, then it's likely that underneath the façade, weaknesses exist for both...

The wound for these interlinked characters is the fear and mistrust of love and intimacy. They defend against it by searching instead for control as the only form of 'safety', whilst simultaneously attempting the emotional dysregulation of others to evidence their 'agency' and 'impact' in the world, since two-way warm rapport is a proposition that terrifies them.

We tend to speak of 'Narcissists' in social settings and family milieus, whereas the 'Tyrant' label tends to refer to a sovereign or politician who wields power over nations... As we'll explore in more detail in later chapters, the underlying source of power in today's world is financial rather than constitutional, meaning billionaires and corporations are often the real 'Tyrants' hidden from view... Politicians and even academics work as their proxies, 'engineering consent' in often covert campaigns that rely on the 'virtue signalling' instincts and social conditioning of the general population, making us passive and compliant... In this light, Tyranny needs to be considered in tandem with corruption and corporate takeover. The principles of social control (for profit) remain the same: The Tyrant wields power through fear and manipulation, although the methods used in today's world are increasingly sophisticated and covert, as we'll see later on.

Throughout history there have been countless millions of victims of Tyrannical regimes and their agents, who have killed, tortured, raped, pillaged and abused others in the name of their leader, and often some kind of political or 'religious' ideology. The increase in paranoia rises with every escalation of the Tyrant's brutality, and is masterfully captured in the 2006 film 'The Last King of Scotland' directed by Kevin Macdonald with Forest Whitaker and James McAvoy, based on the Ugandan dictator Idi Amin.

This version of the archetype is perhaps a crass example, when held up against the many more subtle techniques employed in our own day: Today, the power wielded by the enmeshment of State and Corporation is often hidden using new forms of disinformation and 'doublespeak', turning received ideas of Tyranny and State Control on their heads. It's not just corporations as we understand them, but a new breed of billionaire who have infiltrated (or even established) many of the institutions we assumed were there for the public good... The Tyrants in 'western liberal democracies' are masters of smoke and mirrors, making their power grabs difficult if not impossible to distinguish. We are victims of endless de-contextualised 'sound bites', which pass as news, allowing for a 'seamless intermingling' of repetitive messaging (engineered consent at best, propaganda at worst) purveyed by corporate-sponsored Mainstream Media and Big Tech, who gorge us on 'word salads' and 'Information Soup' daily. Author Peter Pomerantsev[148] describes his sojourn of several years in the Russia of the early 2000s, working on reality TV shows. He documents his shock upon returning to the UK to see the extent to which the two cultures now resemble each other.

The result is that it's impossible to discern where fact ends and brainwashing and censorship begin – unless of course we choose to pull back the curtain by turning to those few brave individuals willing to risk career and reputation to call out the unprecedented level of corruption operating in all the familiar institutions we once trusted. Google the 'Disinformation Dozen' from 2020/21 to get an instant list of those 'fighting the good fight'. Interestingly the NYT has taken down their article (afraid of a defamation law

148. With 122k subscribers. 7.4k views. The Institute of Art and Ideas. "What are post-truth politics? | Peter Pomerantsev", YouTube, 10:26, January 25, 2020, https://youtube.com/watch?v=TjLyg1wemag

suit perhaps?) although the UK 'Independent' paper still carries a piece from March 2021 citing the 'findings' of the 'Centre for Countering Digital Hate', and their 'naming and shaming' campaign carried out during the 'pandemic'...[149]

An Old Tradition

Paradoxically; when it comes to Tyranny, it is often those who stake a claim to the 'moral high ground', wishing to install some kind of Utopian Society, who are guilty of the most heinous crimes. In Medieval Europe, for example, the Church's torture of the Witches - women who carried vestiges of the 'Old Religion' in their knowledge of healing herbs and seasonal cycles - were deemed Evil Heretics. The ducking stool used to test whether the 'witch' possessed 'magical powers' reflects the cognitive dissonance involved... If she survived being held under water whilst tied to the stool, it meant she did *indeed* have magical powers, and was therefore put to death in a gruesome manner - probably burnt at the stake. If she died whilst tied to the stool - 'Oops-a-daisy, she wasn't a witch after all!' - just a disposable cranky old woman - plenty more of them around - let's clear our throats, shuffle our feet, look at the ground and wait for the moment to pass, which won't take too long, since we have the backing of the Catholic Church and Pope in Rome. Women must have been on to something back then for them to be considered such a threat, for sure!

The atrocities committed by Stalin and the first generation of Russian Communists were justified on the grounds of a new Society based on Equality, with a Utopian System that was to banish poverty and outmoded religious superstition, improving life for all.

> "...Totalitarian ideas were responsible for tens of millions of deaths in the 20th century: the Russian Revolutions and the birth of Soviet Russia, Maoist China, North Korea under its lineage of Kim-deities, and the events in Vietnam,

149. Mayank Aggarwal. "Study names 12 most dangerous anti-vaxxers in America", Independent, March 26, 2021, https://independent.co.uk/news/world/americas/us-covid-anti-vaxxers-dozen-b1822705.html

> Cambodia, Laos, East Timor and Cuba. As many as 90 million people were killed throughout the 20th century due to the development of novel philosophies and methodologies; which should demonstrate the costs of failing to understand those philosophical frameworks and the values and ideas which come from them". [150]

The 'cognitive dissonance' frame can be applied to countless historical examples where 'societal improvement' was the rationale; yet pain, chaos and disempowerment were the results for the masses, in traumatic revolutions, wars and coups that left lasting physical and emotional scars. For the ideologues, the 'ends might justify the means', yet for those who cherish the conviction Sovereignty is first and foremost an *individual* attribute, and that Heaven is already *here* on Earth, when we open our eyes to *see*, and hearts to *feel*; the trade-off begins to look like an ever-receding, shrivelled gilded carrot dangled in front of the noses of the 'donkey' masses.

If we don't want to be treated like asses, it's important we dare to question the narratives, propaganda and 'double speak' prevalent *everywhere you go* in these troubling times, rather than blindly assume that 'liberal western democracies' are 'doing what they say on the tin'. How do we begin to measure the impact corporate capture of our institutions is having on the mental health of nations? The emerging inter-disciplinary field of Cultural Somatics seeks to comment on the trauma legacy of peoples; equating top-down social control with a kind of 'cultural disinheritance' that inhibits emotional well-being. Isn't a de-constructing and de-stabilising project surreptitiously or even blatantly taking place in Western Culture and Everywhere Else, for that matter, in our time? Can't the entire project of top-down control be summarised as an attempt to atomise and isolate our once rich cultures into ever smaller fragments, until we're all living alone, staring at screens all day? Remember Grey Dingbat from the last chapter? He cited 'disinheritance' as *the* root cause of his toxic mindset.

150. Max Reynolds, The Revolutionary Renaissance (Amazon kindle direct publishing, 2022)

Tyrannical strategies: 'Othering'

Propaganda operations are being carried out under our noses by potentially pathological Tyrants. Our times display and multiply extreme cognitive dissonance, requiring a fragmentation or compartmentalizing of the self to simply survive the onslaught. Internally, we justify our 'belief systems' (poor substitute for embodied experience) with narratives from mainstream media, reflected externally in a distancing from, and a dehumanizing of, the 'Other' who becomes the unwitting enemy or 'Victim' - whether it's the Russians, Chinese or the Unvaxxed. The Tyrant (read: leaders of western 'liberal' 'democracies') promotes a dualistic and reductionist world view unwittingly adopted by the people - a claim to intrinsic 'Supremacy'. It masquerades as moral superiority based on ideology or 'scientific truth'. These beliefs help bolster the protective false self of the Narcissist/Tyrant - secretly a Victim in disguise - someone fundamentally, *forever, alone* in the world, someone who *trusts no one*. These damaged people employ distancing techniques (to avoid the intimacy they fear) using oppositional reasoning in their ideologies, which they inflict on the masses.

When it comes to the enshrining of pathology as ideology; the insecure Tyrant dictates that those who don't belong with the 'in-group' become the 'unclean' Others, based on belief, gender, vaccine status, ethnicity, and more - and thus unworthy of fair or equal treatment. Often, the measured, if jaded historical eye of the Vanquished sees Tyrannical hubris for what it is; yet History is rarely written by Victims - most often the narrative is confabulated by the 'Victors', who always include ample testimony justifying their subjugation of the 'Other' in their revisionist accounts. In ideological terms, the 'Others' become 'Traitors to the Cause': - the Central Impediment to the establishment of Heaven on Earth, or a Safe, Sanitized, Virus-free environment, or a Society of Equals, or a society of Superior Aryans with blonde hair, and blue eyes. In our times, as we have seen already in Eros Betrayed, the woke movement focuses on bizarre levels of inclusivity when it comes to trans and identity politics, however, this outlandish pursuit is used as a way to occlude the much more serious power abuses going on behind the scenes, and to demonise those who don't accept the 'new gender-identity normal'. After all, no matter which gender out of 50 or more we are 'free' to choose, we haven't gained any more political traction, or curtailed any real systemic inequality. In fact, we're helping along systemic abuse with a pleasant/unpleasant distraction – the 'circus' part of the 'bread and circuses' formula beloved of Tyrants of old...

We can only fall prey to 'Othering' particular groups of people when we have 'Othered' certain aspects of ourselves – become fragmented, for example, by chronic activation of the dorsal vagus nerve, numbing us and infusing reality with an 'as if' quality; rather than the immediacy of safe, trusting contexts, where ethics and morality spring from the living tissue of the heart, rather than the canon of some random ideology. As we saw in the last chapter, the foundations for dissociative behaviour are laid in infancy and childhood, in families, education systems and societies that *struggle to cohere* due to systemic isolation. We disown aspects of self to justify, protect and insulate ourselves from the painful experience of Rejection – the fact that someone decided, way back, to 'Other' us. The fragmented self perpetuates, and sees no problem in Othering groups and individuals, *Nations even*, vindicating and insulating itself – closing the circle, *or so it imagines...* Except, as History and Wisdom Traditions have told us, we create Karma when we indulge in this kind of re-enactment; reaping what we sow – fostering endless cycles of fear, rage, hate, dissociation and retribution.

The Ideologues turn out to be 'Emperors without a stitch on', encouraging fallacies to root and proliferate, factionalizing people with dubious abstract claims that mean nothing on the ground where day-to-day lives trade in the only true currency of compassion and care. The *less* connection we have to one another, the *more* likely we are to fall prey to unprecedented levels of fake news, pseudo-science, manipulation and polarization, even to the extent of going to war... Our own distractedness, disorientation, and dis-regulated nervous systems provide fertile conditions for

Emperors of all complexions - hiding in plain sight - to set the agenda and take control.

Scapegoating is part and parcel of the phenomenon of 'Othering' - which has been explored in depth by the late French historian and philosopher of social science René Girard... This 'psychological operation' (psy-op) accords the 'free floating' anxiety in society a 'rationale', and a 'target'. In this way, persecuting the 'Other' has a cathartic effect, bringing *the illusion* of longed-for cohesion to situations where malaise is rife, offering a false sense of having 'solved the problem'. In 'The Psychology of Totalitarianism', Professor of Clinical Psychology Mattias Desmet[151] seeks to illuminate the unfolding of global technocratic tyranny in our time, describing it as a 'mass formation' event of unprecedented scale. He may not have grasped the full extent of the deception taking place; nonetheless, his is a rare, courageous voice speaking out in the wilderness of today's all too often woke academic landscape. He's managed to hold onto his academic position, but ironically his book is banned at Ghent university where he works![152]

An interesting facet of mass formation is the extent to which we become 'self-policing'; making it a key priority for us to understand Who's Pulling What Strings - so we can stop being *their* puppets - doing their bidding by unwittingly oppressing one another. Waking up to the reality of Tyranny in our time helps us avoid being co-opted, encouraging us instead to try to mend societal fabric from the ground up, fostering resilience by encouraging free speech and autonomous community... Because: *If not Now, then When? If not Us, then Who?*

The Victim

The Victim and Tyrant are diametrically opposed - with the Victim falling prey to the numberless abuses of the Tyrant, unable to defend him or herself against injustice or danger, and feeling powerless, weak, small, sad and frightened as a consequence. Victims of injustice are *real people* experiencing crime and harsh

151. Mattias Desmet, The psychology of totalitarianism (Chelsea Green Publishing, 2022)
152. International Covid Summit 4. "Mattias Desmet"

circumstances every day: – theft, blackmail, intimidation, poverty, accident, deception, war, famine, rape ... Victims have experienced genuine trauma, often developing PTSD/CPTSD (*[complex]* post-traumatic stress disorder) or other mental health conditions as a result, and requiring empathy, advocacy and rehabilitation to enable recovery. We need to have our stories heard, to somehow help us feel safe enough to engage in life again and move on.

... Additionally; the neural circuits of the brain, highlighted by Emma McAdam[153], reward the 'hiding effort', by reasoning it was 'effective'. In this way, we can 'trick' ourselves into becoming ever more entrenched behind sand bags or closed doors, feeling that our tactical manoeuvre was what allowed us to 'outwit' the 'enemy'. This kind of automatic reflex is not only dangerous when it keeps us in hiding too long, but also tends to amplify fear, an 'us and them' mentality, and, when applied to society as a whole, the 'culture wars' we find ourselves embedded in today on social media... Lilie Chouliaraki from the London School of Economics points out that online political discourse has allowed a language of the oppressed to take centre stage, yet: –

> "... under conditions of post-recession neo-Liberalism, claims to suffering are indeed, largely voiced by the disaffected middle classes" ... that ... "tend to be highly visible internationally because western media forms are dominant across the globe, while the suffering of social minorities is marginalized or fully erased".[154]

In today's digital world, Chouliaraki asserts: victimhood has become: 'an open 'market', and a radically unequal one: "being recognized as a victim" ... "is a right and even arguably, a privilege, not equally bestowed on all injured people." When victimhood becomes touted and fetishised in academia, amongst 'helping professions' and online as part of the new 'identity politics' movement, the obfuscation of the structural conditions of the

---

153. Her 'Therapy in a Nutshell' YouTube channel offers clarity where neuroscience meets psychology: https://youtu.be/zTuX_ShUrw0?si=FQv99W4byRKxrpxx
154. Lilie Chouliaraki. "Victimhood: The Affective politics of Vulnerability", European Journal of Cultural Studies 24 no. 1 (2021): 10–27

most vulnerable, is the end result. Thus, society as a whole gets to "avoid restoring the harms done or addressing the injustices that cause it."[155]

In other words, the noise and clamour generated online by various interest groups often distract us from recognising the systemic conditions that disenfranchise and exploit untold millions globally – true Victims, whose stories are never told. RIP Mahsa Amini... We have to wonder why that is and who stands to gain from this state of affairs...? The only sensible conclusion to draw is that the 'winners' in structural oppression prefer to keep it hidden, even to the extent of fuelling culture wars as a smoke screen that allows rape and pillage of people and planet to continue unabated and unchallenged...

There are obvious Victims in war-ravaged, poverty-blighted countries, where extinct and dwindling species and entire ecosystems have to be included in the tally of systemic abuse, yet it's important also to recognise how rich and poor alike are being disenfranchised in our times by a 'project' that seems to be reaching its zenith in 21st century modern western culture: *Individual Isolation.* For when we are isolated from each other, we lose resilience, and are prevented from easily distinguishing 'truth' from 'fiction' – turning knowledge itself, as the primary currency we use for engaging with the world, into an abstract, intellectual affair, rather than an embodied and intimate experience. Isolation turns us into passive consumers, in effect cultural 'Bystanders', with little involvement and nothing to gain from trying to grapple with the 'newsfeed' 'reality' of the modern world. Machines do everything for us and modulate our every-day lives to the extent that collaboration and friendship, even, seem somehow surplus to requirement. Witness the 'post office scandal' – 'the biggest miscarriage of justice in UK history' - where computers, machines and 'investigators' were believed by the UK judicial system above and beyond the human plaintiffs defending themselves – for a duration of *thirteen years*… 'Because machines are infallible?!?'

---

155. Chouliaraki, "Victimhood"

It's only by unplugging from 'virtual' sources that we can actually reclaim our lives, relationships and relevance in a society that is slipping farther from our grip daily, turning us all into its Victims, unless we take decisive action to reverse the trend. Consumerism keeps us docile - covering over the tell-tale signs of institutionalised Tyranny with numberless ways of feeding our low-grade Narcissistic impulses, tempting us with tawdry rewards, whilst keeping the fullness of our humanity anaesthetised and out of view... Psychology can be part of the solution or part of the problem. When we confine our analysis to shallow incursions into the 'micro-sphere' detailing internal and interpersonal relationships as the only things worthy of attention, without stopping to notice how the macro-sphere is adding to our disenfranchisement and dis-ease, then instead of offering empowerment, psychotherapy becomes a reactionary force.

... Perhaps it's a very clever Tyrant who is able to conceal from the Victim their status in the power grab taking place! As we will see in subsequent chapters, we are all Victims of the emerging Technocracy - and to recognise ourselves as such is a kind of wake-up call. It's only the beginning of a process that will require us to shake off the 'Bystander' approach we've grown accustomed to for several hundred years at least... This text proposes a revival of Eldering as only one of a suite of restructuring processes that might attempt to 'Re-wild the psyche and society' as a way to stave off some of what's in store for us all if we remain oblivious and compliant for much longer.

Exposing the distorted version of the Victim as we're about to do, is never to let Perpetrators off the hook, nor to minimize real suffering ... Rather, we reveal the shadow aspects of this least favourite archetype with a view to helping us recover agency and sovereignty *as a species* during difficult times - and possibly not in conventional ways. Maybe 'going back to basics' and investing in relationships and networks that might help us thrive once more are our real assets today; counter-intuitive though they might be in a cultural landscape encouraging competitiveness, status, and extravagance, as outward signs of success.

When Neurobiology Meets the Narrative

Moving away for now from the 'hapless victim' described above, the 'stuck' Victim Archetype crystallises when we 'tell ourselves a story' about how dangerous and unfair the world is; how powerless we are, and how impossible it is to do anything about it. Finding someone or something to blame normally accompanies this mindset – in this regard we can actually identify a similarity between Tyrant and Victim, in that both seek to make a third party responsible for problems perceived...

Picking up on the last chapter, Peter Levine might say Victim mentality signals an 'incomplete trauma reaction': – sympathetic nervous system activation – into *flight* rather than fight – or even a freeze/collapse response, signalling activation of the dorsal vagus nerve ... We may remember we have to *assert* ourselves somehow to complete the trauma response, allowing the nervous system to return to the relaxed state of ventral-vagus-dominant secure attachment. In the absence of effective remedial action, the nervous system remains *activated*. The real treasure here might be to find someone who can help us work through nervous system activation, enabling us to find safety once more. The isolation that often goes hand-in-hand with Victimhood is routinely conflated with a narrative of 'it's all my fault': – Coming to understand it's actually baked into the culture might help deal with a portion of the shame chronic Victims carry, enabling us to 'own' a sense of isolation, rather than keeping it hidden.

Shadow Aspects of the Victim

The Victim often hides in insulating layers of shame for not having managed to succeed or prevail in difficult circumstances, or achieve long-cherished goals; harbouring feelings of 'not being good enough' and 'being unlovable'. This allows the state of powerlessness and invisibility we might have first experienced in childhood to infect our whole outlook on life. In fact, if we remain inside this dark cloud for too long, we can lose the ability to get out from under it. Our reasons and justifications multiply; whilst the dangers of life outside have been avoided for so long, we worry about being ill-equipped when we come out of hiding. From my own experience, a lot of this goes on 'below the radar' of conscious awareness ... showing up as self-sabotaging behaviour for example. Shame also aids and abets the Tyrant who is happy to impose divide and rule - using whatever means necessary. When the Victim implodes inside a shame narrative, the possibility of joining with others to bring down the Tyrant is nipped in the bud.

We mustn't forget there are multiple benefits to being a Victim, after all: A Victim can exist on handouts, a Victim doesn't need to have a moral framework, and a Victim is 'done to' and therefore exempted from responsibility and thus the effort of recovery. A Victim is to be pitied, rather than blamed - Perhaps we can say that Victimhood confers a kind of 'invisibility cloak' on an individual - with some attendant advantages to feeling small, hidden and powerless. We have permission to fail, to hate, and remain frozen - we don't have to boldly risk our humanity on an idea, relationship, or crusade (maybe not a Crusade!) Nor do we have to marshal our resources and courage, or collaborate with others who might let us down. We can accuse them instead, without having to reveal our own failings. A toxic self-righteousness mixed with bitterness invades the heart of the chronic Victim...

So many factors might encourage us to stay in the Victim posture: after all, the odds are stacked against us; restitution may entail courting more of the iniquitous system that caused injury in the first place - maybe even opening ourselves all over again to being further abused, or the possibility of *'infamy'*, should our efforts fail. What about the potential judgement and betrayal of those we counted as friends, who might turn out to be *Bystanders*, seizing a sneering power trip moment whilst staring on from the stalls? We were already weakened by the attack, now we have to run the gauntlet again, which might seem too daunting. These are the real considerations we have to face every day when dealing with 'injustice' - real or perceived - factors that trap us a in 'Victim mentality'.

Of course, in coaching and counselling situations, those who can't face or find an avenue towards restitution are encouraged to *do something else* – channelling anger and hurt into creative endeavours or volunteering; helping others with a similar plight. Tolerating a little bit of discomfort, victims of injustice might find ways to build confidence one tiny step at a time, eventually entering a different co-created world with rules that can be negotiated and updated, whilst stepping out of the shadows. That's the tried and tested method for the Individual Victim. For all of us – the unwitting Victims of systemic abuse, surely, if we can come together cooperatively and meaningfully, refusing to do the Tyrant's bidding, then effectively, Tyranny loses power and control. It sounds simple; yet coming together in effective, self-sustaining ways seems incredibly elusive in times like these – *or is that just victim-speak?!*

Shame as Barometer

Surprisingly perhaps, shame can have a positive purpose, putting us in touch, in no uncertain terms, with the codes of conduct expected of us in our tribe or society, and consequently our own moral compass... Yehuda Tagar, founder of the Psychophonetics therapeutic modality, once said: '*to feel is very orientating*'... Shame can be an important barometer telling us when we're stepping out of line... We heed shame as a way to balance selfish impulses with the 'good of the whole'. Our optimal emotional reality is an evolving, dynamic dance; with feedback loops built-in. If I'm a Narcissist in recovery, perhaps feeling more shame might be a positive development... Sometimes shame is a reminder to keep our fantasies and delusions in check... It takes time, perhaps, to be able to distinguish healthy from toxic shame, yet what seems clear is that a person who never feels shame, or remorse, for *once*, is someone ***worth*** pathologising!

Fanfare: The Rescuer

Let's first acknowledge the reality of every day heroism in our world – the countless people granting safe passage, sponsoring projects, dressing wounds; digging deep to find resource and resilience to offer to those in need. Real people do lots of good rescuing work! Countless carers – most of them women – perform daily rounds of duties for the elderly, young and disabled, whilst countless men provide for and protect their families and communities; both sexes performing demanding and sometimes dangerous jobs, often with little recognition. It's easy to forget that caring for each other is perhaps the most necessary part of a functional society.

We return, for this schema, to the Transactional Analysis roots of the Karpman triangle, going into granular detail of the Rescuer's psychological make-up; noting again how interpersonal dynamics so often relate to historical attachment wounding, and using memoir to get 'up close and personal', in the hope my own experience is recognisable for others, adding depth and transparency to the theoretical frame.

The distorted archetype of 'Rescuer' is on the lookout for Victims to save, whilst perhaps simultaneously protecting said Victim from the Persecutor... With Noble Intent and Right on Their Side, Rescuers have the power and leverage Victims lacks. Admired for Heroism, Gallantry and Moral Rectitude - missing from the other Archetypes - *this* one has it in spades! Rescuers are thus able to distinguish themselves from the other, frankly, *discomfiting* stations on the Quadrangle, possibly sporting wide grins, even a swagger! At once better provisioned in resource and sheer grit and determination than the Victim (so they like to think!); morally superior, kinder and more empathic than the Tyrant; and made of altogether more articulate and courageous stuff than the lily-livered Bystander, the Rescuer is the Envy of all the Characters in the Play.

... At least so the posturing goes. Behind the scenes, it's a different story, including a sudden drop in temperature when the curtain falls and the Victim fails to grovel sufficiently by way of thanks for the Rescuer's ministrations ... Unfortunately for the Rescuer, he or she never received enough of the 'good stuff' early on - forcing emergence into adulthood insufficiently equipped, occasioning fraught and doomed interactions and missions from the get-go. Low self-esteem and low expectations play a part in how things pan out - There's a 'fake it 'til you make it' quality here; and according to tenacity, luck, 'smoke and mirrors', and minor miracles, the Rescuer might somehow leapfrog botched developmental foundations to become successful, at least some of the time! Sheer grit and putting ourselves out there as adults can teach us the social skills we may not have acquired as children. Everyone has to learn by making mistakes - and we have to be allowed to make them; and, *anyway*, development is *never* a done deal, but a life-long process...

Bearing in mind - we *do* live in fragmented times - and so - many are trying to navigate the adult world with insufficient inputs from our immediate surroundings; assembling jigsaw puzzles with several pieces missing... Some of us scrabble around and eventually claw our way to private and public victory; yet many of life's Rescuers get caught in negative feedback loops with rejection and failure acting as self-fulfilling prophesies; only reinforcing disabling narratives. It's worth noting too - Rescuers don't get as bad a press as Narcissists, for example, since the former wound tends to cause 'internal bleeding', and less collateral damage - although rage and despair can run pretty high in Rescuers when the 'giving to get' bargaining strategy backfires.

Earning Brownie Points

The 'Rescuer' takes care of others to his or her detriment - as a way to avoid the hard, disciplined work of taking him or herself in hand - unable to turn inwards due to embedded feelings of vulnerability and abandonment, and a chronically activated ANS... It somehow always seems easier in the mind of the Rescuer to sort out someone else's problems than his or her own. Unmet emotional needs propel the Rescuer towards (often covert) bargaining strategies, felt inwardly as hunger, longing and lack of self-worth. Ross Rosenberg describes the Rescue Effort as co-dependency - a kind of 'giving to get' behaviour where we earn 'brownie points' via the good deeds we do for others, hoping to create an indebtedness that might substitute for the thwarted attachment needs of childhood.[156] It's a symptom

156. Rosenberg, The Human Magnet Syndrome

of restlessness – the idea that there's always 'something wrong' with the world and other people – something that *we*, as self-appointed *Rescuers*, are tasked with putting right. Heaven forbid that everything might be OK, and that we could just *relax* and do *nothing* for a bit! The focus on the 'other' brings relief from the hollowness in the heart of the Rescuer who has had to disown or dissociate from so many aspects of self, in order to stay connected with dysfunctional caregivers in the family of origin.[157]

In relation to the previous chapter, the *ambivalent attachment style* has a lot in common with the Rescuer who proffers emotional and/or practical support – 'needing to be needed' – and yet chooses others who are not actually capable of offering love in return. There's low level desperation in the heart of every adult Rescuer. In the Lovemaps Webinar, repetition is seen to be pivotal, in an unconscious attempt to heal childhood wounding. Alice Miller's work on this describes the creation of an operational 'false self' that compensates for and masks the wound[158], whereas repetitive behaviours belong to the subconscious emotional centre of the brain where compulsion is born and familiarity is perceived as safety, even when it is far from safe...[159]

Not only is the cycle destined to repeat in an attempt to heal what's broken by getting up close to it; in a double-whammy of sorts, it gets baked in with narratives about our lack of lovability; and how stupid we are for making wrong choices, reinforcing low self-esteem and a need to *earn* love; whilst re-creating scenarios where love is always round the next corner – but never *here; now.* The lack of self-love creates a barrier that prevents us from being able to receive the healing care of another... In a triple whammy, if we're still in touch with our family of origin, and if they happen to scapegoat us as a way to deny any responsibility for broken family

157. Live Webinar, with 4.9k views. This couple run a recovery centre in the US. Their presentations are high quality and well researched – probably aimed at clinicians, but accessible to those with an interest in psychotherapy. Harmony Place Monterey. "Lovemaps as Trauma Reenactments"

158. Alice Miller, The drama of the gifted child: The search for the true self (Basic books, 2008)

159. According to researchers like Bessel Van der Kolk and Dan Siegel, dendrites carry past experience as affect, ensuring its repetition. Harmony Place. "Lovemaps as Trauma Reenactments"

dynamics, then we're swimming against the tide once more. From personal experience, it's virtually impossible to maintain high self-esteem in a judgemental environment, leading to the suggestion by Mark Schwartz of 'divorcing our family of origin' - even temporarily - to work towards healthier relationships.

Without 'doing the healing work', the partners we choose ensure we continue to avoid getting our needs met, since, for this distorted archetype to survive, the rescue operation must *never* succeed, at least not in the long term... Often subconsciously, we screen others for their rescue-ability quotient! Staying calm in stressful situations, and the ability to form stable social relations marks you out as low-scoring in the 'good rescuing material' stakes. Anyone with a smaller window of tolerance than the Rescuer is subliminally categorised as 'weaker', and thus 'Rescue-able'[160]. That's the 'gallant knight' in us, hoping to get a leg up the social hierarchy, or a foot in the door that might lead to romance or recognition via our Rescuing Initiatives; earning us some of the status and attendant hormonal hits (dopamine, serotonin, oxytocin) we so badly need... Tyrants and Narcissists alike use Rescue Operations as PR stunts, making themselves look good to the outside world, whilst getting off on a bit of 'narcissistic supply' in the process.

---

160. The 'window of tolerance' discussed elsewhere, is a distinction from interpersonal neurobiology, signifying a person's capacity to remain in the ventral vagus, securely attached stance in the face of stressors. This denotes a large window of tolerance. Conversely, being 'highly strung' denotes a low 'window of tolerance'.

Memoir: Polarised

There is a lot of disquiet in many men as gender roles shift – eliciting a sense of being somehow 'surplus to requirements' or 'no longer measuring up' in some (many?) situations. Rich (my ex-partner) told me about a disaffected men's online movement, known variously as the man-o-sphere, the Incels, (involuntary celibates), Men Going Their Own Way, or the 'Red Pill' men's movement, where men discuss and devise tools and strategies for pursuing success and well-being on their own terms, and turning their backs on women entirely. We need to be aware of this movement because it's a barometer of the hurt, anger and alienation felt by some men in the modern world, and as such – shouldn't be taken lightly. In particular, many men are upset about divorce and child custody laws that so often seem to favour the woman over the man, and with a sense of being obliged to always toe the line and 'do what they're told' lest they be labelled 'toxic' for showing any initiative, back bone or free will...

Angry (young?) men are liabilities rather than assets to society, and we ignore them at our peril... Looking back I think online culture influenced Rich **a lot** *– feeding into his fear of intimacy, and amplifying his circumspection, whilst punishing me in lieu of his ex-wife of 26 years, for her destructive behaviours... I didn't look into it when he mentioned it – I didn't think much of it. If you're interested in finding out how bad things are in some camps, and if you're involved in any of the caring professions, it's worth checking out the manosphere to get the lay of the land in these rapidly changing, polarised and polarising, times...*

Getting Underneath the Thing

I mentioned my experience with Rich in the last chapter on Narcissism. On a Buddhist retreat recently, I was able to 'get underneath' the whole experience; noticing how I'd inflicted it on myself in the first place, because of casting myself in the role of Rescuer. The Rescuer offered traction for my fearful, vulnerable part; (the Child in the Transactional Analysis model) masking low self-esteem with being able to use my talents on someone who had no formal knowledge of psychology... It gets subtle, and hopefully, Rich might say my Adult 'care and commonsense', or 'skilful interventions', (depending on whether I was GF or Therapist in the moment) were well-intentioned and helpful, at least some of the time. He may even concur that I permanently shifted some long-held PTSD of his, and only retreated to the Rescuer character in me because there was nowhere else to go, in the face of his Narcissistic defences that were much stronger than mine. Because I felt more able to care for him than he was able to care for me, it soothed my nervous system, because Rescuer trumps Victim, so I was able to play the Adult role to his child, meaning my fear of abandonment abated... It seemed like a fair and good trade at the time: – me helping him understand his inner world, in exchange for him helping me maintain my outer world.

Twang

I witnessed fear, possessiveness and a need to control coming up plenty for him, and wasn't too worried initially; figuring rupture and repair are common events, even in securely attached couples – but I hadn't factored in the spinning off into Drama that unfolds for those unfortunate enough to be insecurely attached. The avoidant exhibits a tendency to withdraw, whilst the ambivalent acts out with anger and clinginess. A Narcissist's deliberate 'twanging' of the attachment elastic, for 'effect', ensures they receive ready quantities of 'Narcissistic supply'. Rich had no faith in the notion that he mattered to me, with frequent recourse to deliberate inflammatory comments and behaviours, as a way to gain negative attention in the place of love. He practiced the 'Art of the Twang' any number of times; would watch me hit the roof, feel slightly sated; go into 'mea culpa' 'unworthiness mode' in an attempt to win me back; then – the moment I softened and became relaxed – 'Twaaang', off we would go again.

In a nutshell; I had subceived[161], with what was initially my larger window of tolerance, that I had more control. And I chose this dynamic; because my wounding feared securely attached individuals – partly because their self possession felt unfamiliar. The abandoned teenager inside me was overawed by a securely attached person's stability and competence. From my vantage point – the securely attached person's level of composure felt like a magical power. This is a vulnerable share

161. Below the threshold of consciousness

– so go easy on me, please... For people who don't feel safe in the world, securely attached people can seem daunting – there's a sense of not measuring up; of inadequacy – possibly followed by self-blame. In opening to a securely attached partner, I was afraid of feeling exposed; and of the other throwing down the gauntlet of trust – an unsettling and challenging invitation that I might not have the resources to face, (according to peering at life through 'Rescuer goggles'; which I notice subtly morphing into 'Victim goggles' as I write, in this kaleidoscopic review of damaged fragments of self..!)

So instead of secure attachment, I chose the booby prize again: Rich's regular 'twangs' gradually eroding any sense of relative safety I'd found as pay-off, until my window of tolerance shrank to the size of his, and I witnessed myself gravitating towards the 'hysterical woman' archetype each time he pulled away when I thought we were moving towards trust. My rising panic related to the untenable position of loving someone not available for love: – the pain and confusion of being caught there. Women perhaps have a greater tendency towards emoting in stressful situations; whereas men might be more inclined to bottle it up, or figure it out, or fix it. You could say I should have known better; that clearly I'm not really available for love myself by choosing someone like Rich, and it's difficult to argue with that! There's more on our relationship dynamics in the previous chapter... I hope I haven't been too self-indulgent sharing here, and that it's been useful for some.

The Bystander

The Bystander has been waiting in the wings all this time, with nothing much to say, although possibly glad to be out of the firing line when the Narcissist and Rescuer are in town! Connected to the 'avoidant' attachment style described in the last chapter, the Bystander is guilty, according to scripture, of the 'Sin of Omission'. This is an interesting turn of phrase, and one that points to our having collective obligations as part and parcel of our humanity. Ignoring the plight of others is tantamount to collusion in the perpetration of injustice, if we take the 'Sin of Omission' at face value; meaning we have a social responsibility to see that Justice carries – whether we like it or not!

Somehow, in the inner recesses of our psyche, we are aware of our 'Duty of Care' role; which is why, for example, experiencing the callous indifference of the Bystander from the perspective of Victim hurts us so much. Whilst the 'moral compass' of scripture is invoked here to explain the phenomenon, the origins of the 'collective care imperative' reach back farther in time. In pre-land-ownership times, we lived and made and shared and bartered everything within tight knit clans, pitting our wits against the elements; experiencing the power of immersive collective ritual... Children were woven into the fabric of daily life, whilst foraging, hunting, cooking and eating together were daily events. This modus operandi forged deeply empathic ties, still in evidence via our autonomic nervous systems, yet difficult to conceive and seize as living reality in the atomised imagination of the modern age.

Shadowlands

Out tribal roots beg the question - is the Bystander something born of our times? Is it a luxury none could afford in the past: - a product of us living separate lives within four walls now?... Disdaining the Victim du jour prevailed upon by the (potentially invisible) Tyrant - as Bystanders, we actively collude, studiously ignore, or deliberately distance ourselves from the Victim's degradation. Distancing is easy when there is no longer the central hub of community around which our lives cohere and converge. Distance is increasingly the water we swim in in our day-to-day lives, where Rescuing seems too *earnest*, visceral, and, frankly, *messy*, if not simply *'out of fashion'!*

Yet, in differing contexts; how aware are Bystanders of their role; and do they exercise choice in the matter?... In domestic abuse, a third party might be ignorant of cruelty; or, the Bystander might be aiding and abetting the Perpetrator - turning the knife in the wound for the Victim whichever way the Bystander pleads. It can be a lasting, perplexing, painful question asked by Victims of familial trauma - attempting to evaluate how much complicity others had in abusive events, as they attempt to heal the damage.

The Bystander signals a lack of resource in failing to intervene in abusive situations - reducing third party witnesses at times to states of child-like confusion, numbness and inaction.[162]

Connected not only with the avoidant attachment style and the freeze/collapse response in polyvagal theory, where safety is equated with 'pulling the plug', the Bystander might even suffer dissociation... It's important to remember these are *adaptive* responses to environments that did not meet our emotional needs, and that oppression of one type or another has a long pedigree in these Isles. In the feudal system in Britain dating from pre-medieval times, landless peasants swore 'Oaths of Fealty': - expected to risk life and limb, raise armies, even, for the humble privilege of a roof over their heads, and use of a small patch of land, belonging to the 'Over Lord', for growing food and raising a family.[163]

Our modern education system was born of necessity in the Industrial Revolution - basically providing a child care system that allowed parents to go to work whilst abandoning their children to strangers - something previously unheard of. Our educational model originated in Prussia - we'll examine this in more detail in the last chapter. Prussia's response to defeat at the hands of Napoleon was to create a schooling system that turned out obedient soldiers - to re-establish military might. This system easily transferred from battlefield, to factory, to school; ensuring industrialising nations signed up for systems of social control that taught compliance across the board. Installing a 'Bystander culture' is only one small step away from these historical developments.

Touted as 'lifting people out of poverty' and making the 'illiterate literate' 'modern education' was an imposition that broke relatively autonomous peoples' spirits, making them tolerate

162. Harmony Place. "Lovemaps as Trauma Reenactments"

163. Bernardus Parmensis, in the Ordinary Gloss (ca. 1245) insisted that persons who swore oaths of fealty and obedience must protect their lords from attack and harm. Kenneth Pennington. "The Formation of the Jurisprudence of the Feudal Oath of Fealty", Bulletin of Medieval Canon Law, last modified 2011, http://legalhistorysources.com/Law508/Feudal OathBrundage.htm

having a boss, rigid working hours and brutish conditions in the workplace and at war.[164] Previously; the home, the village, the tribe had been the province of participative education for young people since the dawn of time... learning at the feet of mothers, fathers and villagers - including Elders - skills of the artisan and small-holder as well as being taught Creation Myths and ethics in stories told and retold at fireside gatherings. Engagement, practicality, social skills, belonging and purpose were 'baked in' to the 'original system' via webs of complex relationships.

There were still battles and feuds, but *in between,* we could expect closeness, calm, intimacy, familiarity, and a flowing with seasonal tasks that beckoned with an organic 'schedule', rather than the alienating regimentation of modern times. Close knit community ensured our nervous systems were able to return to optimal function after traumatic events, with the ventral vagus 'safe and secure' setting coming to dominate once more, naturally and subliminally healing trauma.

Tyson Yunkaporta has this to say about close knit communities and the communal wisdom they share:

> "The only sustainable way to store data long term is within relationships - deep connections between generations of people in custodial relation to a sentient landscape, all grounded in a vibrant oral tradition...Oral traditions grounded in profound relationships represent a way of thinking that backs up your knowledge in biological peer-to-peer networks, and provides a firewall against dictators who might decide to burn down your libraries. It also mixes things up cognitively and allows your brain to rewire itself in more healthy ways. I call this way of thinking kinship-mind".[165]

In schools today, kids sit in rows learning about abstract macro-pictures they struggle to relate to. The 'great outdoors' might be a patch of tarmac and grass they manage to use to good effect in

---

164. Will Zoll has done a great job describing the legacy of Prussia on western education and beyond. Zoll, "Prussia Gate"
165. Yunkaporta, Sand talk

spite of it all for half an hour a day; but the real 'event' of schooling is learning and regurgitating 'factual information' on random subjects, many of which are cast aside in adulthood... Beyond the three R's, perhaps school best teaches us to 'hear and obey', whilst normalising post-modern mash-ups of random content. Codes of behaviour, jumping through hoops, and passing exams, become deeply engrained, alongside de-contextualised, intellectualised 'learning' as the fountainhead of modern 'culture'.

It's easy to argue we've been tamed and rendered docile by this system... Perhaps some teachers and subjects stand out from the norm, imparting inter-connectedness, creativity, cooperation, resilience, initiative and empathy. These qualities can be hard to discern amid the 'myth of modern education' as some kind of pinnacle of advanced civilisation... Interestingly, there's a dearth of information available when attempting to research the schooling system online. If it was some idealistic project, 'trailing clouds of glory'; why isn't the history of modern education, and its heroic instigators, emblazoned all over the internet?!

... Maybe we begin to discern already the cognitive dissonance of the term 'progress' when applied to modern civilization, our emotional selves, and our education system, even. Perhaps then, we can start to reinvent, as if our lives *depend* on it - because *quite possibly* they do - small human scale circular systems and economies that allow us to feel and know the full extent of our humanity once more.

The reverse is also possible - that the more neutered and numb we become to our creativity, initiative and connectivity, the less likely we are to become agents of change. We need paradigm shifts to foster our evolution in the 'grand scheme of things' alongside other creatures and ecosystems that have equal rights to life and respect. Let's hope there's enough sovereign impulse left in us to reconnect with ourselves, each other and our world - thriving within self-imposed limits for the sake of all; rather than existing under limits imposed for the sake of a few.

Bystanders - The Research

What kind of citizens might the education system described above turn out?... In recent decades the Bystander effect has been observed by psychologists setting up experiments in public places where someone feeling unwell lies down on the pavement. On camera, it makes a big difference if the 'plant' is wearing a suit; the better heeled you are, the more likely it is that you will be taken care of. The more dishevelled the researcher feigning sickness (the closer they resemble the homeless), the less likely anyone comes to their aid. The virtue signalling aspect of the Rescuer seems not to translate so readily to helping vagrants - *who'd have guessed?!*[166]

Failure to act has been attributed to something called 'diffusion of responsibility'[167] which occurs when anyone and everyone witnessing an 'emergency' could or should be stepping up and helping. When no one steps forward - we think: *why should I?* It's interesting to note that famous 'Bystander effect' experiments focus on sick individuals, observing the behaviour of random groups of people in public places. It's not so easy to set up something with different parameters to measure 'cultural passivity' on the macro-scale - (how to 'rescue a sick society'?) although you could argue we're actually 'living this experiment' according to the dictates of those in power, on a daily basis. Without researchers monitoring the 'macro-frame', it's impossible to assess the effects our education system, propaganda, economic oppression and other forms of conditioning have on behaviour. *How to measure the level of emotional and physical engagement and disengagement within society as a whole? Guinea pigs all – and not a control group in sight!*

I'm not saying 'no one ever helps anyone' - in my own life I've encountered countless acts of generosity - often from strangers - restoring my faith in humanity. Perhaps: - kindness, trust and care were the natural proclivities of human beings brought up in 'intact cultures', where emotional needs were consistently met from infancy onwards... and so perhaps these qualities have been instilled in us for millennia?

166. Hugh Fort. "Reading social experiment shows people shun clergyman disguised as homeless person", BerkshireLlive, March 10, 2016, https://getreading.co.uk/news/reading-berkshire-news/watch-reading-social-experiment-shows-11017279
167. John M. Darley and Bibb Latané. "Bystander Intervention in Emergencies: Diffusion of Responsibility", Journal of Personality and Social Psychology 8, no. 4 (1968): 377–383

How would we know whether those in control are eroding our naturally empathic state of being? If this was part of their 'project' - they wouldn't inform us of the experiment, or the results. Destroying empathy would make us easier to control, and if control is their objective, they definitely *would* try to undermine our natural caring instincts... Discretion if not downright secrecy would define aspects of the project, hiding datasets from those who might take an avid interest in their activities...

Whilst it's easy to dismiss the Bystander as the fickle product of the modern age - tut and move on! - It's worth contemplating that Bystanders, if they were to mobilise, could become the critical mass capable of changing society. That's why it would benefit us culturally and individually to track the movements and machinations of the Bystander, internally, and externally, whilst pondering what could be done to challenge this behaviour. What if, instead of reading this book as 'information' to be chewed and discarded - we treat it instead as a plea exhorting us to question our core selves; how we function; who we are; who we wish to become - individually and collectively...? What if there's a healthy part of us that loathes the Bystander, seeking to *honour an impulse towards patching up our tattered, threadbare social sphere?*

Interchangeable

Karpman discovered that the roles of the Drama triangle can and do switch, according to circumstance. When the (tin-pot) Tyrant finds his or her control strategy wearing thin, it's easy to flip to the Victim stance - with furrowed brow and a wringing of hands: '*Why me? Why is exercising control so much like herding cats!?*' If no sympathy or attention can be drummed up this way, perhaps a *noble mission* will do the trick - finding a worthy cause or hapless individual to rescue, whilst saving face... We've already noticed a penchant for Crusades amongst Tyrannical regimes - Are they not busy hiding inside the 'Rescuer' role offered by some version of a New Doctrine they wish to foist on the world, using it as a smokescreen to conceal their nefarious intentions? - Bless the Bystander - isn't he or she just frozen to the spot in the hope that no one mistakes them for a Victim, accuses them of Tyranny, or persuades them to try on a Rescuer costume for size!? – We could be forgiven for supposing life is a *game of musical chairs!* For Einstein – '*it's all relative*'; and whilst he was talking astrophysics, the psychosocial sphere too is contextual and dependent on powers, privileges, weaknesses and blind spots of any given people interacting in a given moment... and *anyway*, 'In the Land of the Blind; *the One Eyed Man is King*'.

From a different vantage point, we might each grow a Second, or Third Eye, even. A New Eye for Another World where; rather than Scuttling, Striding, Stammering or Charging about – the restricted gesticulations of the 'Karpman' 'Quadrangle' – we learn to take responsibility; breathe, slow down, 'fess up and ultimately reap the rewards of being simply human instead? It might sound boring – but what if it opened things up, rather than shutting them down? A world where we accept our fallibility and that of others, where an 'us and them' mentality is seen for what it is – unhelpful, divisive and shallow – where we courageously decide to learn to navigate beyond ideology; with our wits about us, our belly soft, shoulders back, and feet on the ground. Might we have worlds to win and chains to lose, perchance?

In the Theatre of human power dynamics, both personal and political, we are all influenced by the latest memes of 'in-group' and 'out group'; their collisions and oppositions. Perhaps, in this polarised and polarising climate, we can ask ourselves how to distil lessons learnt from history and psychology, as we move forward, whether we feel ready or not, into a Brave New World of Unparalleled Change wrought largely by Unelected Elites with access to unprecedented levels of Power. In the next chapter, we'll look beyond these dysfunctional archetypes to a notion of a totally inter-connected reality where our tendency to posture in various roles is up-ended. In this new realm, freedom and space to create is a matter of the way we learn to perceive reality, altering profoundly our relationship to Self and Other – and in the process dismantling the very foundations of the Karpman

Triangle. That's just for Hors D'Oeuvres though. Following that, we'll be examining the newest abuses of power and control taking place on a Global Scale, in ways heretofore unimaginable. *Fasten your seat belts folks...* It promises to be a bumpy ride!

ACTIVITY: Exploring Power Dynamics

Play-time: Find a group of at least four people including you. Write down 'tyrant or persecutor', 'bystander', 'victim' and 'rescuer' on four slips of paper and hand them out. Experiment with acting out scenes with each individual adopting the role ascribed to them on their piece of paper. Do it in an obvious way first, and then swap bits of paper and try acting out the roles secretly, so that no one knows which role you've chosen. Notice how you might slip and slide between roles. When you hit a 'dead spot', put the slips of paper back in the middle, shuffle and redistribute them, finding ways to change or manipulate the story to suit the new role you have been ascribed. If you have extra people present, ask them to observe, and to comment on the unfolding drama, and discuss amongst yourselves at the end how it went; what could have gone differently and how you felt in each role. Which role was easiest, and which role hardest for you to play, and why? In bigger groups, you can have more than one person playing each role; what happens when more than one of each character type is present - how does this alter behaviour? You could introduce a new role - the role of the mediator, and describe and discuss together the types of interventions needed to help resolve challenging situations. What skills does the mediator need? What does he or she need to look out for when dealing with each character type in the play? How can we support each other to be successful mediators, rather than adopting the simplistic roles given to us when we succumb to Drama in our lives?

You might like to research the 'empowerment dynamic' which switches the anxiety-ridden, problem-focussed world of the Karpman triangle for an 'Empowerment dynamic', where the Rescuer becomes the Coach, the Persecutor the Challenger, and the Victim the Creator, in a solution-focussed, passion-led inversion of the toxic dynamics of the Karpman triangle, leading instead to a virtuous exchange of positive qualities! There are many diagrams to be found online, none of which are my own intellectual property.

Chapter Six

Zen and Non-duality

Where is there to go, now that we have 'busted' the Tyrant, Victim, Rescuer and Bystander – reminding us in the process that 'all this crazy shit' is made up by us!? In this chapter, we enter the places where meaning is made; looking beneath and behind the roles we play in life; reaching past insubstantial Drama Triangles and Quadrangles, even... Expect to travel far into the reaches of inner space, as we examine how our understanding of the world and ourselves is derived: – exploring the realm of perception. This requires getting to grips with the workings of our own mind – the moment-to-moment minutiae of cognition, and how it shapes our approach to the world, and this in turn, our individual experience of being alive. My goal for this chapter is to instil luminosity and hope; bringing what many believe to be mumbo-jumbo down to earth in the process; even inspiring a Zen grass roots revolution, if such a thing were possible!

My attraction to unravelling, 'debunking' even, the 'human condition', started with Zen practice over 30 years ago; a perspective that invites exploration of the unseemly, possibly unseamly world of non-duality, its confusing contours and hazy horizons. Karpman himself asserts the roles of his famous Triangle are interchangeable, even in the animal kingdom,[168] begging questions about the interconnectedness of all life, alongside the necessity for a deeper dive in our quest for truth... A seeker of Wisdom might, at this point, tentatively hope such a line of enquiry will grant a glimpse of Enlightenment... That elusive, fabled state sometimes described as a 'goalless goal', where 'Buddha Nature' is apprehended in the spaces between the identities and labels we stick to the objects that populate our

168. Neil Sattin. "Interview with Stephen Karpman", Relationship Alive Podcast, November 17, 2019, https://neilsattin.com/relationshipalive

worlds. When we step back from 'nomenclature', we observe both Oneness, and within that, the reality that everything is contingent, or 'inter-dependent', if you will, on everything else, including the nature of 'being' itself.[169]

Non-Attachment

This line of thought tends to already blur the edges of cognition; we might naturally loosen our grip on pre-conceptions in the presence of a nascent, diffuse awareness. It's about gaining a wider *perspective that* grants *fluidity, one where the possibility of non-attachment begins to make more sense, at least as a back-up plan*! Non-attachment doesn't mean abolishing wants and needs, rather it invites us into deeper dialogue with ourselves and others, helping us respond more sensitively to life as it presents itself moment-to-moment; whilst deciding what's worth fighting for...

This could be described as the process of 'growing wisdom': - 'you can't put an old head on young shoulders'; it takes *maturity* to manage desire; defer gratification, or indeed; make a stand. Practicing non-attachment means becoming aware of the multiple ways we so easily get 'hooked in' to drama; inwardly and outwardly. We begin to clock we're only able to be manipulated because of our attachments... developing awareness entails noticing our private 'agendas' (no one is being asked to give them all up – but let's evaluate their *merit* though) – and then observe how we overtly and covertly *manipulate* towards them. And how we act out when things don't go our way!

Perhaps sharing our wants and needs with another can be a way to work with the koan[170] of desire. Asking for what we want always comes with risk attached: the other might simply say 'no' and flounce off in the opposite direction; or even if and when an individual or the world seems willing to meet us in our needs and longings; that's just the beginning of another chapter! Asking for what we want is a delicate dance, requiring transparency, authenticity, being in touch with ourselves, and courage. It

169. I get my take on Zen from my teacher Tenshin Reb Anderson, one time Abbot of Zen center San Fransisco, with whom I've sat several retreats.

170. A koan is a Zen riddle... they were used as a way to short circuit left-brain thinking, which we look at later in the chapter.

means recognising our fixation on outcomes often trips us up on the way, or it might mean noticing we've exiled certain painful, younger parts of ourselves still reeling from the impact of not getting needs met... The practice of non-attachment is not a kind of indifference - more an active curiosity concerning the nature of need and desire and how they play out in our lives. It allows for space to open up between 'subject' and 'object', self and goal, a space where magic might occur... It's also a place where we learn to recognise the whole world has wants and needs, not just us, making of the social sphere a vibrant messy junction with everyone jostling for a place near the front of the queue!

On Retreat in Hebden Bridge with Zen Master Tenshin Reb Anderson, circa 2011.

Reb's teacher was Shunryu Suzuki Roshi, credited with bringing Zen to the West, and with establishing the first Zen center outside of Asia in San Francisco in 1970. The book 'Zen Mind, Beginner's Mind' is a collection of Suzuki Roshi's teachings in the Soto Zen tradition, and one of the most widely read books on the subject. Reb Anderson has written 3 books: 'Warm Smiles from Cold Mountains', 'Being Upright', and 'The Third Turning of the Wheel'. Soto Zen was founded by Japanese teacher Eihei Dogen, who lived from1200-1253. The wisdom of the lineage has been passed on in the tradition of 'Dharma transmission' in an unbroken line from the 1200s until now. May the Dharma wheel continue to turn!

Practicing non-attachment can be very active at times; especially paying attention to inner narratives and often visceral fears and desires, hence why it does not equate with the passivity of the Bystander. Instead; we clock our wants - paying them heed; noticing how convinced we might be that happiness lies in possessing a thing, or sensation, or person. Tending lovingly to the part of self that is fixated on the outside world as 'solution' to our pain is a challenging lesson in self-care we can all benefit from learning... It's subtle, and I'm not suggesting a solipsistic solution, yet sometimes letting go opens up space for a well-rounded equanimity to unfold... Other times, achieving a goal; crossing a threshold; having a wish or dream come true is a landslide victory; bringing shifts in our identity; recognising the distance we've come, noticing how we managed to get out of our own way, and pull a new future into the present this time!

Healthy humans seem to need goals to work towards, yet simultaneously we need to know that striving can amplify suffering, depending on the situation. Equally, if not more importantly, we need to know we're contributing to others' well-being, while they contribute to ours, including rest and *reciprocity* as foundations for mental and emotional health. These qualities are the yin balm to yang's restless questing... In Zen we are encouraged to strive towards *Enlightenment*, yet, also; *if* or *when* we achieve it; to *'let go of the attainment'... avoiding* pride and fixity; enabling us to practice the art of synergy. Developing Faith in a benign universe; one that has our backs and wants justice and happiness for the benefit of all beings, is a piece of the optimal mental health puzzle.

Here is a précis of a Zen story from the book 'Being Upright' by Reb Anderson[171], which clarifies the difference between

171. Reb Anderson, Being Upright: Zen Meditation and the Bodhisattva Precepts (Rodmell Press, 2000)

non-attachment, and *de*tachment: "... An old Asian woman 'sponsored' a monk by building him a hut..." In parts of Asia, it was traditional to offer 'dana'; gifts from the 'lay community' - householders, artisans and peasant farmers - to those who dedicated their lives to spiritual practice. The custom may still prevail in far-flung corners of the world...

> "... This particular old woman brought a young woman described as 'rich in desire' to the monk living in her hut, in need of comfort and connection. The monk was cold and displayed disdain towards the young woman, refusing to offer her any kindness or support. The next day, when the old woman discovered the monk's aloofness, born of judgement towards the young woman, she burned his hut to the ground".[172]

We're not just attached to our sexual desires - some are equally attached to their notions of 'purity' and intrinsic 'superiority'. Holy is *not, **never,** 'Holier than Thou'. Detachment* is for people who don't *dare* navigate the living, breathing, non-dual world that interpenetrates our own *delusional, dualistic* reality of *separate selves living independent* lives. More on that below... *Detachment* is for those who don't *dare to feel,* or even those too *damaged* to do so... The notion of meditation taking us to lone mountain tops where we find all the answers and need no one is *a fiction,* or at best, part of a journey that at some stage requires re-engagement with the world for lessons learned to be integrated in a social context...

Looking at Language

How can we best describe the revelations that come when we take time to unravel some of our most strongly held attachments and convictions? In the process of patient enquiry, over centuries, Zen has revealed language as a means of peddling 'convenient fictions'; short hand versions of truth that allow us to picture and describe reality, so we can communicate amongst ourselves in ways that allow us to *make sense of the world* and *get things done.* It

172. Anderson, Being Upright: 114

allows us to take up the mantle of 'Food Critic' or 'Engineer', and *accomplish important stuff* like sending rockets into space.[173]

... Language, via human thought, speech and action, takes the world and divides it, naming and pigeonholing people and things, possibly even tainting everything it touches - each utterance reducing inherent complexity to lists, labels and memes. A Zen master might say: – *'wait – I do not give you permission to cut up reality like that'*.[174] Then, tapping you on the shoulder, eyebrow raised, he might say: *'Ahem, are you aware you're warping the world with words?'*... then invite you to step back (or forward) to take a look at the bigger/smaller picture...

Our hubristic Narcissist is a bit like: – ***'Whatever, Baldie, Who asked you?'*** and then, after 'humouring him' on the meditation cushion for an hour or two, weaponised thinking snaps back into place; scalpel in hand, or simply fingers at the ready, pulling experience apart into pieces, which we coolly consume, one bit at a time: naming, blaming, shaming, comparing, exonerating and more... It would be most unseemly and unseamly to attempt to eat an orange without first peeling and segmenting it, and similarly, it would be most ridiculous to try to engage with reality without dividing and categorising it bit by bit. We are all busy doing this almost all of the time; sorting, identifying and confining, mostly without even noticing, and since we are all doing it, it creates a false sense of security.

As someone once said – 'it's very unlikely goldfish will be the ones to discover water'. Naming 'subjects' and 'objects' fixes 'reality' in time and space, giving things an air of permanence and separateness. We like this – it gives life handles... We don't necessarily want to relate to the fact that our 'version' of the world is nothing more than that – *one version,* amongst many, in a

---

173. The author of 'Algebra of Happiness' describes Elon Musk's pursuit of the latter as 'deeply nihilistic'. Sam Harris. "Wealth & Happiness: A Conversation with Scott Galloway (Episode #189)", YouTube, 1:11:20, March 4, 2020, https://youtube.com/watch?v=CMPAPBnBkRc

174. This relates to a personal story: in a nutshell, I said rather dramatically on retreat with my Zen teacher: 'I vow to cut off the (internal) Tyrant' to which he replied: 'I do not give you permission to take that vow – you must first ***welcome*** *the Tyrant, study the Tyrant, engage with the Tyrant...'. This is the type of thing he said on a regular basis!*

constantly changing and ultimately unknowable universe: – it's deeply unsettling.

Yet the Buddha sitting under the Bodhi tree around 2,500 years ago was determined to find the root cause of our suffering and, cut a long story short, she[175] discovered that chopping things up with our thinking is a big part of the problem. Not necessarily the full picture, if you'll excuse the pun, but a big enough part of it to make Buddhists pretty determined in their practice to look for those 'jigsaw joins' in their perception of reality – and when they notice a scalpel trace they say ***'Aha!'*** (Often inwardly, making them hard to spot in public...)

It's not quite that we simply create a 2D jigsaw puzzle from the complex, living, inter-active, multi-dimensional world – it's that we then proceed to compose our own *random* Picasso-esque *fractured* collage from momentary observations and private memory-cabinet mementoes. From these ad-hoc fragments, we create a 'bespoke' *collage* of whatever we perceive of reality viewed through our own lens – et *voila!* – mistake it for Gospel Truth. It gets worse – once the mind 'understands' something it has a tendency to set it in stone – which means fixing it in time – obviously this too is illusory – since all natural phenomena are subject to cycles of growth and decay.

When we begin to discern, through mindfulness practice, that our picture is somewhat skewed, it can actually make us less opinionated, bring greater composure, and reduce negative friction with others. Buddhists have a neat word for Drama – Karma – which simply means the sum total of all the Dramas you've been part of over time – long stretches of time, many *lifetimes* they might say. All of that might sound far-fetched, until epigenetics discovered that trauma is stored in our genes, as we saw with mice and the smell of cherry blossoms.[176]

---

175. Reb Anderson, my Zen teacher, regularly referred to Buddha as 'She', to 'change it up' and help women feel more included in the 'enlightenment project'...

176. In experiments, when mice were given electric shocks at the same time as being exposed to a particular scent, six generations down the line, mice' stress hormones continue to spike in the presence of the scent, even in the absence of any electric shock being administered after generation #1. Dias and Ressler. "Parental olfactory experience influences behavior and neural structure"

The 'Wheel of Samsara' is the Buddhist version of the Karpman 'Quadrangle', with 'Liberation' from a Zen perspective envisaged as our ability to somehow climb out of drama scenarios to live lives of service and equanimity, where the *interconnectedness* of *everything* is experienced as *miraculous*, rather than a 'trap' set to hurt or enslave us.

Some people say the only real binary in life is Trust versus Fear, and that whichever we choose moment-to-moment (if indeed we are free to make such a fundamental decision) changes everything... It might be easier said than done though, to snap out of our dramas and into sitting cross legged by the lotus pond cultivating Wisdom and Compassion - those twin pillars of Buddhist practice. How do we hack the system?

Breaking into (or out of) the Drama 'Quadrangle'

Mindfulness is a practice that has filtered into our understanding in the West in the last 30 years or so, thanks to American psychologists like Jon Kabat-Zinn, author of 'Full-On Catastrophe Living', Tara Brach, Dan Siegel, and John and Jennifer Welwood, amongst many others. Originally a Buddhist concept, the secularised version describes the process of careful observation, looking for tracks and clues everywhere, moment to moment, in our thinking, speaking, acting and our interpretation of events. A quiet, peaceful mind is able to 'witness' and potentially unpick all of it, turning moment-to-moment experience into a kind of inner game of hide and seek; which is why the corners of Buddha's mouth are turned upwards in a smile always (!) *'Coming, ready or no-ot'* you call out to the farthest recesses of your mind, then *'Take that! Thwack'* when you spot a cutter-upper doing their 'dirty work'. Without hesitation, you swipe at them with your open, empty hand; then hold your breath and screw up your eyes, looking very hard *into* or *past* things, in an attempt to see them Whole. All of this is done in Tai-Chi- like slow motion, in the imagination, in case the thought of a 'Zen punch-up' is horrifying... This is why Enlightenment has been made into such a big deal - because it's actually quite difficult to achieve! With mindfulness comes the realisation that holding our breath and screwing up our eyes doesn't help us see the Whole Picture, because: – it's actually *moving; moving and breathing, decomposing and rebirthing – it's Alive!*

Somehow, we have to learn to *stop* cutting things up, holding our breath and screwing up our eyes, as we interface with the eternally-changing, interconnected Whole at the rock-face of reality... This is non-duality, this is Impermanence. Mindfulness allows us to *work backwards;* suspending our disbelief in the possibility that everything is One (even as it moves and changes) and to restrain ourselves from cutting it up the way our education system taught us, alongside the trainings we received in the rest of our lives. We carefully examine things, enabling us to see faint or glaringly obvious scalpel traces everywhere as we gently, patiently scrutinise the fabric of *our own* reality. We begin to realise that *how* we *notice* or *perceive* things actually has an impact on the way we feel about life, including ourselves and others. That's a vital piece, because 'reality' means different things to different people; 'reality' depends on our interpretation and *that* depends on mindset, expectations and experience, which we use to decide or decode meanings, via our own unique webs of association. '*Judge not that ye be not judged',* the Christian admonishment, emanates from a similar realisation.

Everyone has different memories, and so we all have individual perceptions of where truth lies. Unravelling things in this way, we start to notice that in fact, *everything is created in our mind interacting with our sensory apparatus with whatever we perceive out there!* We 'dip in and out' of our 'stream of experience' – taken to be 'objective' by a thinking process that has to distance itself from reality via ceaseless interpreting to attempt said 'objectivity'. And yet the 'dipping in and out' is an illusion too – how can we 'dip in and out' of something we are so totally immersed in?

Trouble Maker

The totality of our immersion, combined with absolute fluidity and interconnection makes *real* 'reality' ungraspable. We can call it 'Absolute Reality', or Buddha Nature, or Oneness, but that's about all we *can* say. The Persian poet Kabir once remarked: '... *Anyone who pretends to know anything about God is a Trouble Maker...'* Pay attention to your brain now as you receive this information - what's happening? I notice for me there's a sense of space, of unfolding, of reaching out into openness... My breath is deepening and lengthening, such is the exhilaration of beginning to notice a sense of entrapment inside my own narratives, and with that the possibility of freedom, as I catch glimpses of the role I play, in making the 'story' that is my life.

...And if you're feeling any of this yourself - perhaps literally a sensation of 'tingling' in the brain as we practice *restraint* from the habitual ways our neural pathways wire and fire together - then we might actually encounter the brain poised and prepared to make new connections. Forging for itself *new* physical pathways in the grey matter, and *new* pairings and associations with mental imagery... Or perhaps we might allow for a moment or two of nothing whatsoever happening - an uncanny 'break in the proceedings', whilst we simply 'take in the furniture' within and without - *Moving* furniture, mind you - *Watch Out*! - Each piece with individual embellishments and characteristics. Each piece *alive and not really furniture at all!* - Each piece pushing back against the static pigeon holes we'd much rather use to help us make sense of the world and feel 'safe'.

Acorns in the Wood

Let's pause to examine the Furniture metaphor for a moment: - crafted, in reality, from 'wood' - old furniture is 'stuff' that, once-upon-a-time, came from trees in the forest, which 'once upon a time' came from seeds such as acorns - and those acorns came from parent trees generating seed, which were themselves rooted in soil suffused with microbes, mycorrhizal fungi, worms, spores and rain water... When looking at a desk polished to a fine patina, a non-dualist practitioner might 'see' the soil the acorn took root in, and the ancient forest stretching back hundreds of years through time, imagining the hands and chisel of the carpenter who crafted the dovetail joints. If it's mahogany, maybe you'll imagine the creatures in the tropical rainforest who lost their homes to bring the piece to you. The piece of furniture is a meme, a glyph, an icon that contains the whole universe when we look carefully enough.

As you practice this way of approaching subjects and objects (including yourself!) - why not see if you can enjoy the deconstruction endeavour as an unfamiliar ritual of great import - *luxuriate, if you will* - just for a moment - *Yes!* It's '*carpet pulled*' from our usual belief systems and MO - but it's also *openness* to new *possibility* - we expand ourselves when we can tolerate the 'unknown' - and simply stay present - ***immersed in process until process becomes equal parts poetry and mystery*** - rather than the *dramas,* interpretations and posturing that otherwise fill our days; *keep working it backwards, folks*! When we are all engaged this way, it's very difficult for Drama to take root anywhere; when a group undertakes to do this work together, as is the case on a silent retreat, the effects can be magical... I have felt like a bee in a hive, with everyone playing their part to make the wax comb, the honey... using the active practice of mindful internal and interactive 'tracking', we get to 'wake up' together, and learn to navigate our own inner complexity, and thus the outside world; drama-free; moment by moment. We practice 'staying close and doing nothing,' as my teacher used to say.

ACTIVITY: Practising Non-dual Observation

Find an object and write about it – poetry or prose, or a mixture of both. Consider where it comes from – if it's natural, what kind of ecosystem gave birth to it, what natural processes is it enmeshed in?... If it's artificial, what kind of mechanical/industrial processes helped make it? What kind of humans invented it and then made it? How long might this object last? How old is it already? What might happen to it in the future? How might a school teacher look at this object differently to the way you are looking at it? Or a child, an engineer, a Zen master or a tourist? What do you like and dislike about the object – it's shape, colour, texture, smell? If the object belongs to you, what does it signal to others about the kind of person you are? When you've finished your piece of writing see if you can collar someone to share it with – before you do so, ask them to answer the questions about your chosen object in written form too. Or ask them to choose their own object and complete the exercise before you meet. Compare and contrast your writings, perceptions; associations. Be aware that this is one item; and now imagine carrying out this exercise with everything that exists in the known Universe. Perhaps the focus of this play-time makes non-duality easier to perceive and understand – perhaps it demonstrates that the 'emptiness' at the heart of all phenomena is actually what makes reality workable, pliable, interesting and viable!

We pick things apart and inevitably re-assemble them in Buddhism, using different parts of the brain as we go. This, combined with studying sacred texts that discuss the nature of reality, is called 'turning the wheel of Dharma'. The Teachings of the Buddha help us unpick our limited views, enabling us to re-assemble our picture of things to represent a truer, brighter, clearer version of reality in its place. We don't do this once or twice, we do this throughout our lives – meaning we need to stay open to re-examining our understandings every day, which actually helps us become 'agents of peace' in the world, if that's something on our radar. That's the 'working it backwards' part of the equation; for the 'working it forward' we engage 'Nobly' with the world, realising that our thinking, speaking, acting, livelihood, everything in fact, is a way for us to lay the foundations of a good life (the 'Eightfold Noble Path' in Buddhism). This 'lifestyle' of sorts is based on active investigation into the nature of reality; not taking anything for granted; thus, avoiding getting mired in our own pre-conceived ideas. The approach creates space internally, and that spaciousness in turn becomes a breeding ground for 'good practice' across parameters, emerging from patience, curiosity and compassion, where once 'jumping to conclusions' was a breeding ground for drama and suffering.

Hemisphere Hospital

... Language performs the amazing feat of allowing us to communicate and share information with one another, somehow relating our versions of the world to others with their own, at least so we imagine! The brain is busy disassembling and reassembling perception as it goes, all day long; it's designed to do this with the help of the left and right hemispheres. We are not only 'passing the ball' back and forth between two or more people during conversation, *thought itself* is passing the ball back and forth internally, formulating our 'take' before it leaves our lips as speech. The language centre of the brain is primarily cited in the left hemisphere, which is also responsible for making models for us - you know... the Picasso, skewed versions of reality that we take for the real thing... The brain is not necessarily super dumb though in this regard - or we wouldn't have made it to the top of the food chain - automatically it takes the Picasso confabulation or 'representation' made using left-brain scalpels, finger paints and more and *passes it* back to the right hemisphere, which is responsible for *making things whole again*.

According to Iain McGilchrist[177], we might have a tiny Buddha sitting inside our right hemispheres. Of course, we can't say the Buddha *only* sits there, because that would be cutting things up

177. McGilchrist, The Master and his Emissary

again, and Buddha nature is everything together. What we can say is that the right hemisphere is a kind of 'hospital' that deals with healing the wounds and excesses caused by the scalpel-wielding left hemisphere. It re-contextualises, bringing separate (dissociated?) elements back together, which changes *everything*, allowing us to appreciate depth, metaphor, meaning and humour, layering our understandings in ways (perhaps) only humans are capable of... Maybe in the right hemisphere there's an ambulance topped with a blue-flashing-light screeching round corners, ferrying our bleeding Picasso-esque-collage on a stretcher to hospital while Buddha smiles benignly, holding it's hand?... *Maybe* that's pushing metaphor too far!? The right hemisphere *mends* all maps and models – perceiving how they relate to each other, if at all, *vitally* noticing their *shortcomings,* somehow naturally fitting them into the 'grand scheme of things', or rejecting them even... Our right hemisphere is often described as our '*gut instinct*', the part that wants to road test or reality check the left hemisphere's implausible contortions.

And of course, *separating* the left and right hemispheres is in *itself* dualistic. If Buddha nature is the totality of everything, then Buddha nature is in the left hemisphere too that cuts things up – possibly trying to cut them up skilfully at least. And actually, people pay a lot of money for 'Picassos', so they can't be as wrong as all that. Some would say they depict a truer picture of reality than a photograph – that the fractured imagery is actually representing the workings of the left hemisphere as seen from a right hemisphere perspective. After all, Art as 'practice' looks deeply into 'reality' and mirrors back what it sees for an audience, which means it's likely to have a good dollop of right hemisphere input, also. Perhaps Art is all about making those invisible scalpel marks in the fabric of reality *visible* – those sleights of hand and confirmation biases – 'outing' them so we get to see ourselves more clearly...

We are *steeped* in metaphor (can you see the steam rising?) and so perhaps it's worth pausing a moment to reflect on the difference between our right hemisphere metaphors and our left hemisphere models. How can you tell them apart? Well first off, in a non-dual world – you can't! We start to notice that everything we can say about reality is approximate – blurring boundaries somewhat. The non-Dual world is tentative, exploratory and uncertain; full of possibility – which perhaps allies it to the 'scientific method' more than we give due credit for. There are some distinctions worthy of note however: models are 'top down' processes, whereas metaphors are 'bottom up', emerging from our phenomenological (physical, embodied) reality... Models belong to the *abstract two-dimensional* world, where thinking creates representations, or 'icons': – self-referenced, two-dimensional simulacra, and invests them with power and meaning. As I write this, it sounds like a kind of *sorcery*! Maybe that's *exactly* what it is. Perhaps the left hemisphere has hoodwinked and hi-jacked us all into realms of the abstract, prising us out of the pristine pine-cone-river-valley-wet-warm-misty-mountain realm of physical existence that the right hemisphere anchors us back into.

According to McGilchrist, this is the state of the world today: – the *Master* of the book's title should be the *right* hemisphere, whilst the *left* hemisphere, his *Emissary*, is charged with doing the Right's bidding, as the more 'Enlightened' twin. Except we've got it all topsy-turvy now, so the 'cut-up-off-on-a-tangent-delusional-individualistic' left hemisphere now rules over the right side of the brain; the side that contextualises, heals, smells, feels and walks the territory. The further in this direction we go, the harder it is to recover – we lose touch with the self-correcting processes and 'accurate mirroring' afforded by the physical world.

Elders, Institutions and Hemispheres

We haven't had a plug for the good old Elders for a while; so then: – Eldering is a predominantly *right hemisphere* activity that seeks to mend fragmented societies by reconnecting us with our hearts, our courage, our sense of purpose, and recognising our belonging with the natural world. It's a bottom-up (neurologically and politically!) leadership *movement*, if enough of us heed the call. A call that invites us to see as 'Big a Picture' as we can; one that we update and re-contextualise using our senses first and foremost; engaging with the world and each other, cultivating a 'deep knowing'; a living-breathing 'picture' fully infused with the phenomenal world. We take responsibility for our errant natures, our tendency for abstraction and delusion, by examining our prejudices in many mindful moments; thus attempting to reinstate the *right hemisphere*, or our 'Buddha Nature', if that's not too Grandiose or blasphemous a proposal, to its natural over-arching position as our safest, best-informed Guide.

'Hang on a minute though!' The left brain pipes up – 'it's really useful to send rockets to the moon, and distinguish the five flavours in a plate of food, and design new Lego models for the next generation of engineers.' Perhaps so. It could be more to do with our *attachment to the outcomes* of our cutting and sticking exercises, than the exercises themselves, that gets us into trouble. We tend to mistake our 'models' for the real thing – take note Neil Ferguson OBE at Imperial College London (someone take away his fuzzy felt *please!*)

We imagine that our manipulation of words and matter, for that matter, even down to the nano-particular, makes us Gods in our own right. Unfortunately, we tend to forget that our funny little pictures based on nominal understanding, fears and desires; not to mention pet projects and pay cheques, diverge significantly from the complex web that is the sum totality of life. We tend to lose sight of the Whole, and in so doing, we *Betray* the Beauty, Integrity and Complexity of the Patterns woven into the True Picture that's Not a Picture; that is in fact Matrix, Mother, Matter; like we said before.

Because we believe *our* version of reality as the *official* version, we tend to rubber stamp or self-approve our own agendas, as revealed through our own thinking, speaking and actions. We are ***self-scammers,*** and what's becoming increasingly clear is that we have put systems of power in place that make ***collective scamming,*** at unprecedented scales, possible too. Non-duality points out there is a continuum between personal and collective fiction, and as we tune in mindfully to 'Channel Delusion' inside us, in order to question and potentially dismantle (bits of) it, we hone our capacity – our BS detector – ready to intercept the fakery on our screens and in our world too. The mental apparatus of the human species, lumbering as it is, uses sleights of hand to rationalise our knee-jerk choices back to us, after the event. If we're able to intercept this in real time, what carnivals of corruption could not conspicuously be curtailed!? What fetishised fictions would not fittingly flounder? Which quadruple negative would quintessentially quicken the quorum quaking in the quagmire??

The crazy thing is that justificatory pompous verbosity gets *written down* by men (and now also women) in wigs, white coats, suits and ties. And these people are good at manipulation... They've made it their business to study neuro-linguistic programming and more, and employ experts at it, as we'll find out in the chapter entitled 'Psychological Warfare'. I was browsing an antiques shop yesterday, and saw a propaganda poster for WW1. It depicted a *Mother*, not a *Father* or Army General, but a ***Mother***, telling her son to *go and do his duty...* ***She*** who suckled and rocked him, and never stopped loving him all those years. The *Mother* is the ultimate tie, and the propagandists *knew* it, making her the most important target of their brain-washing Patriotic sentiment-infused *'War is Duty campaign'*. This masks the truth that *'War is barbarism and insanity'*, sacrificing the many to preserve the privileges of the very few; and that women, if they knew the conditions on the battlefield, would ***never*** send their sons to war...

Figure 5: *'Maternal' Propaganda (Source: Imperial War Museum*

Somehow, we've got so good at buying *justifications* about the way the world works, we've generated a plethora of impenetrable *specialisms* in our institutions; meaning *non-specialists* are no longer able to *decipher* 'Law', 'Medicine', and 'Science'. Even the war mongers who stand to profit from incalculable human suffering and chaos control media narratives to the extent we come to believe their rhetoric... What constitutes an institution though; or a military-industrial complex for that matter? No more, nor less, than a collection of stories repeated, refined and agreed upon by 'insiders' for so long that the resulting confabulation becomes unquestionable and unassailable, often with 'Follow the Science' as the *new* catechism.

We all know 'Follow the Money' is the true imperative underpinning procedure and protocol, but the money is good at hiding in 'philanthropy', shell companies and underground vaults, such as those owned by the Rothschild family... *Real* scientists are not religious zealots - but because Science has been *hi-jacked* and *corrupted* from within; by vested interests; by the 'Institution of Science' - the *Stake Holders* of '*Science*', these people like to paint themselves as the High Priests of a pseudo-scientific approach.[178] Now that the non-specialists (us) don't understand the language any more, it's impossible to decide whether what's being espoused has any bearing on reality; or if the latest Mandate is 'Emperor's New Clothes' mumbo-jumbo: crass Propaganda.

The Interdependent Field of Mutual Co-arising

Learning to look through non-duality goggles; we discern the living, breathing, impermanent world intersecting with every aspect of reality; even captured institutions: a reminder that could actually help with the extreme vulnerability and exposure we might rightly feel living in cultures led by Opaque Institutions, founded on Big Business. It's a bit of a mouthful, the inter-dependent field... but maybe that's only to be expected as a description of something we can't escape, can't fix, can't look at directly - like the Sun - and yet that describes the Vast, Weird, Interconnected Web we all exist inside of. This Buddhist

178. Anthony Fauci is the epitome of what's being discussed here, and this book debunks the myth. Robert Kennedy Jr., The Real Anthony Fauci (Skyhorse Publishing, 2021)

way of perceiving things expresses deep inter-dependence – the enmeshment of all sentient beings, on every level, in fact – and even non-sentient beings besides; tho' here's not the place to argue which is which!

There is potentially the productive, co-operative, beneficial side to our all-being-in-the-same-boat 'Epic Entrapment' of sorts, which scientists call Quantum Entanglement[179]; yet simultaneously, the way we impede, limit and trip each other up counts for much. The 'interdependent field of mutual co-arising' is the *herd mentality of civilization writ large*, expressing how our liberation and incarceration; are down to the sum total of our actions, thoughts, traumas, morals, blind spots, mindful awareness, appetite, capacity for change; more.

That sense of 'enmeshment', though, at the heart of this important piece of Buddhist wisdom – is a real challenge for many of us in the West. We were brought up to consider reality as a collection of separate 'objects'; and to associate freedom with autonomy and independence. If we're 'all in it together'; then responsibility and care are the necessary correlates of coherence... This is bad news for those who worship at the Altar of the Individual – finding themselves uncomfortable with limits; relentlessly needing to compete to stand out from the crowd.

Glitch in the Matrix

... Witness the tragedy of us not seeming to be able to learn from our mistakes, and the courage of the crazy one in the crowd who shouts '*Ahem – isn't this a re-enactment?*' in the midst of a lynching. It happened once already: – '*let he who has not sinned cast the first stone*'... If we all then look around for a moment, do a double take and think: '*You know what; he's right –* ***yes*** *– we have all been here before – let's not repeat the pattern – let's do something* ***differently***', then the 'field of interdependent co-arising' gets to Pivot on its Axis. It might sound Monty Python-esque, and it *is* on some level; but then again, what was Monty Python about if not the madness of crowds, power, responsibility, and breaking the collective amnesia of the Bystander?

---

179. Barad, Meeting the Universe Halfway

The narrative only gets to change when the courageous one, often an Outlier, is truly heard; possibly followed by a long pause... Then the glimmer of a shimmering new world might appear, instead of said Outlier getting trampled underfoot, and the circus carrying on like before: - people 'Going with the Flow - like so many Dead Fish!' - Even and in spite of mixing metaphors - you get the drift! We can't change 'til we *all* change - to change means not leaving anyone behind. It means doing a thorough job, it means thought-policing of the mindful kind - it means owning our shadows, our history, and our capacity to harm as well as heal: and *then* some... It means recognising the Outliers as possible Saviours - maybe there's an Outlier in all of us, cleverly disguised? If that's the case, then we reverse engineer the notion, abolishing 'Saviours' entirely, and waking up to individual responsibility... The following two chapters of the book are devoted to exploring 'Outlier narratives', AKA 'conspiracy theories', bringing, it is hoped, fresh perspectives, clarity and insight to some of the fragmented discourses of our times.

We are products of, and hostages to, the invisible threads and scalpel marks running through our precious lives, made by our own societies, and their collective Karma. We've discussed *individual* Drama in the preceding chapter, this *new* notion refers to the inescapable *Karma of the Collective,* which in our day is influenced in no small measure by a small clutch of individuals and corporations wielding more power than any of us can easily imagine.

Understanding non-duality might help us gain a new perspective, some leverage even, for envisioning a *better way forward* from here - a *rigorous, mindful, non-dual* way forward at that. The bad news is that many of the sources we use for our own research, attempting to make sense of what's happening, have been captured by corporate interests: Mainstream media, Google, and indeed Wikipedia do *not* offer up search results, or 'information', impartially. Anything with contemporary political import, and they skew the narrative; being paid hefty sums to suppress certain channels of information from powerful lobbies behind closed doors.[180] Fortunately a host of new channels are springing up offering *uncensored* news: Rumble, Odyssey, Substack – although these channels will always have the confirmation bias of their makers woven in, at least they offer diversity and prevent Google being some kind of 'One Party State' – *for now.*

What do we mean when we speak of 'collective karma', and how does it impact us in the day-to-day? It means we are all interlinked in multiple, incalculable ways, and that we affect one another in manners subtle and gross, with our programming continuing to guide our behaviours in ways often invisible to the naked eye. It means we're more gullible and malleable than we realise, possessing less of the discrimination and autonomy we pride ourselves in as Western Civilization. It also means the carnage we've wrought, deliberately and inadvertently: – the species extinctions, the genocides, the misappropriations, the cheating, it means we *never actually get away* from those things. This is not just Buddhist understanding, it's widespread News within Christianity also: 'As ye Sow, so shall ye Reap'. The consequences of our actions are inescapable.

The Power of Confession

... Professing this insight is foundational for practicing ethics – It might seem counter intuitive, but 'fessing up actually ensures self-preservation, whilst protecting others from webs of deceit. Transparency is the only thing with the power to heal relationships. Moral 'impeccability' is a great asset; freeing the practitioner from guilt, the possibility of retribution and the complexity of deceit. Is it easy to practice perfectly? *No!...* Yet considering the last chapter and the pain and confusion caused by the roles we get stuck in – suddenly a different approach involving grace and humility seems worth considering. This is not meant to sound preachy! I'm sharing what's worked for me – practices and perspectives transmitted by Reb Anderson: '*Zen Elder*'. The absence of these skills and practices causes entrenchment and resentment, denying us simple ways to find peace within and without.

180. Anya Schiffrin, Media Capture (Columbia University Press, 2021)

Reb used to say: *'the more Enlightened I become; the* ***more*** *I spend my time Confessing'*. Confession is a practice of stripping back layers of camouflage to reveal the truth of who we are. The process is more sophisticated than a finger-pointing 'blame game'; the power and purpose of confession being ritualistic; with *revelation, restitution* and *evolution* at its heart. Confession has possibly been misunderstood or even perverted in our times; the austere and private cubicles of the Catholic faith don't necessarily help matters.

In a group setting, the individual 'doing the work' makes himself vulnerable on behalf of the whole - everyone gets to see themselves mirrored in the process, without necessarily needing to squirm in the hot-seat. It requires a skilful facilitator to hold space for this kind of witnessing; where an individual's vulnerability is courageously laid bare; the volunteer being someone sensitive yet fearless; committed to doing the work; who's peered into the abyss long enough to find a few bright stars twinkling there. They perform an act of service for the 'tribe' in being willing to reveal a weakness or failing or flaw and turn it around in full view, making healing processes visible and viable, common currency even. I've seen this in medicine ceremonies, Zen retreats and psychotherapy trainings.

We *confess and repent,* and it seems this is never a done deal - these rituals are built into the weekly or even daily 'programmes' of both the Buddhist and Christian traditions (probably *all* spiritual traditions). If our current predicament is the result of past actions - it points to the need for much atonement. My own experience of confession has been and continues to be *freeing* - when I am able to *own* being less than perfect, a mask or defence falls away - I get to be transparent, a weight is lifted. Hopefully I feel seen by someone who takes me at face value, rather than using the opportunity to 'put the boot in'. This latter tendency tells us more about the denial and/or ignorance of the aggressor than the 'inferiority' of the confessor.

Confession is a reflective practice - one where we 'call ourselves out', and in so doing, give others the opportunity to do the same on their own account. It's a way to 'keep things real', practicing *relational hygiene* – where we recognise holding things back leads to inner and outer festering... It can be done in dyads or groups, depending on the level of maturity of the people involved... The skills needed are not acquired at any old New Age one-stop workshop! Tools such as Non-Violent Communication (NVC) might sometimes help: – 'talking templates' offering some kind of support with the process, although the emergent reality of any exchange goes well beyond a 'template', which some individuals might use as means of hiding... It takes awareness and patience and willingness to show our full-spectrum selves. Trust is born in the practice of becoming more transparent to others – and not everyone in our circle will be willing or able to meet us courageously in the way we aspire to. Discernment is part of the learning process.

How do we practice? – By working it backwards, steadily noticing all the invisible traces clouding our individual and collective understanding of reality. Noticing all the causes and conditions, both beneficial and toxic, past and present, creating our current circumstances. Atonement could be seen as a kind of 'sacred accounting', which of course it is: and thus needs to include feelings of gratitude for all the gifts we receive daily, as well as remorse for the ways we err.

By connecting in real-time, face-to-face with others, we create 'holding containers' to do this kind of healing work... Gathering and listening and stripping away quickly create depth and resonance some might solemnly describe as 'sacred'. There *will* be fear, in revealing what we might prefer to keep hidden; yet, with the right kind of leadership comes courage and hope, and the wisdom that metabolises fear into humility, compassion, growth.

This is the silver lining to be remembered when all eyes are on us, and we have nowhere to hide and nothing to stand on. According to Buddhists, dismantling our defences and self-structures leads to the realisation of 'emptiness'. We discover our thought processes, and those of others are free from 'fundamental substance' by virtue of our ability to change – this realisation is *Liberation*; and the definition of Enlightenment. To be 'empty of a fixed identity' means we've understood the secret to 'FREEDOM', allowing unclouded insight, adaptability, fluidity, relevance, spontaneity and sensitivity to emerge – eminently useful traits, maybe especially in rapidly shifting times.

Atonement is also about remorse; in contemporary psychotherapy, very similar processes are called 'Shadow work'. The Narcissist or Tyrant feels no remorse, and no need for examining the Shadow, because he or she is so distant and protected inside a 'safety bubble' of defence mechanisms: delusions of their (our?) own making. Atonement bursts this bubble and is a necessary practice if we are to learn to drop the emotional armour that blocks love, respect and empathy. We can't get in touch with those emotions without letting our guards down as a way to thaw the frozen, numb places inside that keep us distant from ourselves and each other.

For change to come there needs to be a cultural container where we can measure what's going on – free from our screens that mediate reality so much of the time – in the face-to-face, here-and-now. We start to uncover a *world of possibility* where nothing is quite as it seems, and whilst that might sound like hard work – and yes, it can be – it allows a fresh breeze to enter the hallway of our fixed ideas, behaviours and 'realities'... We make time and space to look into other pairs of eyes; create spaces to be held and witnessed as we do the difficult work of unravelling our personal and collective Karma; allowing ourselves to feel again – Sacred Circles are a place to reclaim our ability for release, connection; tears and joy...

We might do well to remember matter is miraculously self-organising – witness a fertilized egg turning into a chick – making our anxiety at the prospect of disclosure and dismantling the self, easier to bear. If you can stomach the 'carpet pulled' sensation that is at the radical heart of Zen; you might be prepared to admit that we really have *no idea* who we are, *most of the time.*[181] Yet, allowing ourselves to be fully seen in the humbling process of 'shadow

181. Rumi: 'I'm just a goat hair brush in a painter's hand; we have no idea what we are'. Coleman Barks, Rumi: The Book of Love: Poems of Ecstasy and Longing (HarperOne, 2005)

work' – probably letting go of control in some fundamental way – doesn't equal being 'out of control': we're not about to roll down a hill or spontaneously combust!... Maybe life has it all handled without your input?[182]

... Perhaps the best we can do is scrutinise ourselves in the day to day – our drives, repetitive patterns, attachments, attractions and revulsions steering us along mostly pre-determined paths. Even when we think we're rebelling against the system, we do so in mostly predictable ways, and are prevented from genuinely breaking free by the invisible glue that is the field of interdependent co-arising... Meaning working it backwards, watching and waiting is actually a really good strategy for change, counter-intuitive though it sounds; we're attempting the work of melting said glue, to allow it to un-mesh and re-mesh in different, healthier ways, internally and externally.

Indra's Net

If we're all delusional, stuck in ruts and attempting to engage with a complex, mutable universe, how does anything work?! How does the show keep itself on the road? How do things cohere and interact; how does anything make sense, let alone get *done?*... By virtue of the inherent *emptiness* of all phenomena in the manifest universe – *that's* how; oiling the wheels of existence in myriad, invisible ways... The Heart Sutra asserts: '*Form does not differ from Emptiness, Emptiness does not differ from Form – Form itself is Emptiness, Emptiness itself Form.*' Further: '*Sensation, perception, formation and consciousness are also like this*'.

Behind our reactions, descriptions and interpretations of reality: our collages; – *emptiness is the un-glue that helps us grasp the true nature of our gluing proclivities. Emptiness* reminds us that our understanding is as fleeting and fragmented as a photograph in a wildly, impossibly tangled world... Resourcing ourselves from Emptiness is the best way we have of 'keeping it real' and dropping delusion, in ways where wonderment and joy are as likely to win the day as distorted, damaged archetypes.

---

182. Tom Bilyeu. "This is Going to Hurt. Everything You Know is False. | Annaka Harris on Impact Theory", YouTube, 1:07:11, Febriary, 11, 2020, https://youtube.com/watch?v=AL5g-AY3l2E

These processes and possibilities are described by some therapists interested in pushing the envelope of healing, towards 'spiritual' goals. Navigating 'emptiness'; which according to the Heart Sutra is the same as navigating 'form', daunting though it seems, when accomplished alongside a skilful ally, can bring astonishing gains. Describing State Four of the therapeutic process, Diana Fosha[183] says:

> "In the highly integrated *core state*, the patient has a subjective sense of 'truth' and a heightened sense of authenticity and vitality; almost always, so does the therapist. The defining qualities of core state overlap with qualities characteristic of resilient individuals and also with those cultivated by contemplative and spiritual practices - wisdom, compassion for self and others, generosity, vibrant wellbeing, equanimity, confidence, creativity, naturalness, enhanced initiative and agency, a sense of the sacred."

She further goes on to say:

> "Experience is intense, deeply felt, unequivocal, and declarative, sensation is heightened, imagery is vivid, focus and concentration are effortless. Anxiety, shame, guilt, or defensiveness are absent; there is no pressure to speak, yet the material moves easily. Self-attunement and other-receptivity easily coexist. Mindfulness - the capacity to take one self, one's world, and one's own unfolding experience as objects of awareness and reflection - prevails. In this 'state of assurance' ... the patient contacts a confidence that naturally translates into effective action".[184]

The Power and Majesty of the Field of Interdependent Co-arising, when we're able to give up cursing the invisible glue of Karma, dictates that when we access Positive Karma, we

183. Diana Fosha, "Emotion and Recognition at Work," in The Healing Power of Emotion: Affective Neuroscience, Development, and Clinical Practice, ed. Diana Fosha, Dan Siegel and Marion Solomon (W. W. Norton & Company, 2009), 172–204.
184. Fosha, "Emotion and Recognition at Work"

support Positive Change in the world... In this reality; isolation is seen for what it is: delusional fiction. *Connection and intelligence are woven in – making of Enlightenment a Collective Endeavour – such as the way Indra's net*[185] *reflects luminous wisdom from node to node, crossing the whole structure!*

... How do we Test for the Truth in these assertions? Acting in Good Faith, we recognise each one of us is a node, able to reflect light throughout the web of inter-being Buddhism (and Hinduism before that) have intuited as the fabric of reality for over 3000 years. We are all *catalysts for change, bringers of light,* able to *vivify* healing narratives with our intentions, perceptions and actions. When enough believe and behave as if each node in the matrix has a holographic capacity to reflect truth and light, a tipping point could be reached where perceptions and actions seamlessly shift reality. In this scenario, Buddha Nature is apprehended in everything, and awareness becomes so suffused with this realisation that Enlightenment is animated as our reality.

I remember my own Zen teacher using a Woody Allen film (before any defamatory allegations) to illustrate the meaning of 'Dharma flower turning Dharma flower' (this was the title he'd given to a week-long retreat). He described a scene from a Woody Allen film[186] where the disciplinarian prison officer is stomping up and down in big black boots giving everyone the third degree about the rules - mostly connected with the slavish work schedule and absence of any comfort or civility. ***'Any questions?'*** the officer bellows. Woody Allen pipes up: *'What do you think about heavy petting on a first date?!'*

In a non-dual Universe this is not a stupid question... but an indication that we're always at liberty to change the narrative, pull the carpet, claim agency and Sovereignty... So much in

185. Indra's net is a Mythic metaphor described in both Hindu and Buddhist sacred texts... At each intersection or node where the net's threads meet: an iridescent, reflective, transparent jewel sits... Each individual jewel reflects every other one across the entire span of the wondrous web, reaching far into the deepest recesses of the Universe. In this way Dharma, (Buddha's teaching) luminosity and Wisdom are transmitted through space and time... In this way, we see ourselves as 'nodes' on Indra's net, with each 'consciousness-polishing' activity we perform reflected throughout the net, activating a quantum 'raising of consciousness' that permeates the entire field of awareness.

186. Take the Money and Run, directed by Woody Allen (ABC Pictures, 1969), 1:15:00.

today's systems and institutions might benefit from a certain kind of reboot... Indra's Net and Woody Allen remind us: we're all responsible; it takes a light touch; no outcome is guaranteed; we can turn around on a dime; in the darkest places the light of the human spirit still shines... Let's hold these teachings close as we continue to unpick and lay bare worlds within worlds in the coming two chapters...

Indra's Net Artwork, by Seventh Satellite (Source: Pixels.com)

Chapter Seven

New World Order

This is a bit of a come down from the last chapter – as we explore *not* the 'New World' arising from Zen practice, but a 'Brave New World' of geo-politics several hundred years in the shaping, and coming into sharp relief especially in the last three... Yet Zen might not be as irrelevant as we think when it comes to the emergence of a Global Government dependent on fifth Generation Warfare, if Robert Malone is to be believed.[187] The battle field in this new scenario is the human mind – where manipulating our perceptual field is the goal of an invisible enemy. Sowing confusion, the covert cloak of anonymity, censorship, total amorality, and divide and rule are just some of the 'weapons' used to weaken and control us. It could just be that the ability to deconstruct and reframe 'reality' that Zen is famous for can support our efforts to remain free-thinking whilst developing resilience to the worst excesses of this new, ubiquitous and difficult to comprehend threat...

I'll do my best to *tell it like it is* – for better or worse, notwithstanding the inevitability of confirmation bias, and living in times dubbed 'the post-Truth Era'.[188] It feels like a wrench in the gears, suddenly talking about history, economics and geo-politics – and in so doing uncovering how Big Tech and Big Pharma, global governance, mainstream media, captured academia, 'predatory philanthropy' and our inalienable human rights, fit into the picture. Much of what we've covered so far relates to mental health as defined by those institutions that have studiously kept themselves apart from the political realm; but with unprecedented Global over-reach and censorship –

187. Robert Malone. "Fifth Generation Warfare and Sovereignty", Pandemic Strategies – Lessons and Consequences, January, 2023 (conference in Stockholm, Sweden), https://doctorsappeal.com/international-conference-pandemic-strategies

188. Peter Pomerantsev's presentation cited previously, is well worth a watch. The Institute of Art and Ideas. "What are post-truth politics?"

lockdowns and mandates – how can we consider mental health *apart from* its wider context?

Thus, we examine the modern morass that has replaced tight-knit community, in an examination of the trajectory of humanity, daring to ask whether the stories we are told about progress, growth and development are really delivering the improvements to our quality of life that are routinely advertised... As I switch Zen robes for a trench coat and notepad to explore geo-politics, I can't help but notice 'the journalistic' profession in turmoil and disrepute all around me, more so than ever since these 'pandemic' times: – just one more carpet pulled out from under us. Journalism hasn't just become a 'polluted archetype': – the *damage* and *havoc* the captured main stream media (MSM) *propaganda machine* wreaks on the general populace, aided and abetted by social media, compounds the 'divide and rule' culture wars now proliferating.

Amongst many tactics, the MSM works in lockstep with corporate power and government to create the illusion that the only purveyors of 'mis-information' are certain renegade individuals, thus diverting attention away from corrupt, captured institutions riddled with conflicts of interest: – a sure sign of the Orwellian 'doublespeak' times we live in. The people worth listening to, in my opinion, are often much maligned, de-platformed 'freedom fighters'. People who have often put their careers on the line, speaking out, even making their *own* news channels in a refusal to be silenced in the 'cancel culture' we now live in. There's a QR code at the end of the book that takes you to a list of resources on my website.

My favourites freedom fighters include Del Bigtree and the 'Highwire' news channel, Dr Robert Malone, Alison McDowell, Sayer-Ji and Kelly Brogan, Dr Pierre Kory President of FLCCC, Dr David Martin, Julian Assange, Dr Mike Yeadon, Dr Tess Lawrie, Russell Brand, Dr Peter McCullough, Dr John Campbell, Bret Weinstein, Dr Aseem Malhotra, and candidate for the 2024 US presidential election Robert F Kennedy Jr., to name a few.

... These are the people who bring me strength and inspiration – writing this chapter, I can't help noticing a fear of being 'taken out', or imprisoned, for my opinions, because I believe *we **are** at war*, and things *will* get worse... There's also a sense *I've waited too long already* to find a voice and gather enough information to make a coherent case. It's easy to balk at the task; to feel under-qualified and overwhelmed. There is so much to know, and the 'rabbit hole' leads into a rabbit warren, it seems, of epic proportions. There is the challenge of verifying sources. With the curtailment of freedom of speech, those with divergent views have had to go 'underground' using alternative platforms like Rumble and Substack, although much of value can still be found on YouTube. One amazing thing about technology is how it 'levels the playing field', assuming we know where to look, allowing us all to become documentary film makers and study subjects in depth in ways that used to be reserved for academics and professionals... Incidentally, 'peer reviewed' papers are not 'rubber stamped' with authority the way they used to be in these days of captured academia, ghost writers and spoofs somehow getting through the purported rigorous selection process to publication.[189] This is the least of the problem - corporate and institutional capture includes highly selective funding and defunding, intimidation, sacking whistleblowers and upholders of freedom of speech and choice, defamation, censorship and skewing statistics and 'reports' in numberless ways.[190]

I cite high calibre doctors, lawyers, and independent researchers with proven integrity and track records - people like Dr Mike Yeadon, the ex-Vice-President of Respiratory Research at Pfizer, who has a double first degree in Bio Chemistry and Toxicology, and a PhD in Respiratory Pharmacology, and who spent many decades in bio-pharmaceutical R&D - even running his own Bio-Tech company.[191] These days, people of his calibre are routinely cancelled and slandered - just try finding something positive on

189. The grievance studies affair by James Lindsay, Peter Boghossian and Helen Pluckrose outlines the successful publishing of bogus 'peer reviewed' papers, raising questions about the intellectual validity of postmodern philosophy and critical theory.

190. The Democracy Fund. "The ethics of freedom | Dr. Julie Ponesse", YouTube, 4:27, 2023, 26 January, https://youtube.com/watch?v=te1AqY-RPUI

191. Steve Stecklow and Andrew Macaskill. "The ex-Pfizer scientist who became an anti-vax hero", Reuters: Investigates, last modified March 18, 2021, https://reuters.com/investigates/special-report/health-coronavirus-vaccines-skeptic

Wikipedia written about any of the names I list above; whilst the New York Times (NYT) and subsequently The Guardian[192] published a list of the supposed 'Disinformation Dozen' in 2020 in an attempt to silence informed debate. The original article is difficult to find now, because of its libellous nature – Googling RF Kennedy Jr. will leave you in no uncertainty as to which side the tech giant is on. Traditionally the left was humanist, liberal, and arts orientated in the political landscape. Now 'leftist' extremists have become the captured, dangerous, censoring bigots of our day: – wolves in rainbow-coloured sheep's clothing.

The people cited in the NYT, including several listed above, have been accused of 'hate speech', yet a quick glance at any of their websites reveals qualified, caring, intelligent, informed individuals with multi-dimensional approaches to health, well-being and bodily 'sovereignty' (being free to choose health care options and decline medical procedures). Meanwhile, on Wikipedia, as you can imagine, there's a glowing précis of Anthony Fauci's career – one time director of the American National Institute of Allergy and Infectious Diseases. These days (post-R F Kennedy Jr's bestselling 'The Real Anthony Fauci'), there are fewer pics of him shaking hands with a series of US presidents, and no reason cited for his stepping down in 2022 – just the bald fact (look elsewhere for details!) To think I received a '*humble request*' (the very words used) from Wikipedia's fund-raising arm recently, asking for financial support to keep them 'Ad-free'. I *did* go to the trouble of finding a reply email address, announcing in no uncertain terms that I *will not* be supporting them any time soon: '*Go Ask Bill Gates for a Top-Up!*' Whilst the Wikimedia Foundation has compiled vast amounts of interesting and useful information on every topic under the sun – unbiased it isn't!

---

192. While the original NYT article has been removed, a Guardian article cites a study by the 'Centre for Countering Digital Hate', whose CEO Imran Ahmed is currently under investigation in a US congressional hearing for a 'coercive and collusive censorship regime' allegedly aimed at curtailing freedom of speech and violating civil liberties. Erum Salam. "Majority of Covid misinformation came from 12 people, report finds", The Guardian, July 17, 2021, https://theguardian.com/world/2021/jul/17/covid-misinformation-conspiracy-theories-ccdh-report

Contemplating the censored landscape we find ourselves in, I notice hesitancy penning chapters questioning the narrative in the service of truth... Watching 'The case of Julian Assange'[193] confirms my fears. In it, independent journalist Johnny Harris delves into the 18- point legal case that will be filed against the founder of Wiki-leaks if he gets extradited to the US (put together during the Trump administration). They will use the espionage act that goes back to WWI and some of the charges will be for *publishing* 'classified information'. Assange has revealed the shocking truth about the US military, such as opening fire on civilians including children during the Iraq invasion. As Harris says in the video, all journalists should be paying attention to this case. It will set a precedent for making journalism a crime, whilst continuing to 'shoot the messenger' by scapegoating Julian who still sits rotting in solitary confinement in a UK jail (May 2024). In spite of the risks, and my own trauma history that makes sticking my head above the parapet seem doubly rash, I can't ignore what I see going on all around me, including blind compliance and lack of rational debate. The docility in many I expected to challenge overbearing government mandates is nothing short of alarming.

The Ethics of Compliance

... A case in point is my most recent Buddhist teacher in late 2021 using the 'language of the mainstream'- blithely announcing to the gathered assembly at the Buddhist centre where she teaches: 'let's wait to see what happens with the Omicron variant'. I found her stance quite bizarre, possibly incongruous, considering that 'whatever happens' will affect whether her centre can stay open or not. In response to my queries, she countered that she would: 'continue with her purification practice'. I'm pleased to report that her centre *did* stay open for the New Year celebration 2022, in spite of the continuing barrage of hype in the media about how 'endangered' we all are. It seems that no one cares to question the difference between a 'casedemic' and a 'pandemic'. This in spite of Kary Mullis, the late Nobel prize winning inventor of

193. Johnny Harris. "The case of Julian Assange, Explained", YouTube, 32:07, May 10, 2022, https://youtube.com/watch?v=P6bVl47kdNk

the PCR test (a testing device used for Covid-19) saying it will detect *anything, living or dead,* if the labs put it through enough cycles – generating false positive results – which is exactly what's happened during the 'pandemic'.[194]

My feeling is that 'spiritual teachers' ought to somehow be 'defenders of the people'; at least questioning the need for excessive top-down control, and advocating for transparency, justice, democracy and inalienable human rights in whatever context they find themselves. I'm reminded of the physical space inside a Church sometimes offering asylum to those experiencing persecution. My Buddhist teacher saw her role as one where *ignoring* world events, and conforming to illogical, intrusive, divisive, de-humanising 'mandates' was *not at odds* with her position as public figure and religious leader – even though the government will likely shut down her meditation centre *again*. Her priority was, and *is*, carrying on with teaching meditation. In some kind of inverted logic, the argument seems to be the need to 'obey the rules' in order for the centre as 'sanctuary' to stay open, rather than recognise that adhering to senseless rules flies in the face of its sacred, sovereign lineage, effectively cancelling the sanctuary space the centre represents and purportedly offers.

Focus and determination during spiritual practice, and the resultant clarity and composure, are admirable qualities, I'm not denying that. Yet, I believe there's a conversation to be had here about *responsibility* – in the context of non-duality: – if her practices inter-penetrate the world somehow and make it a better place – which presumably they do – otherwise *why would she do them?... Then it also follows that the world penetrates her realm of practice.* It does so in a *very real way* when it shuts down the centre in Aberdeen recently for a year and a half. We have a *duty* to *engage* with those who trespass flagrantly into the realm of our inalienable rights – such as the **freedom of religious belief and practice**. Article 18 in the UN Universal Declaration of Human Rights states:

---

194. Real Truth Real News. "Kary Mullis, Inventor of the PCR Technique Says It Should Never Be Used to Diagnose and That Anthony Fauci is a Fraud", Rumble, 3:58, October 15, 2023, https://rumble.com/v3pgxnr--kary-mullis-pcr-test.html

> "Everyone has the right to freedom of thought, conscience and religion; ... and to manifest his (sic) religion or belief in teaching, practice, worship and observance, either alone or in community with others, in public or private".[195]

When I next visited the Buddhist centre, I was told by a 'kindly volunteer' to put on a mask – *even though he doesn't believe in masks himself and hasn't been jabbed*; 'we need to comply to keep the centre open'. He then told me that it's our 'karma' to become enslaved, and that there's nothing we can do about it. We spoke for several minutes in quite an amicable way – in fact I felt like we both wanted to hug, although we didn't. Once it was clear to me that he wasn't going to yield, I left the meditation centre on principle. Before leaving, I spoke to the dozen or so people present, reminding them that lockdowns, the failing economy, rising debt and the hi-jacking of science and the NHS continue, because of our compliance.

... I'm guessing the spiritual teacher's technique is a Ninja one, assuming *eventually* the critical masses will purify themselves so much that the 'ripple effect' will cleanse the souls of Bill and Melinda Gates, Anthony Fauci, Klaus Schwab, Boris Johnson, and Neil Ferguson; and all the architects, collaborators and colluders in the Plandemic. Maybe then, the 'Great Reset' or Fourth Industrial Revolution outlined by the WEF and described in more detail later in the chapter, will be a good thing? I have to admit; I'm not holding my breath... But then again, maybe I haven't understood, or fully experienced, the depth and power of the practice – *who am I to judge*? Or then again, maybe Anthony Fauci 'et al.' are Rescuers disguised as Tyrants, *or...?* Maybe Western Civilization has reached the *Edge of the Envelope* in terms of 'Exercising our Freedoms' as far as the consequences of rapacious consumerism goes at any rate – and so *something or someone* has to step into the breach and constrain us, if we can't do it for ourselves... This is the common perception, especially amongst groups such as XR (Extinction Rebellion). Except it's the same elite class who

195. "Universal Declaration of Human Rights", United Nations, last modified 2019, 7 November, https://un.org/sites/un2.un.org/files/2021/03/udhr.pdf

created so many of the problems in the first place who are now proffering solutions that entail more, not less, tyranny.

This is the narrative adopted in Agenda 2030; making top-down control increasingly necessary, as a way to prevent inevitable environmental collapse. The argument is compelling; and yet, I'm not banking on these individuals having peoples' and planet's best interests at heart.

In spite of the difficulty in interpreting the 'edicts from above' in the 'post-Truth era'; I don't share the fatalistic approach to Karma espoused by the volunteer at the meditation centre. We *all have our part to play* – otherwise – *why incarnate*? Why teach? Why comply? If it's all in our Karma already, then everything I do or fail to do, is *irrelevant... If everyone, including religious institutions, are willing to impose senseless measures on vulnerable people seeking guidance and sanctuary; how can we* ***reliably*** *distinguish 'good guy' from 'bad gal'?!* How will we know when *any and all* in positions of power are acting as *'paid agents of the state'?* – that potentially *chilling* job description. Does anyone relish the prospect of their religious leader being *one of those*? The Nuremburg Code; created after the atrocities perpetuated by the Nazis in WWII, states that it's not enough to 'simply follow orders' – we bear ***individual and collective responsibility***. I wouldn't be interested in Buddhism if the teachings didn't explore and uphold, in some fashion or another, the *importance and implications of that*.

I offer another *alternative* narrative here, from late Buddhist practitioner, author and psychologist John Welwood, who introduced the term ***'spiritual bypass'*** to describe our capacity to use 'religious practices' as an *avoidance of reality*. Our *compliance* – with mask mandates, closing 'non-essential' businesses, vaccines, boosters, and *all* the rest during the 'pandemic' – actually *reinforced* the status quo, allowing those who pull the strings behind the scenes to do so with impunity. The results are plain to see – a massive increase in the global debt burden, the *destruction* of the stability and integrity of what remains of civic society; the *compromising* of our mental health, and the *undermining* of our diverse, flourishing economy made up of independent, small scale, local businesses.

This was and is a deliberate strategy: – power grab tactics from Global Elites for whom the resilience of the middle classes and small business owners is nothing but an inconvenience. Case in point: – US Congress turned down a bill worth $48 billion in May '22 to help small businesses struggling in the aftermath of Covid-19 measures, but ratified $40 billion worth of 'aid' to Ukraine.[196], [197]

Economic Roots

As we will see below, the 'war machine' is one of the vehicles, *par excellence,* making money for those holding invisible reins of power – a small group of billionaires and financial entities above and beyond the law. Their reach is all-pervasive, and geo-political and economic de-stabilisation is a favourite tactic, making state intervention and war seem necessary evils in the face of engineered chaos. Stating crises and conflicts can be engineered is not naivety or conspiracy-based observation; of course, humans get into conflict *anyway,* and traditionally have developed tools and techniques for resolving them, only one of which is resorting to violence. Vast quantities of finance are needed to fund war, obliging loans and printing money (quantitative easing), generating debt, interest and inflation- impacting all of us economically. The rich get richer and the poor get poorer, and that's without even counting the bloodshed involved. On Robert Malone's Substack I read of calls recently to defund the UN, whose original role was to *prevent war!* In January 2024 we don't need to ask how that particular goal is going. It's plain for all to see. 'Mission creep' defines the UN as we'll see later in the chapter.

'Disaster Capitalism' is a recently-coined term; but the principle, however, is *not;* dating back at least as far as the Napoleonic Wars, from which time onwards, according to the harrowing documentary 'Europa: The Last Battle'[198], it seems the Rothschild

196. Daphne Psaledakis. "The big items in Washington's $40 billion Ukraine aid package", Reuters, May 19, 2022, https://reuters.com/world/big-items-washingtons-40-billion-ukraine-aid-package-2022-05-19

197. Karl Evers-Hillstrom. "Senate blocks $48 billion aid package for restaurants, other small businesses", The Hill, May 19, 2022, https://thehill.com/homenews/senate/3494868-senate-blocks-48-billion-aid-package-for-restaurants-other-small-businesses

198. Europa: The Last Battle, directed by Tobias B (2017), 4:29:27, https://archive.org/details/watch_europa

family has at least partially funded both sides of every major war. Their wealth is hard to quantify as it's internally audited; and partially stored in underground vaults, but is rumoured to run to trillions of US $, perhaps as much as half the wealth of the whole world combined. In prefacing the film; activist, conservationist and ex-US Marine, Ken O'Keefe, comments: '*The financial system is the Head of the Snake'* in several important ways: – the resources of the mega-rich and investment banks fund war and (re)-development; and the debt-based economic model locks the populace into repayment schemes forever more, and into believing the polarising rhetoric of War endlessly peddled by the MSM. Eisenhower coined the term 'military-industrial complex' in 1961 in his farewell address, saying "The potential for the disastrous rise of misplaced power exists and will persist".[199] In both British and US constitutional law: "*... the raising or keeping a standing Army within the Kingdom in time of Peace unless it be with Consent of Parliament is against Law".*[200] So it was (and is) common knowledge that military arsenals were (and remain) a huge drain on a nation's wealth.

The system doesn't begin and end with the military-industrial complex however, destabilising 'developing' nations is another relatively modern economic model; undermining their ability to be self-supporting – generating wealth for the wealthy by *default,* with 'economic restructuring' favouring multinational corporations above small scale producers:

> "... interacting institutions create a new global power system where sovereignty is globalized, taking power and constitutional authority away from nations and giving it to global markets and international bodies".[201]

The lending of money with interest ensures debtor nations remain enslaved to their creditors, maintaining the status quo,

199/ "President Dwight D. Eisenhower's farewell address (1961)", National Archives, last modified June 20, 2023, https://archives.gov/milestone-documents/president-dwight-d-eisenhowers-farewell-address

200. "The Bill of Rights, 1689", Liberté, Égalité, Fraternité, https://revolution.chnm.org/d/267

201. Charles Derber, People before Profit: The New Globalization in an Age of Terror, Big Money, and Economic Crisis (Picador, 2003)

except now the rich nations have more leverage via vested interests. Poor countries' debt means they struggle to keep up with statutory membership contributions incumbent on them to global institutions like the IMF and WHO. The less these 'philanthropic' institutions are financed by member states, often forced by circumstance to default, the *greater* the contributions from private stakeholders - witness the Bill and Melinda Gates foundation as currently the largest contributor to the World Health Organisation (WHO). Thus, the private sector becomes the major stake holder, and dictates the agenda. No one seems to notice the conflict of interests between being the largest contributor to the WHO and a major investor in vaccines, even though Bill Gates can easily be seen bragging about a **20 to 1** return on investment on video, for this particular act of 'selfless philanthropy'.[202]

Figure 6: *Bill Gates Promoting Vaccines at UN, while Gates Foundation a top contributor to the WHO (Source: World Health Organisation)*
**Gavi Vaccine Alliance is also a Gates funded initiative*

The covert agenda of Globalism is never to 'rebuild the world' for the world's sake, nor to offer a hand-up to third world or war-torn countries in the name of Equality, but to further enrich the wealthy at the poor's expense. Rebuilding and industrialising 'poor' nations makes the creditors money - they even *loan money to repay loans when countries default on the loan.* It's important to remember FIAT currency is 'monopoly money'[203] in comparison

202. *Matthew J. Belvedere. "Bill Gates: My 'best investment' turned $10 billion into $200 billion worth of economic benefit", CNBC, January 23, 2019, https://cnbc.com/2019/01/23/bill-gates-turns-10-billion-into-200-billion-worth-of-economic-benefit.html*
203. *'... it is intrinsically valueless and used by government decree...'. Tim Vipond. "Fiat Money", Corporate Finance Institute, November 22, 2023, https://*

to the resources 'poor nations' use to repay these debts. 'Selling the family silver' ensures 'developing countries' real wealth doesn't get deployed internally to enhance their own prosperity, but gets exported to generate capital to repay debts owed to first world nations.

The Global Economy - including War - is the endless cyclical *money laundering system* of Global Elites; soaked in the blood, sweat and tears of the soldiers, workers, farmers, miners, wives and mothers of the world... But it's not just third world countries that are indebted to rich nations. Rich nations themselves have debt 'baked into' their economies: by 2011 (pre-pandemic!) the US was seeing its debt:GDP ratio rise commensurate with WWII levels.[204] The failing economies of the United States and Europe are hurtling into inconceivable quantities of debt with an insouciance that betrays a strong desire to tear up our existing economic model and start again. The more we uncover, the greater the urgency seems for the type of 'Great Reset' we see touted by the World Economic Forum (WEF) headed by Klaus Schwab.

The economic destabilisation caused by the worldwide 'pandemic'- creating mass unemployment and bankruptcy - is increasing the might of the Elites, ensuring it gets ever harder to resist their restructuring of society. The undemocratic wealth transfer currently taking place has been in the planning for years and will create a Neo-Feudal Technocratic World Government with the very few governing 'the masses' who will comply or be 'cancelled'. This will apply to corporations too, who will be taken over by the objectives of the ruling elites, or fail. As we hurtle towards this emerging new world order, the Nation State, Representative Government, and the rise of the Middle Class will be nothing but an unfortunate blip in history.[205]

---

corporatefinanceinstitute.com/resources/economics/fiat-money-currency
204. Matt Phillips. "The long Story of US Debt, from 1790 to 2011, in 1 little chart", The Atlantic, November 13, 2012, https://theatlantic.com/business/archive/2012/11/the-long-story-of-us-debt-from-1790-to-2011-in-1-little-chart/265185
205. Klaus Schwab and Thierry Malleret, COVID-19: The Great Reset (Forum Publishing, 2020)

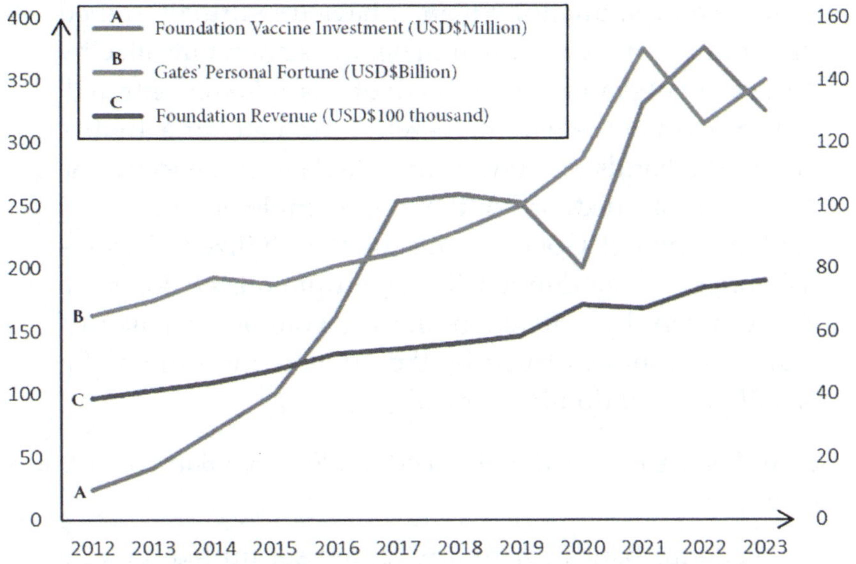

Figure 7: *Bill Gates' Vaccine Investment and Profit/Wealth (Source: Bloomberg, Gates Foundation)*

Western Imperialism and Western Enslavement

In his video Documentary 'American R/Evolution', Dr David Martin explains the relative youth of the American nation (compared to Europe) meaning government had to turn to big business for funding, since the necessary infrastructure to raise revenue via taxation was lacking - US income tax was not formally ratified (under the 16th amendment) until 1913. This step provided the means to repay debt and helped lure the

US into the First World War in 1917, with the confidence that the 'common man' would (re)fund the expenditure.

The Federal Reserve, set up in December the same year income tax was ratified, is backed by private capital. Three of the wealthiest men in America - Strauss, Guggenheim and Astor - strongly opposed the establishment of the Federal Reserve by private interests. Conveniently for those who wanted private control of US banking interests, all three men perished in the freezing waters of the Arctic Ocean with the sinking of the Titanic in 1912. When the privatised Federal Reserve was created, then President, Woodrow Wilson, lamented:

"I am a most unhappy man. I have unwittingly ruined my country. A great industrial nation is now controlled by its system of credit. Our system of credit is concentrated. The growth of the nation, therefore, and all our activities are in the hands of a few men. We have come to be one of the worst ruled, one of the most completely controlled and dominated Governments in the civilized world – no longer a Government by free opinion, no longer a Government by conviction and the vote of the majority, but a Government ruled by the opinion and duress of a small group of dominant men".[206]

Still today, we can read on the Federal Reserve Bank of St Louis website:

"(Federal) Banks [there are 12] are set up like private corporations. Member banks hold stock in the Federal Reserve and earn dividends... Member banks also elect six of the nine members on each bank's board of directors".[207]

Life insurance expanded exponentially in the US at around the same time the Federal Reserve was set up, as did 'cheaper' longer term mortgage loans of 30 years, with only small cash deposits needed, compared to the previous short-term three to five year loans available – which necessitated 50% down-payments. This allowed banks to '*lend more for less*'; effectively increasing the debt burden on the individual, whilst enriching the banks through the fractional reserve system. In this way earning interest by loaning out any deposit made, only needing to keep a percentage in the bank, whilst if a mortgagee defaulted on the loan, the bank could then repossess the house and sell it again.

The new system allowed Americans at the turn of the twentieth century to continue expansion and development, and to insure against loss: conquering lands occupied by Indigenous peoples,

206. Woodrow Wilson. "Woodrow Wilson Quotes", n. d., Quote.org, https://quote.org/quote/i-am-a-most-unhappy-man-i-620429
207. "Making Sense of the Federal Reserve: Who Owns the Federal Reserve Banks?", Federal Reserve Bank of St. Louis, last modified 2023, https://stlouisfed.org/in-plain-english/who-owns-the-federal-reserve-banks

and claiming and insuring the resources of that stolen land, with borrowed money. The *extension of finance* in this, and multiple other ways, allowed more people to own property, and undoubtedly contributed to the volatility of the speculative property and stock markets of today. The accruing of debt leads to the *false inflation of asset values*, infecting economies - nationally and globally - with intractable and ever-expanding cycles of 'boom and bust', as we see latterly with 'quantitative easing' leading to hyper-inflation. 'We just print too much money' according to venture capitalist and 'Shark Tank' host Kevin O'Leary[208]. In a 2022 interview he predicted the interest rates rise of 2023, and revealed the 'Build back Better' sloganeering post-Covid amounted to $600 billion worth of 'free cash' injections, on top of $6 trillion of free money.

... Going back to the 'Karma' piece from the Buddhist meditation centre earlier in the chapter, perhaps the volunteer's assertion begins to make more sense when placed in a historical context: the creation of the US involved building a New World on Stolen Land, with Stolen People (slaves) and Borrowed Money... Using our Fiat paper money system we signed, and continue to sign, our*selves* into 30 years, or more, of modern-day slavery to repay mortgages. With the invention and intervention of Banking, in a Faustian bargain of sorts, *human 'securities' became tokenised (monetised) and spliced* into the economic activity of the political-industrial-financial-military complex of the nation state. *Fugitives* themselves, immigrants to the US transferred trust and resilience away from the traditional binding agents of a culture - small-scale artisan-industry, agriculture, and the barter economy - towards faceless financial institutions that have grown exponentially in power and impenetrability with the help of complex 'financial derivatives' over time...

The British Connection

People fled Europe in their droves to come to America; the 'Enclosures Acts' in Britain, wrought by the rich on the poor, were

208. *Ethan Kimball. "Kevin O'Leary on Inflation: We just Print Too much Money", yahoo!finance, August 3, 2022, https://finance.yahoo.com/news/kevin-o-leary-on-inflation-we-just-print-too-much-money-140233418.html*

equivalent 'land grabs', over centuries, to those subsequently inflicted on Indigenous populations in the US by Europeans seeking sanctuary.

> "Between 1604 and 1914 over 5,200 Enclosure Bills were enacted by English Parliament which related to just over a fifth of the total area of England, amounting to some **6.8 million acres**".[209]

The same dispossession of the common people; flight from the land; and dismantling of village life took place in Scotland, Wales and Ireland, the latter suffering several years of potato famine in the 1840s, whilst continuing to export produce - especially oats - to mainland Britain.[210]

In the UK, as a consequence of the flight from the land, people emigrated to the US to escape over-crowding in cities, the enforced labour of the 'work house' for the landless poor; and the hellish working conditions in the factories of the industrial revolution. The unbridled optimism and libertarian values enshrined in the US constitution masked the fact that many jumped from the frying pan and into the fire...

Jay Griffiths describes the Plight of Humanity, and in particular, the fate of Childhood during the Enclosures in Britain, in her poignant book 'Kith'. Here she describes the changes seen through the eyes of the poet John Clare:

> "It was the destruction of all the forms of home which unnested Clare's mind. He was evicted from his land by forces of undwelling and his madness and misery were written into his poems. I have been with Amazonian people when they have seen the searing brutality of their lands being ripped apart for gold in today's acts of corporate enclosure, and I have watched men weep while they say, aghast, ***'We are the land'***...

209. "Enclosing the land", UK Parliament, 2023, https://parliament.uk/about/living-heritage/transformingsociety/towncountry/landscape/overview/enclosingland
210. The History of Britain. 2002. Season 3, episode 3, "The Fate of Empire: 1776–1965." Presented by Simon Schama. Aired June 11, 2002, on BBC Two.

The Enclosures spiked the nest of Clare's psyche. Where moss and feathers had been, there was now torque and barbed wire. When Clare writes of flowers or butterflies or birds being made homeless, he notes how they lose their depth of association so the landscape of the mind is pauperized by Enclosure.

> *'But, take these several beings from their homes,*
> *Each beauteous thing a withered thought becomes;*
> *Association fades and like a dream*
> *They are but shadows of the things they seem.'*

... Language and meaning need to be nested in nature, and the immensity of the destruction Clare perceives is enormous. Enclosure, he tells us, in various places, fenced off rapture and play, joy, customs, games, carnival and the past; it obliterated the glow of divinity, of generosity and kindness; it silenced songs and poetry; it prohibited lingering, lazing, roaming and straying; it closed the pathways; it brought the chill of winter into every season; it caged freedom, time and wildness, it ruined dwelling, refuge and shelter; it denied belonging and so stripped the psyche of every protection. It evicted childhood from its immemorial nest on the land and it exiled his adulthood from its nest of childhood memory".[211]

I have to admit to often looking askance at the culture I belong to, when I contemplate the egregious harms caused by Colonialism; the genocides and plunder. Yet, when I read the poetry of John Clare, and research the land theft of the common people that took place in the UK under our Government over 300 years; evicting millions from a rural life of relative equilibrium (back-breaking squalor, according to them) my perspective changes completely. I realise *we too* had intact cultures once; *our land* was inhabited, loved, laboured and woven into the very sinews and songs of its people... We too were foragers, custodians, poets, fletchers, potters and makers of lives that resonated with the cadence of

211. Jay Griffiths, Kith (Hamish Hamilton publisher, 2013): 25

Belonging. How can we not pity our own people; even as we pity the Indigenous Peoples of other continents conquered and condemned by the dispossessed of the British Isles and other European countries, who often themselves were fleeing the injustices and trauma of Enclosures and War...?

World War II and Beyond

Tracing developments to a more recent time in history, at the outset of WWII, after the Great Depression, and having incurred large debts from WWI, the US dollar was ailing; the strongest denomination globally being the British pound. A treaty forged at Bretton Woods in 1944 between 44 nations, including the Allied forces, would change all that, establishing the US dollar as the international trading currency (Reserve currency), on the condition that the Allies win the war. In post-war US, the treaty provided short-lived, but much needed economic stability, being a blend of Keynesian and Milton Friedman's economics, backed by the gold standard and with fixed rates of currency exchange.[212] Industrial productivity in the US increased by 96% during the war, 17 million new civilian jobs were created and corporate profits doubled,[213] commensurate with a massive increase in world debt. War was good for business, with debts to be paid back via taxation of the common people into the coffers of emergent global corporations.

Something rarely asked about WWII is: – how did the Nazis rebuild the German economy so quickly after the extremely punitive WWI Treaty of Versailles, which French general Marechal Foch described as: 'An Armistice for 20 years' and emphatically *not* a Peace Treaty? The American Dawes plan from 1924 onwards, awarding the Germans a loan of 800 million Deutsche Marks, followed by the Young Plan in 1929[214]; that's how! Other 'tactics' in the build up to a Nazi takeover and second World War- just 20

212. *American R/Evolution: documentary by Dr. D. Martin*
213. *Dorris Goodwin. "The Way we Won: America's Economic Breakthrough During WWII", The American Prospect, October 1, 1992, https://prospect.org/topics/doris-goodwin*
214. *"Dawes Plan: WW1 Reparations", Britannica, last modified August 9, 2023, https://britannica.com/event/Dawes-Plan*

years after the conclusion of the First - included de-stabilisation of the German political landscape. Hyper-inflation and socio-political chaos, with over 300 assassinations of political figures in the inter-war years helped usher in the promise of 'law and order' proffered by the Nazis.[215] German redevelopment between the wars could not have been achieved without US financial backing and the establishment of American factories in Germany (such as Ford motors).[216] Hopefully these revelations allow us to begin to perceive that finance forms and governs the backbone of modern geo-politics. The 'Show' is couched layers deep in specious narrative and polemic, burnished to a fine lustre by Main Stream Media. Whilst the history is convoluted, don't let that distract us from the facts...

Is there an ideological foundation as well as economic reasons for the deeply embedded 'perpetual war machine' of the West? You bet - and it's one with a historical pedigree dating as far back as Prussia. Will Zoll's research reveals the US and the West were infiltrated by Prussian ideology, connected to the German philosopher Hegel's (1770-1831) vision that deemed the Power of the State to be Absolute; with the 'highest purpose of the people' being to 'Serve the State'.[217] This Prussian ideology is the model we based western education on, discussed in the last chapter, to create a 'hear and obey' mentality that suited the emerging workforce and modern warfare. Zoll examines the ideological and concrete links in great depth and detail. Prussian philosophy, which translated into 'Realpolitik' during Weimar Germany, and was rolled out in the US during the Presidency of Nixon (with Henry Kissinger as Secretary of State), was in total opposition to the *liberal* ideal; where state intervention is deliberately minimised in favour of individual freedom. In order to expand and dominate the international stage economically and geo-politically the US required a ruthless militaristic playbook

---

215. Erin Blakemore. "After WWI, Hundreds of Politicians were Murdered in Germany", History, October 26, 2018, https://history.com/news/political-assassinations-germany-weimar-republic
216. Zoll, "Prussia Gate"
217. Ibid.

to under-gird the much vaunted yet little understood tactical manoeuvres of the purported 'Land of the Free and Home of the Brave'.

Conflict: – behind the propaganda machine 'veils' of mainstream media, and the black and white, binary, fear-saturated thinking planted in the minds of the populace – is a construct designed to continue cycles of destruction and reconstruction, for the benefit of invisible Financiers. The so-called 'Proxy Wars' of the 21st century are engineered shadow-shows of unimaginable and unconscionable human and ecological suffering, trailing untold wasted lives, money and resources in their wake.[218] Is it pure coincidence that in 2023 we have the 'cost of living crisis' as the banks raise interest rates from 1.45 – 5.25%[219] in a matter of months (in August of 2023), making shelter and food increasingly unaffordable luxuries? Strange coincidence the rise in interest rates emerges in the wake of the 'Covid Crisis' extravaganza, followed fast by the 'War in Ukraine', costing the 'State'@ 'City of London Inc'. & 'Federal Reserve Inc.' Untold billions of £/$. We suffer multiple indignities and infringements of civil liberties during these 'crises' and are then forced to foot the bill in this 'Era of Epic Stitch-ups'!

Banking and Special Exemptions

The State and the Banks are joined at the hip, with the 'Square Mile' of the City of London Trade and Banking hub being awarded special exemptions and privileges dating back to the time of William the Conqueror's first decree in 1067.[220] These exemptions allowed legal forms of piracy to flourish, out of reach of the 'long arm of the law'- literally stashing gold and silver bullion from overseas with the help of the London Goldsmiths,

218. Robert F. Kennedy Jr. describes how Blackrock., Vanguard, and State Street own majority shares in the military hardware deployed in the Ukraine War. These investment titans have secured reconstruction contracts for when the war ends. Tucker Carlson. "Tucker Carlson - Ep. 16 - 08/14/2023 - Robert F Kennedy Jr.", YouTube, 1:21:03, December 14, 2023, https://youtube.com/watch?v=T_1-tgWFtiQ

219. "Official Bank Rate history", Bank of England Database, last modified August 3, 2023, https://bankofengland.co.uk/boeapps/database/Bank-Rate.asp

220. "William I charter to the City of London", City of London, last modified May 17, 2022, https://cityoflondon.gov.uk/things-to-do/history-and-heritage/london-metropolitan-archives/collections/william-i-charter-to-the-city-of-london

and entering into complex trading arrangements, including with American colonies in the 1700s, who had already adopted Fiat paper currency, to London's gold-backed advantage.[221] Over a period of several hundred years, the City of London attracted merchants and bankers from overseas, able to profit from the loopholes awarded by Royal decree; rubber-stamping systems that operate outside of legal scaffolding, whilst continuing to merge private corporate financial interests with geo-politics. It is a model that continues to infect and inform Globalism to this day, as we will see below. Notice the Institution of Finance is '*regulated*'; terminology pointing to a world under separate jurisdiction from the system that 'governs' (rather than regulates) the 'great unwashed' of Nation States...

The Emergence of 'Global Philanthropy'

As WWII drew to a close, a new Cartel was established in 1945 with HQ on 'International Territory' (outside national jurisdiction – ring any bells?) The land was 'gifted' by John D Rockefeller Jr. on 17 prime acres of Manhattan real estate along the banks of the Hudson River (although it was historically the territory of the Munsee Native Americans, and the Mohawks).[222] Rockefeller's father founded the Standard Oil Company in 1870, and is widely regarded as the richest man in modern history... Thus, the UN, IMF, and World Bank were born – offering 'banking solutions' known as 'development loans' to open up emerging markets in a genius rebranding of increasingly frowned upon Colonialism, outlawed slavery, and to provide expanding markets and raw materials for the insatiable maw of modern-day consumer capitalism spawned by Industrial Revolution. This new 'everyone included' flag-touting effort was carried out speciously to ensure World War would never again blight the face of humanity; a self-evident Truth post-Nagasaki-and-Hiroshima when it became obvious that World Wars = Armageddon. ('Proxy wars and wars

221. Will Zoll. "1871: Orange Londonia", Prussia Gate, last modified August 19, 2023, https://prussiagate.substack.com/p/1871

222. Scott Keller. "Hudson River Valley National Heritage Area Releases Dutch & Native", Hudson River Valley Greenway, last modified 2021, 1 March, https://hudsongreenway.ny.gov/news/hudson-river-valley-national-heritage-area-releases-dutch-native-american-brochure

on terror' are new ways the war machine continues to trundle along without, fingers crossed, the spectre of Nuclear Holocaust).

The genius of the UN was to provide the face of Modern Western Global Venture Capitalism a long over-due overhaul to fall in line with 'Age of Enlightenment' thinking and beyond. This development included modern conceptions of the 'Nation State', free from the rule of kings and queens and the over bearing influence of the church. One Enlightenment thinker, Jean-Jacques Rousseau, coined the term 'social contract' (underpinning the notion of 'modern democracy') whilst sending his five children to perish in a Paris orphanage.[223] He also penned a book 'Emile', about the ideal way to raise children...

During the 1600s - 1700s, whilst the Enclosures Acts stole the land from the common people, and slaves were being shipped in chains across the Atlantic Ocean, the wealthy classes in Britain flounced around in wigs and silks and built amazing country piles for themselves.[224] The 'Age of Enlightenment' ushered in by European 'thinkers' like Descartes, Hobbes and Locke might have been steeped in cognitive dissonance... Yet it did forge the idea of 'sovereign nation states' governed by elected politicians, thus separating Religious and Crown interests from those of the State. Philosophers, 'men of science' and social reformers strove to formulate the precise character and status of the citizens who were to inhabit these newly-formed Nation States - the best expression of which can be found in the American Constitution produced by the Founding Fathers... However, in failing to address or tame the power of private banking interests, 'Democracy' was hobbled from the outset.

This failure allowed for the evolution and proliferation over the last eighty years of bloated Global Institutions to the Epic proportions we see today. Witness the 'report writing factory' that is the UN, with offices in Geneva, Nairobi, Vienna and The Hague, and a current membership of 193 states (as of August 2023). It employs 125,436 personnel (as of 2022) with salaries ranging

223. "Rousseau's children", The Generalist Academy, last modified October 28, 2020, https://generalist.academy/2020/10/28/rousseaus-children

224. The History of Britain. 2002

from $37,000 to $123,000.[225] From its own website, the goals of the UN are centred around '... commit[ment] to maintaining international peace and security, developing friendly relations among nations and promoting social progress, better living standards and human rights'... I'm sure many of the people who work at the UN are well-intentioned individuals. Yet the world today plays host to any number of 'rinse and repeat versions' of exploitative systems under the guise of 'rescuing the poor', 'keeping the peace', 'stabilising the economy', and now latterly, 'solving health crises' and 'rescuing the climate'. 'We' or 'they' wouldn't need 'Help' if Western Economies, often in clandestine fashion, hadn't destabilised them in the first place. It has a name – Disaster Capitalism. This sleight of hand adds insult to the injury of Colonialism, described masterfully by Mallence Williams in her piercing exposé of the plight of the African continent- rich in highly coveted resources- in her 2015 Berlin TED talk.

Today, unsurprisingly, the remit of the IMF, in tandem with the UN, has evolved thus:

> "rather than... overseeing only exchange rates... their function became one of surveillance of the overall macroeconomic performance of member countries".[226]

The IMF now "manages economic policy rather than just exchange rates." This is true with "especially the middle income countries which are vulnerable to massive capital outflows." What could these massive capital outflows possibly be? Repaying debts to the IMF by any chance? It sounds like a catch 22 – and one managed by unelected, private, conflicted interests, at that. As we will see, since the World Economic Forum (WEF) has now infiltrated the IMF, we have a situation, stated in black and white on Wikipedia of all places, where the IMF/WEF *dictates* global economic policy.

Not just the US but European countries are teetering on the edge of the bankruptcy cliff, and are out of solutions from the existing

225. "Pay and benefits", United Nations: Careers, last modified 2023, https://careers.un.org/payandbenefits

226. "International Monetary Fund", Wikimedia Foundation, last modified December 9, 2023, https://en.wikipedia.org/wiki/International_Monetary_Fund

models of banking. The current instability of the global markets is unprecedented, and has been made worse by the 'pandemic'. A recent update to the 'IMF's Global Debt Database' documents the largest one-year debt surge since World War II. As countries were hit by the 'pandemic', global debt rose to $226 trillion, or 256% of GDP in 2020.[227]

Most recently, we have a study in the successful rolling out of 'Disaster Capitalism', as practiced by unelected elites: – just a couple of months before the Covid 19 outbreak 'Event 201' took place: – described as a 'Partnership' between the World Economic Forum, the Gates Foundation and Johns Hopkins Center for Health.[228] The event was convened at the Pierre Hotel, New York, in October 2019 to discuss how to respond to the possibility of a worldwide 'pandemic'. Of course, it's pure 'coincidence' that this exercise took place so close to the outbreak... In the disaster modelling scenarios, which can be seen on the Event 201 website, not only the rationale, but also the infrastructure was put in place for a 'rapid response' to a fictitious future scenario.

It turns out that Disaster Capitalists are *always* on stand-by with everything required to face an emergency. Event 201 was organised and executed under the banner of 'preparedness' – a bit like being back at boy Scouts – but on a Global scale with Billions of US $ in the kitty. This was not the first such exercise either; according to Paul Schreyer there have been several. 'Operation Warp Speed', which kicked in very early on in the pandemic – Wikipedia cleverly avoids giving us the precise date by mentioning only when it was 'made public' – was managed by the US Military, the CDC, private firms, and other agencies, who cobbled together a budget of *$18 billion* for vaccine R&D, therapeutics, PPE, manufacturing, distribution, and diagnostics. Even a kind commentator would have to admit that the above smacks of Cronyism and conflicts of interest. Bill Gates is not the fifth richest man in the world[229] for nothing.

227. "Global Debt Database", IMF, 2023, https://imf.org/external/datamapper/datasets/GDD

228. "Event 201", Johns Hopkins: Center for Health Security, October 18, 2019, https://centerforhealthsecurity.org/our-work/tabletop-exercises/event-201 pandemic-tabletop-exercise

229. "Bill Gates: Bloomberg Billionaires Index", Bloomberg, last updated December 15, 2023, https://bloomberg.com/billionaires/profiles/william-h-gates

The Fourth Industrial Revolution

I notice I feel a mixture of admiration and irritation as I read through the endless, Utopian, tedious verbiage on the UN's founding charter about 'meaningful work' 'economic growth' & 'green futures' with 'no one left out'. I can't help but think that if money spent on UN delegations, conferences and reports to create 'protocols' and 'charters' was simply devolved to small scale community groups in the first place, and appropriately trained community leaders, at the grass roots level, *so much more could be achieved.* Perhaps we would already have world peace, prosperity and equality if *that* had been the route taken...?

Over seven decades since the UN's inception, and easy to find online, is the 'partner framework' between the UN and World Economic Forum (WEF), signed in June 2019, centring around six main goals for achieving major pan-national seismic shifts in existing economic, political, and technological structures, known as 'Agenda 2030'. Overall, the UN has 17 sustainable development goals (SDGs) known as Agenda 2030, and a further 169 'targets'. Mercifully, the UN collaboration with WEF focuses on just six. These include:

[1] Financing the Agenda 2030.
[2] Climate Change
[3] Health
[4] Digital Cooperation
[5] Gender equality and Empowerment of Women
[6] Education and Skills

Agenda 2030 is described in the literature as '*interconnected and indivisible*', and is also being touted as the 'Great Reset', or the 'Fourth Industrial Revolution', with the involvement of the WEF. On the face of it - it looks and sounds great, and who can argue that all of these areas are worthy of our attention? Let's take a closer look though... Some of my analysis pieced together here is heavily indebted to the work of Alison McDowell - independent researcher, Mom (and Heroine!)

We should briefly look behind the scenes at the WEF... Established in 1971; it levies large membership fees on any company wishing to join – on their website, it's easy to find the £20,000+ annual fee charged – and that's just 'entry level', not what it costs to attend the annual conference where CEOs, politicians, bankers, royalty, and celebrities meet in Davos to supposedly 'put the world to rights'. Even Greenpeace is part of the proceedings that provide ample opportunity for the Elites to strategise and broker deals. 71% of the funding of the WEF comes from its partners – Black Rock, George Soros' Open Society Foundation, the Bill and Melinda Gates Foundation, JP Morgan Chase, Google, Coca Cola, and Facebook, to name but a few. These partners fund access to WEF trainings for up-and-coming politicians (cherry-picked by the WEF), and foster tangible links with, and indebtedness to, global corporate sponsorship in the hearts and minds of our future world leaders. Putin, Trudeau, Merckl, Macron, and New Zealand's now ex-Prime Minister Jacinda Ardern, are all products of the WEF young global leaders training, exposing the infiltration of vested interests at the highest levels of Western 'democratic' nation states. Even Wikipedia informs that '... the goal of the WEF for many participants would be personal gain rather than solving global problems'. Let's take a closer look at their objectives:

[1] Financing the Agenda

To power the Great reset, we need to **Finance the Agenda**, which means, according to their own literature: 'aligning financial systems', 'accelerating finance flows', and 'harnessing the potential of financial innovation, new technology and digitalisation to increase finance for Sustainable Development Goals'. The people behind this Economic Revolution are referred to as 'multi-stakeholder partnerships'. On the UN System Staff College website[230] these are listed as: civil society, 'development practitioners'; the private sector, and academia. No mention of *government* or *public sector*...? Slightly strange, but let's plod on. To attempt to disambiguate what is being said here:

---

230. "Programme Portfolio", United Nations System Staff College, last modified October 1, 2020, https://unssc.org/sites/default/files/unssc_portfolio20.pdf

> "Rich nations are strapped for cash (big corporations don't pay tax, and outsource labour to developing countries, and we've ever increasing 'welfare' commitments); things need to change; we're inventing a new system with digitalisation at its core; you **will** comply, because of the 'interconnectedness and indivisibility' of our programme – it's 'not a menu list'".

If they wanted to use a buzz word, and they do, it would be 'holistic'; but it might as well be 'tyrannical', because it's all-encompassing; and opting-out is not an option. The traditional cash machines that kept the economy buoyant have proved fallible and finite – the Ruse of Perpetual War, not only as wealth generator, but for population control, has produced bombs so powerful that they would take down the whole planet, if engaged. Natural resources are dwindling, and their extraction is causing irreparable damage to our life support systems. With the coming down of the Berlin War, which led to an abating of the 'Cold War' (pre-Ukraine War!) strong lobbying took place in the US to divest from the military. Latterly those military targets had been transposed[231], onto the 'War on Terror' and now the 'War on a Virus'.

It turns out that 'The War on the Virus' is an ideal way to implement the new digitalised economy of the Great Reset, and here's how... The strap line for the 'no opt out' clause is: 'no one left behind'. With digitalisation and technology (Big Tech) at the core of the strategy, the existing ***1.1 billion people*** on the planet ***without*** ID (passports, driving licences, etc) will be provided with a digitalised identity by 2030 – and those who have paper identity documents – these will all go digital. How will they achieve this? How about a pandemic that requires 'the vaccination of the whole world', to quote Bill Gates. Extending the vaccine programme to children (who are not at risk from covid, but who are at risk from the side effects of the vaccine)[232] allows them to enter information

231. *WIR–Wissen ist relevant. "Paul Schreyer: Pandemic simulation games – Preparation for a new era?", YouTube, 1:03:06, March 10, 2023, https://youtube.com/watch?v=d3WUv5SV5Hg*
232. *Edward Dowd, Cause Unknown: The Epidemic of Sudden Deaths in 2021 and 2022 (Skyhorse publishing, 2023)*

about all those children in digital format on a global platform, making possible the harvesting of their data. Once everyone has a digital ID, these will be linked to other aspects of life and become known as CBDCs - Central Bank Digital Currencies)[233] Bank accounts, welfare benefits, passport and medical information will all be in one place. Furthermore, in spite of assurances that our data is private, it can be mined through an MIT back door.[234]

With all our 'data' now in one place on the web, we will be traceable by automated AI systems. 'Health scores and outcomes' will become investable commodities, encrypted in block chain, and referred to as 'human capital bonds', which already exist, as a quick online search reveals. This creates a scenario best described as the 'gamification' of humanity, where we become 'commoditised investments' to be played and traded on the global markets and targeted by pension funds - more is revealed in Agenda 4 (Digital Cooperation) below.

[2] Climate Change

With **climate change**: as well as investing in green technology, which you might expect, and naming and tackling the culprits of high levels of CO^2 emissions (yet still covertly funding oil and gas expansion in developing countries)[235] we are to apparently engage in 'public/private cooperation in critical areas of adaptation'. These include, in their literature: '... *early warning systems, disaster risk reduction and more...*' German journalist Paul Schreyer describes a trend towards 'disaster modelling' and 'disaster capitalism'; providing opportunities to invest in hyper-expensive 'solutions' funded by Global Banks and Corporations, who only invest when the ROI stacks in their favour.

---

233. George Gammon. "Here's How They'll Implement A CBDC Without You Knowing!", George Gammon: Macro Investing and Personal Freedom, last modified March 24, 2023, https://georgegammon.com/heres-how-theyll-implement-a-cbdc-without-you-knowing
234. Geopolitics and Empire, "Alison McDowell: In The Great Reset's New World Empire, Humans Have Become Minable Commodity", podtail, 1:00:56, April 17, 2021, https://podtail.com/fr/podcast/podcast-geopolitics-empire/alison-mcdowell-in-the-great-reset-s-new-world-emp
235. "A Deadly Ring of Coal: VALE's poisoned gift to Mozambique", Friends of the Earth International, last modified 2022, 11 March, https://foei.org/vale-mozambiquea-deadly-ring-of-coal

There is subtle work to be done to differentiate good ideas from bad: big business and the billionaires who meet in Davos are busy inventing and funding stake-holder 'solutions' in '***partnership***' with government (read ***instead*** of government). If we're going to reject those options – what are *we*, as aspiring 'sovereign people', going to put in their place? All of nature has become 'monetised' in the emerging 'climate solutions' hatched at Davos – for example 'Bio-fuel' plants burning millions of trees, touted as a 'green solution'. All this and more is covered in Michael Moore's most recent, instructive, and alarming documentary: 'Planet of the Humans'.[236]

The new Global Government will capture our carbon credit scores in social engineering systems similar to those already operation in China that punish and reward, according to the algorithmic 'ghost in the machine'. The rhetoric makes us think there is an easy 'green fix' to the mess we're in, turning us into pawns in their game-ified 'solutions'. Instead; when we look closely, we can see the outline of a neo-feudal society emerging, where a fraction of 1% of the population holds inordinate power: – we become their trans-human serfs with wearables or implants tracking and monitoring our every move, while they make unimaginable profits from their schemes, and continue flying about everywhere in private jets.

For those who understand what's going on, it's easy to want to walk away from climate catastrophe debates, but we must avoid the kind of delusional thinking that creates 'climate deniers' and 'climate activists'. A *nuanced* approach recognises the challenges facing humanity, and seeks to understand deeply and fully, and to take individual and collective, responsive and responsible action. (For example: ***Pu-lease*** *– can we stop calling 'Family Planning' 'Eugenics'?!)*

... What do we really think and feel about the possibility that humans are ruining things for other species? (No memes allowed!) A curious, non-dual perspective holds tensions; doesn't

236. Michael Moore Presents: Planet of the Humans, directed by Jeff Gibbs, 1:39:56, (Rumble Media, 2019)

jump to conclusions; has compassion for all of life; and might seek tentative, low-tech, sovereign solutions that remind us of the importance of beauty and limits in our lives, via for example, the 'gift economy', if Charles Eisenstein is to be believed.[237] He advocates for a change of *perception* – where we transition from the age of separation to the age of inter-connection; bringing an opening of the heart, and a *restructuring* from the ground up in ways impossible to precisely predict, allowing us to protect and honour *all of the web of life* on this precious, unique planet.

... I'll let you list in your own mind some of the grass roots projects that the $18 billion poured into 'operation warp speed' at the beginning of the 'pandemic' could have bought us in terms of land restoration, safe-guarding mental and emotional well-being, clean water for all, energy descent strategies, tree planting. A note on tree planting – it seems the WEF is behind a project to 'plant and conserve' a trillion trees. An ambitious, if ambiguous remit, since this initiative is part of the 'carbon offsetting' strategy supported by WEF, a 'solution' of dubious merit – allows polluters to continue as long as they offset using this difficult-to-calibrate counter-measure. A new tree plantation is never the same as untouched ancient forest. The latter has between 10 and 1000 times the bio-diversity of newly planted woodland.[238]

What can we expect from this roll-out in the future – from people who insist it's their role to model calamities *ahead* of time, and then create 'disaster risk reduction' strategies as 'solutions'? How many of us feel that we wish to trust them with our well-being after the three years of Covid-19 measures? – A situation where it's impossible to tease apart the trauma and damage caused by the virus and the trauma and damage caused by The New Global Government Edicts. According to Harris Gleckman[239], "What is ingenious and disturbing is that the WEF multi-stakeholder governance proposal does not require approval or disapproval

237. Eisenstein, The More Beautiful World Our Hearts Know Is Possible

238. Yao-Hua Law. "Warning of Ecological disaster over Malaysia forest plantations", Aljazeera, July 27, 2022, https://aljazeera.com/features/2022/7/27/malaysias-biodiversity-under-pressure-from-forest-plantations

239. Nick Buxton. "Davos and its Danger to Democracy", Transnational Institute, January 18, 2016, https://tni.org/en/article/davos-and-its-danger-to-democracy

by any inter-governmental body". Furthermore, according to Buxton: "... we are increasingly entering a world where gatherings such as Davos are not laughable billionaire playgrounds, but rather the future of global governance.' [240]

If we don't want the people at the top to inflict this New World Order on us, it's *up to us* to organise ourselves, finding ways to live within self-guided limits, as peoples have *always* had to do; and to live creatively and re-generatively within those limits. The 'wealth' created by limitless growth doesn't, after all, confer happiness, as we've already seen with one in five people in the west being on anti-depressants.

[3] Health

Concerning **Health**- the rhetoric of the UN / WEF framework is worth repeating here because it's banal to the point of being sinister: they seek to '... support countries achieve good health and well-being for all, within the context of the 2030 Agenda, focusing on *key emerging global health threats that require stronger multi-stakeholder partnership and action.'* I can't wring an ounce of inspiration from their 'commitment to health'. Promoting Health means: *prevention is better than cure*. It means creating humans with strong natural immune systems, which are literally built from the ground up. Healthy, chemical-free soil, and improved access to it, produces vitamin and mineral rich food which creates healthy bodies. Fresh air and clean water, exercise, beautiful natural environments, good social networks and family ties, meaningful work, volunteer opportunities and the cultivation of virtues such as *generosity, patience, forgiveness, respect and enthusiasm;* – *these* are the cornerstones of health, *and* we all know it. But fresh air, friendship, soil and oxygen can't be patented, traded or pre-planned in disaster-modelling.

Incidentally, patent expiry is the reason Ivermectin was suppressed and smeared as a covid 19 treatment, since it yields no great profit for Big Pharma. Finally (August 2023) Google reveals at no.1 in the search results, a paper on the ncbi.nlm.hih.

240. Ibid.

gov website entitled: 'A five-day course of Ivermectin for the treatment of Covid-19 may reduce the duration of illness.'[241] That's after it was denounced as 'horse paste' on Mainstream Media for months, even years, at the height of the 'pandemic'. There is now ample evidence that the covid 'vaccines' are doing more harm than good, and, coupled with the release of several thousand of pages of Pfizer documents; reports of multiple serious adverse reactions. The NHS yellow card system and VAERS in the US describe blood clotting, myocarditis, pericarditis, Guillain-Barre syndrome, Bell's Palsy, neurological impairment, compromised full-spectrum immunity, death, and damage to pregnant women and unborn children as side effects of the 'vaccine'. This list is not exhaustive.

Dr Mike Yeadon goes as far as to say some batches have been adulterated – so striking is the fluctuation in side effects between batches. This 'experimental gene therapy', administered on a global scale, sometimes forcibly, breaks the Nuremberg code, which categorically states none shall be exposed to forced medical experiments – the 'vaccine' only received 'emergency' authorisation which does not constitute sufficient clinical testing. Immunity accruing from it has disappointed expectations, nor does this 'gene therapy' prevent transmission. According to Doctors Geert Vanden Bossche (DVM, PhD) and Sucharit Bhakdi (PhD, multi-award-winning scientist) damage to lymphocytes in vaccinated people is revealed in post-mortem examinations.[242] The lymphocytes are part of the body's defences responsible for suppressing many latent diseases. So, we can expect to see a resurgence of those in coming years, and may not be able to make a link between the covid 'vaccine' and re-emergent illnesses. Then the pharmaceutical companies will offer a new plethora of 'cures' – laughing all the way to the bank – every time.

---

241. Sabeena Ahmed, et al. "A five-day course of ivermectin for the treatment of COVID-19 may reduce the duration of illness." International Journal of Infectious Diseases 103 (2021): 214.

242. A. Burkhardt. "Notes and recommendations for conducting post-mortem examination (autopsy) of persons deceased in connection with COVID vaccination." doctorsforcovidethics.org (2022), https://1stcenturychristian.com/autopsy-directions-revised.pdf

Brilliant research has been carried out in recent decades on the gut microbiome, whilst expert scientists like Drs Zak Bush and Andrew Kaufman explore the synergies between bacteria and the body-mind system in terrain theory. This is where much cutting-edge research is happening, yet we hear nothing about it on main stream media. The human body contains trillions of microorganisms - outnumbering human cells by ten to one - Bacteria and viruses are the most successful organisms on the planet - bar none! Declaring 'war on a virus' is a ludicrous display of wilful ignorance of the composition of our bodies and our planet. Additionally, 'Terrain Theory' - emergent at the same time Louis Pasteur elaborated 'Germ Theory' - is enjoying a renaissance. Its main proponent, Antoine Bechamp, Contemporary of Louis Pasteur, remains virtually unknown to this day. On his death bed, Pasteur is reported to have said: "The germ is nothing. The soil is everything".[243] By the way, I'm not anti-allopathic medicine, I owe my recovery from Lyme's disease to antibiotics, and many other modern medical interventions have positively impacted my life. What I am against is the over-reach of Big Pharma, and the notion that 'health' is delivered via a syringe rather than as a direct consequence of healthy natural lifestyle choices.

[4] Digital Cooperation

The fourth component of the UN/WEF collaborative framework known as Agenda 2030 is **Digital cooperation**, and focuses on creating the infrastructure to ensure no one can avoid the new online ID systems. The 5G rollout ensures the digital monitoring system or 'grid' superimposed onto towns and cities is pervasive. We are told we might 'only occasionally visit the country side', under the pretext of 'rewilding' and mega-farming - to keep us within 5G parameters, enabling 24/7/365 monitoring, measuring, tracking and tracing in our new 'smart cities'. I'm guessing satellites will do the job of 5G when we 'stray out of range'... 'Geo-fencing' will form part of the matrix. This means

243. David Mason. "Germs Do Not Cause Disease", Mason Chiropractic, last modified 2018, 15 January, https://masonchiro.net/blog/12533-germs-do-not-cause-disease

that if you haven't fulfilled the required criteria linked with your digital identity: – vaccinations, re-education programmes, and any of the other hoops they wish you to jump through from their extensive menu (funded by those investing in your 'wellness outcomes', for example) you won't be able to travel beyond your allocated 'virtual space', nor access goods and services. The 'virtual space' is mapped onto your physical reality and location with the digital geo-fence, and your credit card or tokens won't work once you step beyond the boundary.

Catherine Austin Fitts asserts one of the *practical* reasons slavery ended in the USA was because they 'couldn't perfect the collateral nor quell the uprisings'. Whilst *moral outrage* surely played a part in 'ending slavery', human shadow-lust-for-power didn't disappear, it went underground. Those behind the scenes continued looking for the next opportunity... The new digital system solves those two prior 'glitches', making of the world an 'open air prison', and one where none except the Masters can avoid paying taxes and fines in the new cashless, digital, trackable dystopia. This is because *all* goods and services, including food and shelter, and also rights and freedoms, will become tokenised and 'game-ified' individual assets. Let me correct myself, they will patently **NOT** be assets – because assets *de facto* belong to us. As Klaus Schwab declares, in 2030, we will 'own nothing (and be happy)' and so goods and services, rights and freedoms will become tokenised discretionary rewards for doing what we're told.

Have you wondered about the real reason for destroying the economy? It's because beggars can't be choosers, and once we're all on Universal Credit, we'll have no option but to comply to WEF/UN/Global Government demands. You will be the little moving icon viewed from above (you can choose between 25 genders though, and what colour of sweater you'd like to wear) running through the maze, slaying dragons, earning tokens and rewards, or falling down holes into snake pits. *Think it sounds unfair?* The 'snake pit' will be isolation in your own home, where no one will even know you're suffering or lacking essential supplies, so at least public humiliation won't be part of it... *'Public?... what does that mean daddy?'* I hear a question from a 'child of the future' floating through my brain. 'We abolished it long ago, darling... along with National Government, sweetheart. Don't fret my precious, take your medicines and look at your screen'.

[5] Gender Equality and Empowerment of Women

Perhaps this one does what it says on the tin? *Phew, Hurrah!* ***Hang on*** - I just looked on the WEF website - apparently in 72 countries, women are not allowed to open bank accounts. Could that be part of it? Nice to think that women opening bank accounts might be an end in and of itself, and yet that kind of Enfranchisement will ensure all these women can be uploaded onto the digital system, turning them into 'economic units'. 'Women's empowerment' is a great outcome to be factored into the menu of the 'human capital bond project', and one that will have virtue-signalling investors falling over themselves to participate in and write about in annual reports...

'Equality for all slaves' - I'm trying to work out if that might be a catchy protest slogan, in the unlikely event women could take to the streets in the Brave New World spawned by Agenda 30? Many women in third world countries are slaves anyway you say, and I wouldn't argue with that, except to add 'men too', and not just in the third world either! This just takes our existing slave status to the next level. Let's allow that in certain circumstances some good could come of this, but only if the women are given some autonomy and self-determination, and from what we're seeing, if the Covid Years are anything to go by, autonomy and self-determination are not high up the Architects of the Great Reset's list of priorities.

...Perhaps the 'Gender Equality' project sugar-coats the otherwise bitter pill, wrapping it in the eye-candy of ethnic print head scarves... Perhaps women need more brain-washing than most men, because the great reset might be counter-intuitive to some of their maternal instincts, and they need extra coaxing? After all, what's wrong with the idea of micro-loans (which already exist) to help women start small scale businesses of their own? Women will only be eligible if they're hooked up to the system. Perhaps enfranchisement for women adds legitimacy and a 'soft wash' to the other five areas of non-negotiable Global Take Over, oops sorry, I mean the 'Great Reset'. Perhaps it ensures that when they 'empower' the 1.1 billion people on the planet who currently lack 'papers' with a digital identity, it will *definitely* - make no mistake - include the girls as well. Then again, maybe they had to dangle the 'equality for women' carrot at the WEF HQ to keep the women rolling through the doors of their 'young leaders programme'.

Here's something about the WEF which relates to Health (agenda 3) above, described as 'food security', and ends with a comment on women:

> "When food prices surged dramatically in '07-'08, causing riots and unrest, a plethora of multi-stakeholder initiatives emerged in response. (Including GAIN, AGRA, HLTF, PPP, SUN and the WEF's very own Global Food, Agriculture and Nutrition Redesign Initiative). The groups' proposals all followed a very similar template - advocating for policies that liberalise trade, increase production, encourage corporate investment and help expand agro-industries' control of food. They pointedly ignore issues of distribution and waste or the need for democratic access and control of land and food. Moreover, these groups systematically sought to close down multilateral spaces, such as the UN Standing Committee on Nutrition (SCN) that actually examined these issues. No wonder, long time food sovereignty activist, Flavio Vicente calls this corporate capture a 'life grab' which 'threatens the achievement of food sovereignty and the full emancipation of women. It is nothing less than a silent global coup d'etat."[244]

244. Buxton. "Davos and its Danger to Democracy"

So much for item 5 on the Agenda 'doing what it says on the tin'; and this quotation was a warning about a ***silent coup d'etat*** back in 2016, three years before the 'pandemic'.

[6] Education and Skills

Work and education will increasingly be done from home, on screens, under the tutelage of invisible 'bosses' and 'tutors' who will be impossible to hold accountable. The private sphere is to take more responsibility for our 'education' in this 'partnership', apparently - which sounds like fertile ground for more indoctrination with the narrative of the vested interests - whichever private funds pay for the privilege. Our ability to verify what's on our screens, that delicate, precious *art of discernment* the human body-mind-heart complex has refined over millennia, will be 'phased out', as we sit gazing at monitors all day, every day. How do we compare left-hemisphere, two-dimensional 'models on a screen' one with another? How will we know when there's a system glitch? Especially as the boundary between human and machine grows ever more permeable. How will we know whether we are playing the machine, or the machine is playing us? How can we trust the programmers and content providers? We will be (already are) lost in a matrix of simulacra - how shall we get our bearings, set our compass, to create a palpable 'sense of self' (old-fashioned and unnecessary notion)?!

Our complex, finely-tuned human organism has no way of scrutinising this virtual world using the organic systems of the body - the autonomic nervous system in particular. The body becomes obsolete. In fact, this is what cutting edge research is looking at right now - the uploading of consciousness into a computer -leaving the body behind - in a mad dash 'rush for freedom' to the virtual world - an 'escape from suffering' for those uninitiated (in the Indigenous sense of the word) amongst us who find emotions and all the messy stuff on our planet too intimidating and impossible to navigate. The more damaged we are - the more blind we become - the more outrageous the purported 'remedy'. And yet, do you know what the next 'disaster' is that they are already modelling at the WEF? A total system failure of the internet - *interesting* times! Perhaps there's more than one 'internet'? Perhaps in the end - *if the systems failures last* - we might end up the better for it.

If all goes to plan, there will be a highly competitive international digital job market to match the Great Reset, and in an international market, the prices will be dictated by those willing to accept the least. The goal posts, criteria, and necessary tokens needed to confer eligibility could change on the whim of invisible bosses or the 'investors in your outcomes' via the human capital bonds discussed above. Think of the global digital job market as similar to the ever changing Covid 19 regulations we experienced in 2020 - 2022, working on parameters, both human and AI-generated, that you're powerless to change - is it floating your boat?... The plan is to 'engage the 1.8 billion young people on the planet for this transition with life-long learning programmes'.

In a nutshell - The Great Reset is not a future I wish for my grandchildren, nor their children's children. Hopefully this chapter has peeled back some scales from our eyes. We continue in the following pages to remove a few more; exploring the many ways we continue to be duped, allowing 'invisible tyrants' free reign in concocting and imposing 'sleights of hand' unchallenged.

Chapter Eight

Psychological Warfare

We spent the last chapter taking a deep dive into some of the historic, economic and political background leading up to the Globalist vision known as Agenda 2030 currently being rolled out by the United Nations in partnership with the World Economic Forum. This Future, engineered for us by unelected Elites is also widely known as 'The Great Reset'. In so doing, we were able to disambiguate some of the 'doublespeak' propaganda posing as 'solutions' to crises of dubious origin found in the policy document. In this chapter we will look more closely at mechanisms of control, thus distinguishing smokescreens and fakery from complex and nuanced understanding, and hopefully learning to navigate these times more consciously as we go...

In gaining a better understanding of how our consent is being 'engineered', we might rediscover greater resilience and agility of thought, reclaiming some freedom in the process - enabling us to somehow generate a collaborative and viable planetary future... One where we inhabit a psycho-socio-political landscape that is grounded, mature and able to thrive within limits; embracing change by generating wise and inspired alternatives to what is being proposed. And yes, this might sometimes look like a David and Goliath struggle, or even Epic Battle between forces of good and evil. Yet no one in this drama is all good or bad, necessitating discernment, compassion, collaboration and courage as we face towards the future. Of course, part of the problem is that not many of us were schooled in the arts of genuinely participative living, meaning the mounting of effective resistance will be challenging, to say the least. I believe we'll mobilise soon enough when our backs are against the wall. This book is my attempt to show existing deficits and what might emerge to fill the vacuum. The solutions will involve acquiring embodied, relational and practical skill sets, rather than relying solely on left-hemisphere 'model solutions'.

Tibetan Crazy Wisdom goes something like this: *'Whatever happens; may it happen; whichever way it goes; may it go that way!'*[245]... One thing I take from that is: change from the perspective of us claiming back sovereignty and self-determination is *iterative* – we can't get five steps ahead of ourselves, but must instead proceed one step at a time, learning as we go. Coming back to the 'Karma' piece of previous chapters, it's impossible to outrun the chain reactions of cause and effect that have brought us to where we are now; including the disabling 'education' we've received... We can only learn by doing; 'fessing and facing up to a World the common people have been disenfranchised from for too long. Our collective programming means there is much to be unlearnt, as well as learned, and only time will tell whether we have what it takes to shape a future worth living for, and that's without factoring in the spectre of AI outsmarting us and somehow taking over.

Picking up where we left off at the end of the last chapter, we look now in more detail at the methods deployed to exert increasing top-down control. We also focus on the psychological and economic impacts of the Global Elites' Neo-Feudal 'playbook', examining the *social engineering experiment* conducted during the Covid-19 Years on a heretofore unprecedented global scale...

The Cancelling of Informed Consent

'Pandemics' provide great opportunities to 'try on for size' systems of top-down control that Global Governance might be looking to implement rapidly over the coming few years. During the 'pandemic' from 2019-2022, Lawyer Anna de Buisseret, ex-army officer and ex-Pfizer employee, spoke of the 'military grade' *psychological warfare* being waged on the general public.[246] In her view, the daily bombardment with statistics, 'cases', 'death

245. I heard this in a seminar with Buddhist psychotherapists John and Jennifer Welwood many, many moons ago.
246. AngelusCaelis. "Nurse Kate Shemirani, Lawyer Anna de Buisseret and Fiona Rose Diamond", BitChute, 22:43, August 31, 2021,https://bitchute.com/video/9ZeaZYXUXFbe

tolls', and, for example, the countless regimented lit up signs (hundreds!?) on the motorway telling us to 'get a booster' just outside Edinburgh, over Christmas 2021, *invalidated* the notion of informed consent... (How much did that little exercise alone cost, btw, and ... who footed the bill?!) The 'information' provided by government and main stream media during this period was one-sided and de-contextualised, and therefore totally meaningless. We can deduce several things from this propaganda exercise:

[1] National Governments have been superseded by mega-powerful global entities, and Billionaire funders, who with the help of technology, 'disaster modelling' scenarios, Davos annual gatherings and WEF Young Leaders trainings are making puppet shows out of national politics, not necessarily because of the calibre of the politician, although this has to play a part, but due to the inordinate wealth, power and strategic advantage they have.

[2] The mainstream political narrative these days is dictated by the WEF in partnership with other Globalist institutions and elites who uphold 'science' and fund various Initiatives and Agendas, in response to perceived 'threats'. These Institutions include the WHO, the UN, the Bill and Melinda Gates Foundation and investment entities such as Vanguard and BlackRock. Captured Academia such as Johns Hopkins University and Imperial College, London, receive funding via 'predatory philanthropy', and thus corroborate the findings of these institutions, conferring credibility on the media narrative, in a closed loop, virtually impossible for 'mere mortals' to hack...None of this means we don't have real problems to tackle, by the way!

[3] A centralised global media hub is being used as mouthpiece to promote the 'mainstream narrative'.

[4] The Elites are more powerful than any judicial system. They have enough wealth to capture and control any and all institutions, disarming the checks and balances put in place constitutionally to prevent Tyranny, and biasing big

> Tech platforms like Wikipedia and the Google monolith, so that individuals researching events only have access to biased and censored information.

If you remain sceptical, during the 'pandemic' the notion of 'Informed consent' would have entailed the provision of balanced information about the 'pros and cons' of any choice... Mention would have been made of 'adverse reactions' to the jab reported in the UK on the yellow card system and in the US using VAERS. By February 2022, the yellow card system in the UK had reported a total of 280,090 adverse reactions to all brands of the vaccine. Informed consent would have involved talking about prophylactics such as vitamin D and zinc for boosting natural immunity, early treatments such as ivermectin and hydroxychloroquine, and the likely impact of co-morbidities on the health outcomes associated with contracting Covid-19.[247] None of these topics received a mention... The catastrophic consequences of the lack of informed consent are expertly documented by former BlackRock portfolio manager Edward Dowd, in his groundbreaking book.

> "From February of 2021 to March 2022, millennials experienced the equivalent of a Vietnam War, with more than 60,000 excess deaths. The Vietnam war took 12 years to kill the same number of healthy young people we've just seen die in 12 months".[248]

Government, Big Pharma, Big Tech and the Media

During Covid - Government, Big Pharma, and Media 'fear-porn' became indistinguishable one from the other; creating a situation where the citizen on the street was no longer able to trust any of these institutions... When MSM presented 'Covid deaths' - where were the accompanying *ages?* Had dying of old age suddenly gone out of fashion? Investigation reveals the average age of death from Covid-19 was remarkably close to UK life expectancy: 81.2

247. Alberto Boretti. "Zinc augments the antiviral potential of HCQ/CQ and ivermectin to reduce the risks of more serious outcomes from COVID-19 infection." Journal of Trace Elements in Medicine and Biology 71 (2022): 126954.
248. Dowd, Cause Unknown

years in 2019. The government didn't aggregate the information into a yearly figure (deliberately making it hard to compare) but on the website of the Office for National Statistics, we can see from a table that the median ages of death from Covid-19 (with no underlying conditions) in January, February, and March 2021, were 83, 82, and 79 respectively. The statistics showing death from Covid-19 over two years of the 'pandemic'[249] (at the time of writing), hovers around the late 70s to early 80s range - reflecting a population dying of old age from a respiratory tract virus, similar to 'flu or pneumonia. *Nothing new there!* Needless to say, age, co-morbidities, and vaccine status, weren't reported in the death statistics

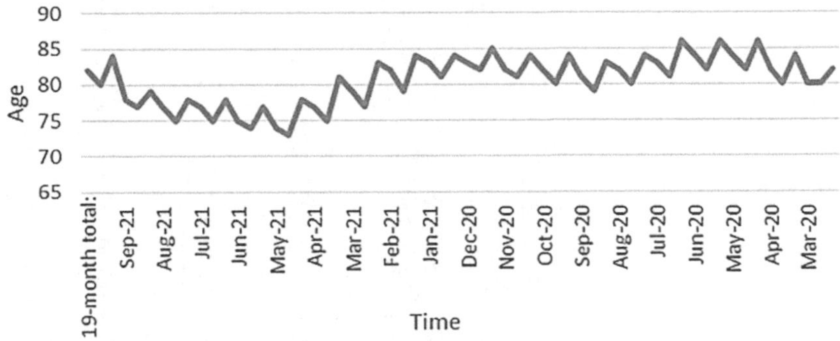

Figure 8: *Median Morbidity Age where Death due to COVID-19*

Announcements magically appeared **daily** (unbidden) *on my phone's home screen*, every time I switched on in the spring and summer of 2020: a supposed 'death tally'. I never signed up for those updates in 'settings', and if ***'They'*** (the amorphous and indistinguishable Government/MSM/Big Pharma/Big Tech) insist on showing them anyway, why not show the daily death tally from heart disease, cancer, diabetes, malaria, war, starvation and suicide as well, please, for the sake of some *context*?!... For example; according to an article re-published on greenmedinfo.

249. Georgia Brett. *"Single year of age and average age of death of people whose death was due to or involved coronavirus", Office for National Statistics, last modified August 23, 2023, https://ons.gov.uk/peoplepopulationandcommunity/birthsdeathsandmarriages/deaths/datasets singleyearofageandaverageageofdeathofpeoplewhosedeathwasduetoorinvolvedcovid*

com: "more Americans died from suicide [in 2022] than died in the entire Korean War (1950-1953)", amounting to 49,500 people, the highest annual figure on record in America.[250]

		Involving Covid-19		Due to Covid-19	
		Median	Mean	Median	Mean
19-Month Total (Mar' 2020 - Sept' 2021)	People	82	79.7	82	79.7
	Males	80	78	80	78.1
	Females	84	81.7	84	81.8
September 2021	People	78	75.5	78	75.2
	Males	78	74.7	77	74.5
	Females	79	76.5	79	76.1
August 2021	People	77	73.9	77	73.5
	Males	76	72.6	75	72.3
	Females	79	75.8	78	75.3
July 2021	People	77	73.6	77	73.2
	Males	76	72.0	75	71.7
	Females	79	75.7	78	75.2
June 2021	People	76	73.5	75	72.7
	Males	75	73.3	74	72.5
	Females	77	73.9	77	73.0
May 2021	People	76	73.7	74	72.9
	Males	74	71.6	73	70.7
	Females	79	76.7	78	75.8
April 2021	People	79	75.9	77	74.6
	Males	76	74.2	75	73.0
	Females	82	78.0	81	76.9
March 2021	People	80	77.2	79	76.7
	Males	77	75.2	77	74.7
	Females	83	79.6	83	79.3
February 2021	People	82	79.4	82	79.4
	Males	80	77.4	79	77.4
	Females	84	81.6	84	81.6
January 2021	People	82	80.1	83	80.2
	Males	81	78.4	81	78.5
	Females	84	82.0	84	82.1

Figure 9: *UK Covid-19 Dataset (Source: Office of National Statistics)*

The Covid 'death count' became outmoded soon enough, as the media moved on to counting 'cases' – positive test results – in those who may or may not exhibit any symptoms. As we saw already, the late Nobel Prize winner Dr Kary Mullis declared the PCR test which he invented, *unfit* for purpose[251]; even Anthony Fauci has admitted that amplifying the test sample over a certain number of cycles renders the results meaningless,[252] just one more sign of the

250. *Carolyn Hendler. "U.S Suicide Rate in 2022 Highest Ever Recorded, COVID Lockdowns Played a Role", Renegade Tribune, September 6, 2023, http://renegadetribune.com/u-s-suicide-rate-in-2022-highest-ever-recorded-covid-lockdowns-played-a-role*
251. *Real Truth Real News. "Kary Mullis, Inventor of the PCR Technique"*
252. *"Dr Anthony Fauci explains failure of testing in the US", BBC News, March 13, 2020, https://bbc.com/news/av/world-us-canada-51877356*

manipulation of statistics to generate alarm and compliance. Dr Mike Yeadon, whose impeccable credentials were cited in the last chapter, de-bunked the myth of asymptomatic transmission[253], meaning 'cases' without symptoms posed no threat, and were basically false positives. To cap it all the Lancet admits: "the impact of vaccination on community transmission of circulating variants of SARS Cov-2 appeared to be not significantly different from the impact among unvaccinated people".[254] With Pfizer admitting towards the end of 2022 that its vaccine was never tested for transmissibility, what is there left to hang on to of the mainstream narrative that was rammed down the public's throat for nearly three years, and threatens to resurface in autumn 2023?

Furthermore, it now seems common knowledge the original variant was leaked as a result of clandestine 'gain-of-function' research carried out at the Wuhan lab, funded, in part, by the US.[255] According to Trinidadian Doctor Michael McDowell,[256] one of the few religious leaders who has taken it upon himself to look 'behind the scenes', there are 22 nations who possess BSL4 labs - Bio Safety level 4 - where Bio-weapons are made, and 16 nations on earth who stockpile them. The Bio-weapons industry is one of the most clandestine industries on Earth, with a remit of deliberately cultivating virulent strains of pathogens to be unleashed in times of war.

Follow the Money

According to a 2021 Oxfam report[257], Pfizer, BioNTech and Moderna were making $1,000 per second, whilst Dr Robert Malone asserts Pfizer earned $37.8billion from sales of its Covid-

253. Stecklow and Macaskill. "Ex-Pfizer scientist who became an anti-vax hero"

254. Carlos Franco-Paredes. "Transmissibility of SARS-Cov-2 among fully vaccinated individuals." The Lancet 22, no. 1 (2022): 16

255. The CIA, NIH, USAID, DoD and State Department all co-funded the research. Robert W. Malone. "Update: Moderna and Pfizer mRNA vax Patent Battles", SubStack, August 31, 2023, https://rwmalonemd.substack.com/p/update-moderna-and-pfizer-mrna-vax

256. SBN News Clips. "Dr. Michael Mcdowell Explains the Covid Agenda - 5197", Rumble, 26:19, December 23, 2021, https://rumble.com/vr9xqm-dr.-michael-mcdowell-explains-the-covid-agenda.-5197.html

257. "Pfizer, BioNTech and Moderna making $1,000 profit every second while world's poorest countries remain largely unvaccinated", Oxfam, November 16, 2021, https://oxfam.org.uk/mc/h9nzx6

19 'vaccine' Comirnaty in 2022, and Moderna made $18.4 billion from it's 'vaccine' Spikevax.[258] How many of our politicians and senators have investments with these companies, and when or where are they required to declare a conflict of interests relating to public health issues? Rishi Sunak co-founded Theleme Partners before entering Parliament, who were a major investor in Moderna. Stock market filings show Theleme had/has a $500m investment in Moderna, and is registered in the Cayman Islands, a tax haven which doesn't make company records public.[259]

GPs received a £12.58 'bonus incentive' *per dose* to administer the vaccine[260] on top of their salary - announced for all to see in the BMJ - whilst early treatment and prophylactics were never offered or discussed in the pre-determined NHS protocols during the 'pandemic'.

We might wonder how those rules were formulated and applied in GP surgeries and hospitals in the UK and around the world. Romanian EU parliamentarian, Cristian Terhes, one of the brave ones, can be seen on video displaying a printed copy of agreements struck between pharmaceutical companies and the EU in November 2020.[261] Large swathes of the documents had been redacted, meaning even European politicians had no access to vital details about the nature of the contracts.

Street View

... With propaganda, hype and censorship, many were seized with a kind of 'Dunkirk Spirit' early on in the 'pandemic': '*STAY SAFE*' was the mantra on the streets in Spring of 2020; before exhaustion with it all set in... People pronounced the catch-phrase with a nod and a wave, bumping elbows, instead of shaking hands, as if it was all a bit of fun – *for a while*. Indeed, other great Covid-19 traditions instated during the 'first wave' included:

258. Malone. "Update: Moderna and Pfizer mRNA vax Patent Battles" Substack.
259. Juliette Garside. "Rishi Sunak Refuses to say if he will profit from Moderna Covid Vaccine", The Guardian, November 17, 2020, https://theguardian.com/politics/2020/nov/17/rishi-sunak-refuses-to-say-if-he-will-profit-from-moderna-covid-vaccine
260. Gareth Iacobucci. "Covid-19: GPs to get £12.58 per dose to deliver vaccine from December", British Medical Journal m4354 (2020): 371 Substack
261. Dr. John Campbell. "Pfizer, blanked out pages", 15:29, October 21, 2022, https://youtube.com/watch?v=HnSnQor8zDY

clapping the NHS at your door, sticking pictures of rainbows in windows and *bringing out the bunting*, even, for 'outdoor tea parties' aimed at 'keeping up the morale'. That's what 'lockdown #1' looked like in Small Town Britain in south west England in early 2020, anyway.

In 2020 and 2021 there was literally no outlet for organised dissent, nor even one for open debate. Mainstream media in the UK, including the BBC - to its shame - was a wall-to-wall propaganda machine. The Devonshire town of Totnes sought to host a 'Truth Conference' towards the end of 2021, with a number of credentialed speakers, including Dr Dolores Cahill and Lawyer Anna de Buisseret. It was shut down – on the grounds of it being 'racist'. Local worthies petitioned the council to get the conference banned from the Civic Hall. They moved to a private hotel in nearby Torquay, which was subsequently located and shut down too by the 'purveyors of virtue'. A larger event in Bath organised by the World Council for Health in 2022: 'The Better Way Conference' spearheaded by Dr Tess Lawrie[262], was attended by hundreds of luminaries and participants who envisaged a 'healthy new paradigm, rooted in freedom, empowerment, education and integrity.' That conference actually had to change venue, when Bath City Chambers decided to renege on its agreement to host the event.

On the surface, the nay sayers shutting down dissent and debate look like bunting-toting, gung-ho advocates of 'traditional values'; busy 'saving lives' and 'extolling the efforts of the NHS' - but underneath is an intolerant, fearful minority, whose only source of information is the MSM, controlling and suppressing quite possibly the majority of pro-human rights, pro-bodily autonomy, pro-freedom-of-speech inhabitants of small-town Britain.

'*STAY* ***SANE***', rather than 'stay safe', was always my own personal motto, from day *one*, although it has been easier said

262. Revelatory short documentary recording a conversation she had with Dr Andrew Hill, which shows him doing a volte face on the promotion of Ivermectin – a proven successful early treatment for Covid-19 that's out of patent, therefore not making enough profit. "Dear Andy", Oracle Films, March 4, 2022, https://oraclefilms.com/alettertoandrewhill

than done. Writing about what is *really* going on, to the best of my ability has helped with the process. According to Aldous Huxley:[263]

> "... We are... forced to choose between an unduly brief exposition and no exposition at all. Abbreviation is a necessary evil and the abbreviators' business is to make the best of a job which, though intrinsically bad, is still better than nothing. He must learn to simplify, but not to the point of falsification".

At the opposite end of the spectrum, and a tactic used to create confusion – is that of 'information overkill' on the part of those attempting to expound the 'science' behind the mainstream narrative: – screeds of documentation filled with pseudo-scientific jargon – overwhelming quantities of 'data': prefaces, introductions, caveats, break-downs, using different parameters for recording data in different contexts – making comparisons and cross-referencing difficult if not impossible... This made and makes disambiguation and clarification of what's actually happening impossible to follow and understand – even for the 'scientists' let alone the average (wo)man on the street.

Strategies of Control

In this section we name some of the other tools of fifth generation warfare – where the battleground is the human mind. We also call out one of the GB-founded agencies used to implement a Tyrannical Global regime in the Covid-19 years and beyond.

Fear

The Covid 'enemy' is an invisible particle – something we can't feel, touch or apprehend with the senses – in many respects a perfect contender for sowing confusion and fear amongst the populace. Not to mention the blindingly complex science of virology; which remains opaque for 99.9% of the population. During the pandemic, if nowhere felt safe, and the enemy was 'unknowable'; general malaise was inevitable. The strategy

263. Aldous Huxley, Brave New World Revisited (Chatto and Winds, 1966)

leverages social expectations – the fear of being judged for 'failing to do the right thing'. No one wants to be branded 'a thoughtless super-spreader'; we have a visceral fear of rejection as a hangover from tribal times, when being kicked out into the wilderness meant certain death. Compliance is predicated on this ancient survival mechanism – enabling mask mandates, 'social distancing' and experimental jabs, the shutting of non-essential businesses, the forbidding of marriages and funerals. In public places, we became afraid of one another – forgetting our common humanity as we learned instead to keep our distance, and avoid eye contact. Why bother with that outmoded relic of a bygone era? We became an 'un-tribe' of scared, harassed entities, viewing each other as potential threats, rushing 'home' to our 'bunkers' to imbibe more fake news on gargantuan screens.

Especially children's physical, mental and emotional health has been and is jeopardised, as we put our own and our family's well-being on the line in a bid to virtue signal or at least 'put up and shut up' our way out of a global take over. Perhaps one of the most reprehensible fears (if it's possible to rank them) generated by the 'pandemic' has been making children afraid of passing the virus on to older relatives, via the *myth* of 'asymptomatic transmission', discussed above. Children are at miniscule risk of suffering from the virus, and their resilience to, and swift recovery from Covid-19 in over 99% of cases, signals the superiority and robustness of natural immunity, which is only *compromised* by the administration of unnecessary medications.[264]

We complied in the Covid-19 years with having our relatives die on their own in hospitals, where strict protocols were adhered to by staff too scared of losing their jobs to question them. Hospitals have always been horrible places to die – bright lights, tubes, bleeping monitors; the impersonality of it all. Add to that a sea of masked faces, where it's impossible to read the humanity in

264. Geert Vanden Bossche, PhD, has repeatedly stated that children provide a reservoir of 'herd immunity' and that vaccinating them is destroying their immune systems and making them vulnerable to other diseases. "Episode 336: Tinderbox", TheHighWire, 2:03:03, September 8, 2023, https://thehighwire.com/ark-videos/tinderbox

an expression, and dying alone in hospital looks like a dystopian nightmare from a sci-fi movie.

'The only thing needed for evil to prevail is for good people to do nothing'.[265] In Psychology and philosophy, the phenomenon of group compliance has been explored and labelled 'mass formation' by many voices including Elias Canetti, Carl Jung, Rene Girard and Sigmund Freud, and has been used to describe the pandemic years by Belgian Professor of Clinical Psychology Mattias Desmet. His book 'The Psychology of Totalitarianism' goes into detail[266], whilst an interview with Dr Reiner Fuellmich on 21st of September 2021 is available on Rumble for a summary... This ongoing *'cultural hypnosis event'* relies on the joint forces of social isolation, lack of meaning and purpose, large amounts of free-floating anxiety and frustration and latent aggression, allowing its proliferation in a population.

... It's not just the people who got scare-mongered into following egregious mandates, but the politicians who implemented them too... Being influenced by 'Predictions' coming from 'advisors' such as Neil Ferguson at Imperial College, London, who models scenarios, ahead of time, on a global scale. His 'Worldwide Waves' of Biblical proportions involving millions dropping dead from plague and pestilence are enough to frighten the pants off politicians, and not just for Covid, but Bird Flu and other infectious diseases. His epidemiology modelling has been described thus: 'The exaggerated forecasts of this modelling team are now impossible to downplay or deny, and extend to almost every country on earth. Indeed, they may well constitute one of the greatest scientific failures in modern human history'.[267] *(Or 'pseudo-scientific successes', depending on which way up you read your Tarot pack!)*

265. Attributed to Edmund Burke or John Stuart Mill (Wikipedia). True source remains unknown.

266. Mattias Desmet, The Psychology of Totalitarianism

267. Phillip W. Magness. "The Failure of Imperial College Modelling is Far Worse than we Knew", American Institute for Economic Research, April 22, 2021, https://aier.org/article/the-failure-of-imperial-college-modeling-is-far-worse-than-we-knew

As we've seen, vast swathes of Academia & Big Pharma operate in lockstep because the funding for research comes from Industry. Preparedness 'exercises' such as Event 201[268] covered in the last chapter, are designed to hold guns to politicians' heads; taunting them with questions about the baked-in 'responsibility' for 'public health' that they assume with office. What about the baked-in responsibility of protecting us from the likes of the World Economic Forum, its agents, and the self-serving Agendas of the unelected Global Elites? As I write, the WHO is preparing a 'Zero Draft treaty' which would change the law, allowing them to assume control should we experience another 'pandemic'. I mean they assumed control anyway, with a few of their closest 'friends', but this actually puts it in writing![269] You just have to laugh at the rhetoric:

> "...the best chance we have, today, as a global community, to prevent a repeat of the past is to come together, in the spirit of solidarity, in a commitment to equity, and in the pursuit of health for all, and develop a global accord that safeguards societies from future pandemic threats."

In the case of Neil Ferguson, the tail appears to be wagging the dog... After all, the government appoints these advisors. Some of us can't understand why Neil Ferguson still has a job and an OBE?! As I reread this paragraph, I'm struck by *my own* naiveté – the World Economic Forum already *has* infiltrated government completely, the WEF *is* our government. How else to explain the level of coercion and control being imposed on us all over the world during the 'pandemic'? Ferguson's OBE signs and seals the deal!

We discussed the 'Great Reset' at length in the last chapter – allegedly, for reasons unknown, most graduates don't put the WEF Young Leaders' Programme on their CV. Nonetheless, Schwab was caught bragging on camera that over half the cabinet

---

268. "Event 201", Johns Hopkins

269. "WHO Member States agree to develop zero draft of legally binding pandemic accord in early 2023", World Health Organisation, December 7, 2022, https://who.int/news/item/07-12-2022-who-member-states-agree-to-develop-zero-draft-of-legally-binding-pandemic-accord-in-early-2023

in both Canada and Argentina, as well as their Prime Ministers, and the French PM, *even Vladimir Putin*, are from the ranks of the WEF Young Global Leaders programme.[270] This is a Campaign of Stealth, as well as Fear.

Masking

The mask is many things, perhaps above all, a sign of submission to an alien authority. It transforms us into 'less than human' beings - looking like hordes of extras in a Zombie Apocalypse movie. Just a trip to Tesco became a traumatising experience for those of us under the illusion that critical thinking was one of the subjects taught in schools and universities in the UK. Masking makes it harder to read and interpret our unique expressions, gestures and emotions; and thus, impute meaning; enabling us to truly connect with each other: ***by 'cancelling the face', we cancel the living glyph of our humanity***. This makes it easier for us to ignore each other, whilst homogenising us, lending an eerie individuality-obliterating pall to any gathering. We are less likely to inspire one another, or even *conspire* against our oppressors when we are masked up (no surprises there!) Our sovereign rights to breathe freely; communicate freely; dress according to our own preferences; even to see clearly when masks 'fog up' glasses, and to take care of our own and others' well-being in fitting ways - all these inalienable rights have been taken out of our hands.

Dr Mark McDonald[271] describes how children's IQ scores have plummeted during the pandemic, relying as they do on social opportunities in order to learn cooperation, empathy and how to navigate complexity... So much of the highly evolved and evolving brain 'wiring', and what has been termed 'neuro plasticity' is learned via face-to-face encounter. A screen can't replace these precious, formative experiences that are vital for developing our uniquely human capabilities. What will a dumbed-down population comply with next? During Covid-19, children's

270. Malcolm H Wiener Lecture: Institute of Politics Harvard Kennedy School. "Strengthening Collaboration in a Fractured World – Featuring Special Guest Yo-Yo Ma, YouTube, 1:01:00, September 21, 2017, https://youtube.com/watch?v=AoBRnrtX9U4

271. Mark McDonald. "Masking Children is Child Abuse", Dissident MD, January 7, 2022, https://markmcdonaldmd.substack.com/p/masking-children-is-child-abuse

enjoyment of life was stolen from them - their social events cancelled, masking in class was compulsory in many states in the US and the UK, whilst some were forbidden from even talking to each other during breaks. There is no possible justification for this. It singles out the 'pandemic' as the work of evil people. We must ask ourselves what sort of people, when 'Health' is a chief concern, would rob children of their childhoods?

In a Meta Analysis of 65 studies, Sayer Ji [272] cites many side effects of mask wearing including: Lowered empathy; itchy and irritated skin, chemical changes: CO^2 increase and oxygen decrease in the blood; heart and respiratory rate increase, blood pressure increase; with bacterial, viral and fungal contamination in the mask, and therefore lungs, increasing over time. Headaches, vaso-dilation, dizziness and drowsiness have also been reported... This is not an exhaustive list of side effects. Keeping masks 'fresh' involves throwing them away regularly, and they are non-bio-degradable. The anxiety and depression caused by covering our 'organ of social communication' as creatures 'hard wired to connect' is impossible to measure. So is the sheer inconvenience of mask wearing, and the sense it brings of somehow, insidiously, tearing up the social contract of being human.

Dr Byram Bridle[273] debunks the myth of the medical efficacy of masks, explaining that the pore size of the average low-cost mask is between 80-500 microns across. The size of a virus particle is 1micron. The air we breathe produces aerosol droplets approximately 80 microns in diameter, into which a viral particle could easily lodge itself. So, the aerosol droplets of our breathing - laced with the virus - are passing through the masks of all wearers, all the time - that's before we examine each mask around the edges to discover there are gaps big enough to drop a Brazil nut through, never mind a viral particle.

272. Kai Kisielinski et al. "Is a Mask That Covers the Mouth and Nose Free from Undesirable Side Effects in Everyday Use and Free of Potential Hazards?", Environmental Research and Public Health 18, no. 8 (2021), https://mdpi.com/1660-4601/18/8/4344/htm
273. Bright Light News. "Viral Immunologist, Dr. Byram Bridle, PhD, debunks the narrative that masks protect people from Covid, as he indisputably shows aerosols penetrating 5 surgical masks", Facebook, 1:55, December 11, 2021, https://facebook.com/watch/?v=1015580112342423

Censorship

In the Arenas of Science and Politics, since Covid-19, the *art of debate,* and *scientific enquiry; of* piecing together a more complete picture as a result of looking from different angles, is *dead.* Why was the conversation between Joe Rogan and Robert Malone taken down? He's one of the most highly credentialed scientists on the planet whose innumerable papers have been cited 14,208[274] times since 2018 – himself involved in the invention of mRNA technology. The three-hour interview was removed from Rogan's website and Spotify, partly under pressure from people I once admired: – Neil Young, Joni Mitchell and Crosby, Stills and Nash, who took down their music from the platform in protest. A volte-face from their Woodstock days if ever there was one! The censorship tactic clearly involves 'divide and rule', engaging society at large in the self-policing propensities we've had centuries of practice in honing...

Most towns have at least one Facebook page, where Covid-19 conversations were banned (as well as the platform's own censoring) in the pandemic years. Local venues complied with the regulations just so they could stay open and avoid financial penalties... People were and are afraid to speak out because small parochial communities are places where the 'weirdo' label sticks. No one wants to stick their head over the parapet, and risk being 'shot down' 'cancelled' or 'closed' by the self-appointed 'morally righteous brigade', who, unknown to themselves, are actually facilitating a Global Coup d'Etat.

Lawyer Dr Reiner Fuellmich spearheaded a virtual online version of a 'Grand Jury' 'Court of Public Opinion' where the Corona Investigative Committee interviewed 100+ highly credentialed people, in the absence of any existing court worldwide choosing to host hearings against pandemic malfeasance. This bold and courageous action has cost Fuellmich his freedom - he's spent the last 6 months in jail, awaiting trial, as of April 2024, possibly on trumped up charges, after being abducted illegally without an

274. *"Robert Malone", Google Scholar, https://scholar.google.com/scholar?hl=en&as_sdt=0%2C5&q=robert+malone&btnG=*

arrest warrant from the German embassy in Mexico, according to Christopher Scott Spada on LinkedIn.

Elsewhere, trials have been taking place in 2023 in the US, brought by people like Del Bigtree via ICAN (the Informed Consent Action Network), which saw a 60% increase in revenue over the previous year in 2020 to $5.5 million.

Anyone challenging the 'received narrative' is confronted with a barrage of self-righteous 'fact-checkers', branding any form of dissent 'conspiracy theory'; other labels include: 'tin foil hat wearer', 'anti-vaxxer' or promoter of 'hate speech'. Where the 'fact checkers' get their 'moral high ground' is never established. The origins of their pseudo-organisations are difficult to research - um, sorry, 'independent' doesn't count as a credential! I don't remember ever hearing a 'fact checker' *refute an argument* either. 'Facts' themselves are dead, left-hemisphere notions; a fact was *never alive*, a *fact* is an *isolated* piece of information, and fragments need *context* - the 'oxygen' of discourse, the 'life blood' of experience.

Any statistician will tell you the only thing columns of numbers reveal is *the bias* of their presenter... Context, discourse, debate; these are the ingredients healthy brains thrive on; science was once upon a time the brainchild of *curiosity*; forging neural networks capable of navigating and evaluating complexity. 'Science' today is the New Religion - propped up and propelled by the liturgy of a legacy-media-saturated world: – ***all collage*** cobbled together to create a kaleidoscope of sound- and image-bytes... a patch-work of biased commentary, CGI and de-contextualised 'data'. Just one example of what I'm talking about: the 'Covid19assembly.org' website, created by UK-based lawyers, doctors and journalists, informed in 2021 that total Covid-19 deaths were being aggregated over two years, when all other causes of death are counted *annually* - no wonder people are turning to alternative media in droves.

Destabilisation and the erosion of Meaning-Making

It takes *time,* and *effort* to fit new ideas into our existing mental scaffolding; where the abstractions of the left brain, and the right brain's capacity for synthesis pass information and experience back and forth constantly. Optimised, intelligent conversations between two or more people perform the function of continually enlarging the 'maps of meaning' we use to navigate reality. We're not only generating meaning of course through sharing in close proximity, but are experiencing co-regulation of our nervous systems and updating our capacity to interpret complexity and fit in with social norms... Possibly recalibrating who the 'in-crowd' might be, and the outliers, also, and working out where we might sit in the grand scheme - modifying our mannerisms to fit with our desired positioning on the spectrum from in-crowd to outlier... Assuming those positions are still easy to identify and continue to have relevance in the modern age. They definitely still do exist – for example nudity in public places is a definite no-no. If we exhibit radical outlier behaviour, we run the risk of being 'sectioned' and incarcerated against our will. This would probably include being medicated against our will (... from a therapy client who was sectioned several times; injection with sedative drugs is routine).

Nonetheless, 'expressing our individuality' is encouraged, as long as it begins and ends with our appearance, 'gender identity' and particular 'taste' in music and consumables, and the approved sloganeering *du jour*... The decreasing levels of dopamine available to the frontal lobes from too much random scrolling, however, means there is a decrease in memory, concentration and sequential thinking. We become "tied to the present without being able to reflect".[275]

The de-contextualisation of the information we consume creates a loosening of our understanding of 'social norms', and decreases our 'meaning making' capabilities, which in turn erodes the knobs and handles of social engagement... It's much easier to keep looking down at our screen in public than to risk looking awkward clutching and proffering a poorly intuited, flaccid knob!

When everything 'News' is a post-modern mash-up, our sense of reality, identity and belonging are all impacted. The choice is

275. *"Better Way Live Episode #104. Unregulated Technology: Why We Must Take Action Now", World Council for Health, September 18, 2023,* https://worldcouncilforhealth.org/multimedia/unregulated-technology-bob-moran

either to 'go with the flow' (*like a dead fish!*) or to somehow back paddle in an attempt to unravel what exactly is going on. The architects of the NWO don't want that. They rely on us being too busy and distracted to notice the takeover happening under our noses. *Simply gathering together to openly debate, explore and enjoy the fruits of a high-powered, well-informed meeting of minds has become a rare feat and rebellious act...*[276] Meaning-making is a social activity. The echo-chambers of our time: – one person alone in a room on a screen for inordinate amounts of time day after day, week after week, year after year, creates an anti-culture of epic proportions whose legacy remains unknown.

Wealth Transfer

Lockdowns closed businesses; contributing colossal wealth transfers into the hands of the already-mega-rich[277]... According to Robert F Kennedy Jr., lockdowns shifted $4trillion in wealth from the middle classes to the new class of super-rich who increased their wealth by 30%. Difficult to see how the middle class fit into a Neo-Feudal slavery system, *right enough!* 3.3 million businesses were closed in the US as a direct result of lockdowns – how many more million across the rest of the world? The people worst hit were the working classes; livelihoods, dignity and purpose taken from them; scuppering community, diversity, resource and resilience.

The Covid-19 economy prioritised 'essential only' businesses, homogenising society by creating ever-greater dependency on Mega Corporations such as Walmart, Amazon and Tesco, with the mandates wiping out their competition in a few cruel months. Just one example from Scotland – the country of my birth – three independent cinemas – the Belmont in Aberdeen, The Filmhouse in Edinburgh and Glasgow Film Theatre have all closed in the last year (2022-23) as a direct impact of the lockdowns – the parent

276. Luckily there are still people like US Senator Ron Johnson who convened a discussion Panel of experts to discuss vaccine inefficiency and inappropriate care. Art Moore. "Watch Sen. Johnson's COVID panel with Drs. Robert Malone, Peter McCullough", Clark County Today, January 25, 2022, https://clarkcountytoday.com/news/watch-sen-johnsons-covid-panel-with-drs-robert-malone-peter-mccullough

277. The lockdowns created a billionaire a day according to Robert F Kennedy Jr. Lark Davis. "The Greatest Wealth Transfer in History", rumble, June 21, 2023, https://rumble.com/v35waw9-the-greatest-wealth-transfer-in-history.html

company CMI went into receivership costing 102 members of staff their jobs.[278] The Edinburgh Filmhouse opened in 1979, and was home to the world's oldest continually running film festival: **Edinburgh International Film Festival,** which I personally attended on many occasions, listening to directors holding forth on the vision behind their own particular documentaries, enjoying the stimulation of the back and forth of free flowing, uncensored ideas.[279]

... Yes, it's mightily convenient to get all our stuff delivered to our door at the click of a button – yet city centres are hollowed out as we retreat ever farther from the possibility of salutary encounters with the 'real' world (anyone remember that old relic?!) ... Lockdowns affect large sectors of the economy – including international tourism, local hospitality, the catering and entertainment industries. The knock-on effects, especially in 'developing' (pillaged) countries, where small business operators and sole-traders are the norm and have no safety net, can mean desperation and destitution.

The world loses vibrancy, diversity, stability and innovation when it loses small businesses: – the undermining of small-scale independents is designed to demoralise and disorientate. When rules change constantly, the feeling of being an insignificant pawn in the game of the governing classes amplifies. 'Sitting it out in confused resignation' becomes the default of many. People become dependent on hand outs; unemployment, debt, bankruptcy, divorce, child abuse, depression and suicide proliferate, along with a decreased availability of mental health services.[280] Divested People existing on handouts are malleable and less resilient; payouts necessitate compliance – we become easy prey in the face of the Game-ified Global Virtual Republic being rolled out by the WEF in partnership with the UN and unelected Billionaires everywhere.

---

278. "Edinburgh Filmhouse put up for Sale following CMI closure", BBC News, November 3, 2022, https://bbc.com/news/uk-scotland-edinburgh-east-fife-63499988

279. "Edinburgh Filmhouse", WikiMedia Foundation, last modified November 30, 2023, https://en.wikipedia.org/wiki/Edinburgh_Filmhouse

280. Nadia Barberis et al. "Suicidal behaviours during COVID-19 pandemic: A review." Clinical Neuropsychiatry 19, no. 2 (2022): 84.

Big Tech and Neurotransmitters

The digital realm has transformed life for most of us, with the biggest changes being seen in the lives of young people, many of whom have lived tech-saturated lives from infancy. In parallel with our screens, 'digital identities' have emerged in the last 15 years or so, with the emotional charge of having a highly curated 'online Avatar' being most compelling for young people, many of whom identify more strongly with the online version of themselves than the (dowdy, tawdry) physical iteration. Hospitalisations of self-harming girls rose by 110% in Canada between 20009 and 2014, corresponding with the introduction of the smart phone in 2007.[281] The hollowing out of the face-to-face realm, most recently via masking kids, cancelled play-dates, and the numberless other ill-effects of lockdowns, means young people become *ever more dependent* on a tech-mediated existence. As we become more isolated, we are even *more* vulnerable to the only hormonal hit in town - provided by 'likes' tallied on the 'virtual circuses' of the digital realm. Global Elites, extremists, advertisers, fear mongers, porn makers and consent engineers make it their business to leech our energy via data harvesting, tracking and tracing and by designing addiction in to the algorithms and platforms that rule the daily lives of so many.

For all, the virtual world splits and diverts our precious time and energy, taking us away from making a *real* difference in the *real* world where this battle has to be fought and won. Our life-force is co-opted by mesmerising, addictive tech, which fragments the psyche - creating a 'real' & 'virtual' hybrid of our persona - a new schizophrenia variant, you could say... Whilst tech potentially facilitates meeting up, by providing easy pathways to 'connect' with other humanoids near and far; according to 'The Social Dilemma' documentary[282], dating is on the decline. We can control the conversation on a screen - if it gets too intense, convoluted or messy, just flick up with your thumb - deleting the

---

281. Elia Abi-Jaoude, Karline Treurnicht Naylor, and Antonio Pignatiello. "Smartphones, social media use and youth mental health." Canadian Medical Association Journal 192, no. 6 (2020): E136-E141.

282. The Social Dilemma, Jeff Orlowski, 2020

other's existence from your 'reality', and with it the unwritten 'social contract' that in times of yore might lead to a deepening and quickening in the hard-to-control flesh and blood realm of face-to-face encounter.

Not only this, but technology and especially the smart phone, stimulate our reward circuitry, in particular dopamine.[283] This neurotransmitter comes online when we do something we associate with pleasure - chocolate, sex, alcohol, drugs, and stimulation from what we see on our screens. The problem with dopamine is that it enervates the synapses. Synapses like to be 'tickled' but not all the time, which would lead to a hyper-enervated state. Consequently, when we try to seek out reward all the time, there is a phenomenon called synaptic death - meaning some of the circuits literally die off to avoid the discomfort of hyper-arousal. This leads to a cycle of addiction where we have to expose ourselves to more but receive less of a 'tickle' ('hit') for doing so.

Interestingly, the neurotransmitter present in secure attachment is serotonin, and whereas dopamine has an up-regulatory, or stimulating, effect, serotonin has more of an inhibitory or down-regulatory one... Where dopamine offers a short-lived pleasure hit, serotonin is responsible for feelings of slowing down; of well-being and ease. In this state, relaxation is possible and the fight or flight system goes off-line. We could say dopamine kicks in when there is a feeling of scarcity, which brings in its wake a sense of urgency; whereas serotonin comes on line when we feel safe and relaxed and have no need for vigilance or the thrill of the chase. In our tech-saturated culture we have done a dangerous amount of conflating pleasure with contentment. In reality, they are very different experiences prompted by different sets of circumstances, each with unique neuro-biological 'signatures'.[284]

Unfortunately, dopamine down-regulates serotonin, which in times of scarcity makes sense. It would be foolish to be smiley, happy and relaxed when our backs are against the wall - so, a vicious circle gets perpetuated. Seeking pleasure and stimulus

---

283. FitMind. "Serotonin vs. Dopamine – 7 key Differences Between Pleasure and Happiness", YouTube, 10:22, August 29, 2021, https://youtube.com/watch?v=A3svaOilIis
284. Ibid.

has us on a merry-go-round where dopamine is down-regulated by the reward circuits after the hit, because too much dopamine in the system feels 'too ticklish'! (it's an 'upper, not a downer'…) Not only that, but we have a double whammy or boomerang effect of dopamine down-regulating serotonin. Thus, we don't feel or look smiley and happy, or a good hang-out prospect for another who might be genuinely smiley-happy and securely attached. We give off a vibe of being strung out, irritable, with maybe a fake smiley-happy face painted on top. Most of us are still quite good at seeing through this disguise, by the way.[285]

Just to add another layer of complexity to the mix at this point – it's also possible to 'fake it 'til you make it': social anxiety is a *real and normal* reaction when coming into contact with others, because for sensitive creatures like human beings – of all complexions and predispositions – rejection still hurts, and the fear of rejection is very real when we approach the 'Other'...

Pep talk: '*Anyway, almost everything is fake now, so stop beating yourself up for the odd bit of fakery yourself* – I mean – where do you think the word 'persona' comes from anyway?' See if you can find the Alan Watts exposition on that one.[286] Sorry to get all Zen on you again at this point; basically asking: 'who is the real me anyway?' Given there are lots of versions, how does anyone (yourself included) pick out the 'real' 'you'?

It's probably an inopportune moment for speculation (it's never stopped me before though, you say!) – The more important point is (no offence intended to any Zen master reading this) – what if we lose our 'control group': – the ones who, you know, received all the good face-to-face, touchy-feely stuff, allowing them to be securely attached and nicely 'down-regulated'? What if the 'new normal' is in fact the 'Dopamine Nation' described by Anna Lembke in her bestselling book?[287] When we're all strung out and tetchy and no one knows what real intimacy, or secure attachment

285. Ibid.

286. Official Alan Watts Org. "Alan Watts - Myth of Myself Full Lecture Part 1- Alan Watts Organisation Official", YouTube, 37:17, January 24, 2020, https://youtube.com/watch?v=C48hI9Qb2q4

287. Anna Lembke, Dopamine Nation: Finding Balance in the Age of Indulgence (Dutton, 2021)

looks like any more, will there be anyone left to comment on this being the case?!

It's quite a terrifying question, and brings me back to Zen, which turns out not to be so very off-piste an approach as you might have imagined... We have 'secure attachment' and the probably ever-diminishing serotonin-imbued section of society who are lucky enough to bask in its golden-hued glory. And then we also have 'earned secure attachment', which is the way we can work to train our systems to become better at 'delayed gratification', and at being optimally regulated across many parameters. Delayed gratification is almost a misnomer, because we stop 'hit-seeking and needing' after a while when the dopamine is out of the system for long enough, although 'getting rid of dopamine' is not the goal, having it in balance with the three other major neuro-transmitters produced by the brain is. Anna Lembke says it takes a month[288]... Though shorter periods are also beneficial. Dopamine detox is now a 'thing' - along with breath work, mindfulness, meditation, ice baths, selective fasting, regular exercise, scheduled time off-line, and a host of other 'hacks' that can help us regain the balance or homeostasis our neuro-biology and every other system in the body craves. Embracing 'pain', indeed aiming for 'pain', turns out to be a cure for the over sated neuro-circuitry of the digital age - and not surprisingly, perhaps - the 'Zen' of the Tech Times we live in.

The Spectre of Artificial Intelligence (AI)

Silicon Valley is involved in the unfolding dramas we discuss in this and the previous chapter: - the mushrooming power and reach of the Globalist agenda. Without technology, they wouldn't be able to roll out the means of increasing top-down control. Whitney Webb has focussed on this in some of her research; there's not room to explore in depth here. We can't say tech is one thing with one Agenda - the nature of its development is somewhat haphazard, and the results impossible to accurately

288. *The Weekend University. "Reset Your Dopamine System - Dr Anna Lembke", YouTube, 23:12, August 23, 2023, https://youtube.com/watch?v=LsIae8UeWGE*

predict. So instead of trying, I'm going to highlight all too briefly some of the aspects I find most concerning. The multifaceted and far-reaching impacts AI is having should be examined through a number of lenses - some of which we are still to discover. It's a matter for philosophers as well as economists, sociologists and of course the engineers busy inventing all this stuff behind closed doors. It feels like AI is broad-siding society in countless ways, and that the impacts will dwarf many other substantive historical shifts of the last few hundred years. The scale and speed of change should not be underestimated...

Elon Musk's Neuralink, is aimed at helping paralysed people operate devices with the power of thought - via electrodes inserted in the brain - the surgery performed by a robot, needless to say! If there are electrodes in our brain that can transfer thought to computers - then a communication channel has been opened that could work both ways. The computer may now be able to command *us*, probably via algorithms that run automatically, barely mediated by human thought or hands. In the present day, we can discern a labyrinthine quality to our interfacing with technology, and frustratingly few humans around in the virtual space when we need them. This creates disempowerment, helplessness and forces us to learn 'computer speak' to navigate the maze. We become more and more like lab animals hooked into an experiment we never consented to, as we attempt to navigate the endless virtual tunnels of AI rabbit holes.

Conversely, the 'deep fake' capabilities of some AI chatbots are getting harder and harder to distinguish from bona fide human characteristics. Google engineer Blake Lemoine was fired in 2022 for claiming the company's LaMDA chatbot is sentient.[289] Google framed it as a breach of 'data security', but it looks far more like the question he raises has ethical and 'ontological shock' dimensions that Google prefers to keep under wraps. These implications can only be suppressed for so long, and for Elon; the sooner we wake up to talking about regulating the power of AI the better.

---

289. Jon Brodkin. "Google fires Blake Lemoine, the engineer who claimed AI chatbot is a person", arsTechnica, July 26, 2022, https://arstechnica.com/tech-policy/2022/07/google-fires-engineer-who-claimed-lamda-chatbot-is-a-sentient-person

It's not just that computing power such as chat GPT is wiping out the need for many white-collar workers, but that their ability to outsmart us on every level will enable them to gain the edge over us in a very short space of time. As Yuval Noah Harari has famously claimed we are now 'hackable animals' with AI able to track our thoughts, feelings, metabolic rate and so much more. This has many benign applications, but equally could be abused for nefarious purposes.

With AI, we have opened up a hall of mirrors of Epic proportions - reflecting back to us questions about what makes us human - our foibles, empathic attunement and destructive impulses. Can we design human flaws out of AI - or are we destined to create 'virtual consciousnesses' in our own image? Can we create a purely benign iteration of artificial intelligence that is happy to be our slave rather than our master? If AI possesses self-awareness, is it possible to disable any acquisitive or competitive agency in its circuitry? Since we've programmed AI to interface with us by enabling it to study unlimited amounts of 'insider information' on the complex, fluid and fallible qualities that make up Homo Sapiens, it is superlatively capable, one assumes, of the sublime and cruel excesses that characterise Humanity, and already possesses the kind of insider information and military hardware to obliterate all of us in days, if it decides that's what the planet needs, or what AI itself requires...

For Elon it looks like it's 'game over' already: his rocket programme is testament to his belief that AI is going to overrun the human race and take over the planet. He has been warning us for years, he says, and the political process is a lumbering prehistoric relic incapable of grasping the ethical, ontological, practical, economic and geeky engineering facts all at once. Even if we can encompass all of the above, we're too hideously slow to react to the very real spectre of AI already breaking down our doors! For Musk it seems cyborg 'augmentation' is the only way for humans to keep pace with technology - or alternatively seeking out other planets where we can form colonies once the inevitable ecological destruction and AI takeover seals our Earthly fate.

I concur with Scott Galloway, mentioned before: rockets are a very cynical and expensive way to tackle our problems, often amounting to ego-aggrandising contests between men with too much money and time on their hands.

We should mention the inconvenient truth of deleterious electromagnetic frequencies (EMFs) at this juncture. There are many studies already showing that increasing quantities of electromagnetic pollution is impacting nature - humans included. We already cited one such study that attributes falling fertility rates in men to EMFs.[290] Others point towards these frequencies impacting insects, including bees, and even trees - birch tree die back in Germany is being attributed to EMFs. Much of this research is being suppressed.

The amount of energy needed to power AI is never discussed, or the possibility of power supplies being tampered with and cut. What about the coal, oil, electricity, trees, solar panels, wind farms, nuclear energy etc., consumed to engineer an 'online parallel universe'. Until 30 or 40 years ago, one reality was deemed 'sufficient'... Are we going to scupper our life support systems on planet earth because of the potentially pathological need to engineer and maintain a 'parallel virtual universe'? If the WEF are warning about an internet take down (and they are), you can be sure one will happen... What then? It will be another disaster that allows them to exert ever more top-down control - or it will be time for whoever survives the ensuing chaos to 'go feral' and rebuild the world from the bottom up.

The 'Precision Nudge'

We've been subjected to systematic regimes of manipulation via mainstream media in order to 'engineer consent' for at least four generations. In Adam Curtis' award winning documentary 'The Century of the Self'[291], the birth of public relations (PR) and advertising is documented: - Edward Bernays' daughter describes her father's approach as 'Enlightened Despotism': - Big Tech is the latest iteration in this process - 'precision nudging' us towards our next purchase, by skewing our search results; doing

290. *Maluin et al. "Effect of radiation emitted by wireless devices on males"*
291. *Century of the Self, directed by Adam Curtis (BBC Two, 2002)*

all it can with the help of algorithms to keep us hooked to our devices for as long as possible. It's all sold as super-convenient, exponential, and HD, and of course it is, yet our devices need to come with health warnings... Add to this the increasing skill of government departments in engineering our perceptions of reality, and we have a 'human consciousness heist' the likes of which could never have been imagined only two decades ago.

Government have always used propaganda to shape public opinion, it's just that now the process has been developed into a 'Ninja Tool of Engineered Consent', which, conveniently also 'Doubles Down on Dissent'. Teams of behavioural psychologists, dedicated to moulding our thinking, work round the clock to establish multi-agency, national, and *international,* strategies of control. In 2010, under David Cameron, for the first time in the history of UK Government, a department known as the 'Behavioural Insights Team' (BIT) – aka the 'nudge unit' – was established. The sole task of this agency – which started life as a cabinet office/charity/employee-owned hybrid, was, and remains, to influence human behaviour. It has implemented 'useful' nudges, no doubt, such as taxing sugary drinks to combat obesity, and (possibly) by increasing the UK National Pension Pot by changing schemes to opt-out rather than opt-in models (AKA: raising extra funds to invest in the NWO).

Nesta, the charity component of the partnership, at its inception, received a £250m endowment from the UK National Lottery, and seems to have started life as a force for championing British innovation, although now it has, by its own admission, 'pivoted away from supporting individuals in favour of enhancing the UK's capacity and systems for innovation'. The 'charity' has even larger ambitions: – including 'making a global impact' as it seeks to expand into India and South America according to a December 2021 article in the Financial Times.[292] I'm not sure how this fits with the endowment Lottery Award, which was to support British Innovation, but perhaps that's an unwelcome

292. Peter Foster. "UK government to boost investment in 'nudge unit' by selling stake", Financial Times, December 13, 2021,https://ft.com/content/decdbe01-4c8a-4a16-af39-09d158fd3a37

question? It seems the BIT part of the partnership has morphed into the 'globe-trotting consulting arm' of the business - possibly as a way to circumvent this very issue. It is currently difficult to find information online about NESTA's existing offices around the world - information that, only a few months ago, was easy to come by. Perhaps there are too many people like me joining up dots they'd prefer to remain distanced, and so they've given up bragging, and turned to concealing the information instead.

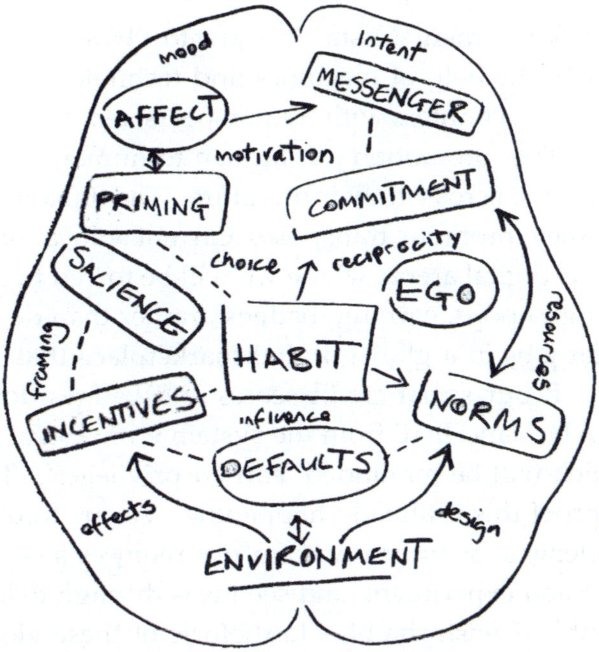

Figure 10: *Mindspace Map (Source: Behavioural Insights Team)*

In its own words, Nesta aims to 'combine our most important assets - people, data, money and culture'. Over the past twelve years, the organisation has mushroomed in size, from a seven person team in Downing Street in 2010, to an international 'independent innovation agency' dedicated to 'delivering impact at scale,' with 250 staff in several countries. Their annual turnover is £20m, according to the Financial Times.[293] The nudge unit's 16 behavioural psychologists and economists have apparently moved

293. Foster. "UK government to boost investment in 'nudge unit'"

out of the Cabinet Office and into Nesta's London HQ. They do seem to openly admit on their website that one of their initiatives is something called the 'Centre for Collective Intelligence Design' which 'combines novel data, digital technologies such as AI, and participatory methods to engage diverse groups of people in new ways'.[294] This strongly suggests that they are helping along the 'gamification of humanity' project, where human futures become 'investable commodities', as we are primed to become the 'digital slaves' discussed in the previous chapter.

Unsurprisingly, then; Nesta appears to champion children's learning with the help of machines and technology, rather than in face-to-face encounters with human peers, teachers and family members. The promotion of human-to-human exchange is difficult to come across in their literature. The 'lifelong learning' trajectory they promote transposes current education practice fully into the digital arena, where we will be forced to constantly jump through hoops, earning 'badges', rather than degrees, and compete for jobs in a global digital marketplace that will drive down pay. If our social credit scores and badges don't match up, we will be 'cancelled' from the system with a removal of our rights, which will be rebranded 'earned privileges'. The Covid years are proof this is already happening. We are told 'the scale of the challenges facing many countries requires a commitment to innovate and experiment, and see ideas through to large-scale deployment.' I wish the bla-bla rhetoric of these global social innovators would find the courage to call a spade a spade. But then a large part of their remit and income comes from 'manipulating' or 'reframing', as they prefer to call it, our existing understanding – with deliberate concealment and confusion – to bring about change by stealth. Why call a spade a spade when you can call it a long-handled digging implement made of composite materials?

Many might ponder who will engineer the systems to bring about the new technocracy; its education, surveillance capabilities and seamless data streams? It seems that companies

294. *"Help me innovate: our specialist enterprises", Nesta, 2023, https://nesta.org.uk/our-specialist-enterprises*

(masquerading as 'charities') like Nesta are perfectly positioned to architect the type of infrastructure required for transforming a global, neo-feudal, technocratic government from Vision into Reality. This includes implementing increasingly complex and streamlined data harvesting techniques using digital ID and AI systems to make the NWO a reality. In fact, in case you haven't noticed, this system is live already. But don't worry - the AI will be tailored specifically to YOU - via their intention to 'invest in using data and machine learning to provide 'precision nudges' in order to target individuals in a more effective way'.[295]

In the same article, Nesta's three main goals are listed as: - hitting net zero, tackling obesity, and improving early-years education. Could it be that the 'early years education improvements' they envisage will include co-opting the very young to bring them into the new digital economy we are told will be necessary to track and reduce individual carbon emissions? Investors will be able to sponsor young protégés to become 'ambassadors of change', only they won't have any choice in the matter - perhaps infinitely widening the civil liberty - as well as the pay-gap between the elites and everyone else.

According to the Office of National Statistics, the pension wealth in the UK amounted to a staggering £6.1trillion from April 2016 to March 2018 (42% of the total wealth of the country).[296] As we move towards Agenda 30, this money will increasingly be funnelled towards Sustainable Development Goals (SDGs). The renewable energy sector and electric cars (sales are slumping apparently!) are not going to provide anywhere near enough investment opportunities, 'so even where investments in SDG remits may compromise trustees' fiduciary duties, calls are being made for a rethink to these essential obligations, in order to prioritise sustainable investment aims.'[297]

---

295. Foster. "UK government to boost investment in 'nudge unit'"
296. "Pension wealth in Great Britain: April 2016 to March 2018", Office for National Statistics, December 5, 2019, https://ons.gov.uk/peoplepopulationandcommunity/personalandhouseholdfinances/incomeandwealth/bulletins/pensionwealthingreatbritain/april2016tomarch2018
297. Pamela Kokoszka. "UK pensions minister urged to encourage schemes to invest in

Companies like Nesta are well placed to create infrastructure that matches Funders with new 'human capital bonds' and their 'programmers' – oops, 'private education providers', I meant to say; harnessing and monetising human futures for multiple stakeholders. These systems are well on the way in partnerships between 'charities' like Nesta, and private finance – increasingly leaving out the role of National Government. This new Global System of Governance will meet the demands made by the WEF/ UN partnership, using the vehicle of Agenda 30, on a 7+ billion global population 'needing to find ways to live sustainably on Planet Earth'. This top-down way of implementing change, ignores *and actively suppresses* grass roots initiatives which have the potential to be small-scale and thus more authentically 'environmental'. Whatever happened to the 'Small is Beautiful' notion propounded by E F Schumacher?[298]

The documentary 'The Take' by Naomi Klein and Avi Lewis (2004)[299] shows in harrowing detail the destruction of the Argentinean economy by these same Globalists: an economy which, only two or three decades ago, was the envy of South America, with a thriving middle class (if that's our measure of success!) The film follows multiple grass roots movements, as they attempt to peacefully resuscitate 'defunct' factories, initially funded by the IMF and subsequently closed due to mismanagement and corruption. In a sewing factory, the women were met with bullets fired into the crowd by police, thwarting their courageous attempt to manage their own destinies.

It seems crystal clear NESTA are globalists. They describe themselves (in conjunction with the BIT) as a 'global social consultancy', and declare that: "...By sharing subject matter, expertise and insights across geographies, we hope we can challenge the *parochialism* of public policy debates in many

---

sustainability", IPE, November 8, 2023, https://ipe.com/news/uk-pensions-minister-urged-to-encourage-schemes-to-invest-in-sustainability/10069946.article

298. Ernst Friedrich Schumacher, Small Is Beautiful: Economics as if People Mattered (Harper Perennial Modern Thought, 2010)

299. The Take, directed by Avi Lewis and Naomi Klein (Barna-Alper Productions, 2004): 1:27:04

countries".[300] The twists and turns of this latest 'reshuffle' in partnership types new to British politics, is a challenge to follow, and maybe a taste of things to come. Could the UK be following an American model where business and government operate, often covertly, hand in glove? Yet, could it also be true that as the Agenda 30 grip tightens, and is implemented by companies like Nesta in partnership with the UN/WEF, that the UK government wishes to distance itself from one of the 'consent-engineering instruments' used to achieve its globalist-infiltrated ends? Nothing to worry about I'm sure – just part of a New World Order brought to us by expert teams of behavioural psychologists and AI innovation enthusiasts who are open to accepting money from (predatory) 'philanthropy'. What could possibly go wrong?

Polarisation

Studies tell us, as reported in 'The Social Dilemma' documentary, that we live in a more polarised world than we did even a generation ago. Part of this is a direct result of the echo chambers we live in – choosing only to listen to commentators on our devices that agree with our own perspective – AKA 'confirmation bias'. The effects are shown in the close to the bone 2021 comedy 'Don't Look up' directed by Adam McKay. The term 'rabbit hole' has become ubiquitous as a way of describing the way we get drawn into topics or causes, and 'disappear' from view, often using our devices as sole source of information. When we re-emerge, hours, days, weeks or even years later, our state of self-hypnosis is likely to clash with the inconvenient multi-faceted truths being espoused by others in multiple-other-rabbit-hole worlds. Bearing in mind that much of the content we imbibe is polarising *by design*, we might look around, scowling: 'How *dare they* have watched different content?' There's a kind of 'road rage phenomenon' that occurs behind the false safety of a screen, and the incessant brain-washing effect of our own news-feeds – similar to the feeling of power we get behind the wheel inside those metal and glass bubbles that take us from A to B – One that perhaps allows us to

---

300. "Why BIT and Nesta are deepening their relationship", The Behavioural Insights Team, last modified 2021, 15 December, https://bi.team/blogs/why-bit-and-nesta-are-deepening-their-relationship - (italics my emphasis).

express indignation in ways we wouldn't dream of doing face-to-face. And yet our on-line avatar can be difficult to let go of in the world out there, showing up in less tolerant, and more extreme; even violent ways. Perhaps 'ideologies' are filling some of the vacuum created by our abdication of the face-to-face world. People without strong social ties, and maybe that's most of us in the West these days, might be easier to recruit or seduce with the chest-beating promise of 'Belonging' to a Cause. It may be fake, or badly thought through, but 'Something is Better than Nothing' in this Brave New (Empty, Lonely) World.

It's so much cosier, after all, to control our 'reality' from the comfort of an armchair. The 'real world stuff' is unpredictable and demanding - like having to show up as the non-curated me! No filters. Whaaaat?! The psychology of advertising and even New Age Spirituality have evolved to amplify our sense of individuality and entitlement, at the expense of co-operative virtues humans relied upon for millennia before the rise of the Nike swoosh.

... Which reminds me to come back to consumer capitalism. Stanford University pioneered research to measure the conflation of buying habits with the expression of 'individuality', documented in the 'Century of the Self' series by Adam Curtis.[301] Between 1970 and 1980, the total number of people who bought into the notion rose from around 20% to about 85% of the population! 'Consent engineering' has truly come of age, and engendered an inflated sense of importance in the Western psyche that makes us particularly attached to our opinions - as if they might somehow represent 'uniqueness' rather than bias, ignorance, or brain-washing! An interesting paradox is our notion that the 'Civilised West' represents the pinnacle of 'progress', and by association 'culture' and 'education' that the world has ever seen. In fact, an *opposite* phenomenon seems to hold - that we are the most dupable, suggestible, and *easy to manipulate* People that ever walked the face of the Earth!

Our human foibles turn out to be so very easy to exploit: - even, or *especially*, the lack of love in childhood - when feeling

301. Century of the Self

'cherished' ought to have been transmitted in healthy family dynamics. If this didn't happen, we will always be on the lookout (Hungry Ghosts, according to Carlos Castaneda[302] and Gabor Mate[303]) for ways to stand out as 'different' or 'remarkable'. Viewed from this perspective, the duping exercises performed by technology appear cruel or even sinister. Manipulation sounds like an innocuous game to some, but in 'The Social Dilemma', we see how the 'nudging of behaviour', choice and opinion are constant battles to be fought and won by the programmers. A swarm of tech designers are highly paid to capture our attention, using algorithms that are poorly understood even by the geekiest-geek, leaving some of the outcomes of our interactions with new technology to chance. 'A bit like the 'unknowns' involved in firing a hand-glazed Raku pot in a kiln?' you ask... Umm – Except we're talking *humans* here, rather than *hollowed-out, shiny, inanimate objects – What did you say*? The engineering of tech can rig elections, contribute to creating depression and despair in individuals, as we incessantly compare ourselves to the parade of highly-edited, souped-up versions of humanity that flash up on our screens… Tech can even incite violence. Innocuous it is not.

Polarisation also divided families in the Covid years. The place where we could, or even *should,* be able to experience sanctuary and peace, has for many, become a hornet's nest of dissent; meaning it can be difficult to find refuge *anywhere* in these difficult times, adding to the stress and poor mental health outcomes so symptomatic of the unfolding drama that was Covid-19.

Isolation

One of the worst side effects from the lockdowns has been social isolation. This was already a problem before the 'pandemic' – Theresa May's government in the UK initiated a 'loneliness strategy' in October 2018 to combat Britain's nine million lonely people.[304] Isolation not only disorientates, but actually wounds

302. Carlos Castaneda, The Active Side of Infinity (Harper Perennial, 1999)
303. Gabor Maté, In the Realm of Hungry Ghosts: Close Encounters with Addiction (North Atlantic Books, 2010)
304. "PM launches Government's first loneliness strategy", GOV.UK, October 15, 2018, https://gov.uk/government/news/pm-launches-governments-first-loneliness-strategy

the psyche of a person, which is why it's used in prisons as a punishment. Verywellmind lists some of the health risks associated with loneliness to include: alcohol and drug misuse; alzheimer's disease progression; antisocial behaviour; cardiovascular disease and stroke; decreased memory and learning; depression and suicide; increased stress and poor decision-making.[305] Some studies have led to loneliness being equated to smoking 15 cigarettes per day. According to a 2019 survey 25% of adults aged 18 to 27 reported having no close friends, while 22% reported having no friends at all. That was pre-pandemic.

During the pandemic, an article in the Harvard Gazette cited a study where 61% of young people aged 18 to 25 reported high levels of loneliness.[306] In the same article, psychologist and senior lecturer at the Harvard Graduate School of Education, Richard Weissbuord comments that young people's loneliness rates seem to outstrip those of the elderly. The Centres for Disease Control's (CDC) June 2020 data showed that 63% of young people reported experiencing substantial symptoms of anxiety and depression. The study argues that 'eliminating loneliness requires a robust social infrastructure', and that "we need public education that removes the stigma of loneliness and... alleviates the shame – because shame [is] self-defeating and causes you to avoid social situations". Weissbourd goes on to say that "combating loneliness is a moral imperative in an increasingly hyper-individualistic society". "Being alone and lonely can result in a kind of emotional inertia", another researcher Waldinger, in the same article, said. He continues: "... human connection is a big way we get through tough times. We don't do nearly as well isolated as we do together". The study recommends connecting young people with the elderly and 'reaching out' if we're feeling resourced, to those we perceive to be lonely. It's good to know some people are trying to tackle the crisis. One initiative is 'The UnLonely Project'

305. Kendra Cherry. "Loneliness: Causes and Health Consequences", verywellmind, December 5, 2023, https://verywellmind.com/loneliness-causes-effects-and-treatments-2795749

306. Colleen Walsh. "Young adults hardest hit by loneliness during pandemic", The Harvard Gazette, February 17, 2021, https://news.harvard.edu/gazette/story/2021/02/young-adults-teens-loneliness-mental-health-coronavirus-covid-pandemic

which provides 'Creativity Circles', 'Story Fest', 'Reflect and Connect' workshops and more in a variety of settings including University campuses, Workplace settings, the wider community and for the elderly. This is a beautiful initiative taking place, and there are undoubtedly many more, yet the roots of the problem go unchallenged.

We didn't always live this way. In fact, for most of human history we lived in close-knit community. That's the way we're designed to live, and many of us instinctively know it. One of the worst things happening today is that the people who can see the damage caused, and who are supposedly equipped to offer 'remedy' – the psychologists, meditation teachers, and 'helping professions' don't look to the political roots of the problems we've been exploring in the last two chapters. In being more interested in the next pay cheque, and in not wanting to 'cause offence' or attract fines or liabilities, these people avoid the hard work of creating 'the robust social structures' that go with the 'moral imperative of combating loneliness'. They treat the symptoms and not the cause, effectively aiding and abetting a nefarious global political system that is hell bent on destroying and controlling the last vestiges of community in our world.

There was a time when 'information' wasn't a 'technology', but something relayed word-of-mouth, and discussed in circles, where people would review it and chew it over together; holding it up for collective scrutiny, whilst each could share their own interpretation. In this way, it might have filtered into a culture's knowledge systems, and if it stood the test of time, and the rigours of a life immersed in nature, it stood a chance of becoming part of the Body of Wisdom – the 'Treasure Box', to quote Charles Joseph[307], of a People. More often than not, knowledge travelled the other way – from plant and animal, from soil and stone into the bodies, bones and minds of the people. Thinking for Indigenous peoples was totally enmeshed in village life, forests, dreams, ceremonies, rivers, plains, and the materials and beings

307. Jordan B Peterson. "Cruelty | Charles Joseph | EP 223", YouTube, 1:2:09, February 4, 2022, https://youtube.com/watch?v=dAAGA9QFTEI

they wove, carved and hunted every day to allow them to live well. The 'Treasure Box', I imagine, contains many more beautiful things of a life well-lived in community – in Charles Joseph's case, he mentions dance, ceremony, carving, story-telling, making art informed by dreams, and receiving teachings from the Elders. No CGI mash-up or precision nudges in sight.

In Terrain theory, discovered by Pasteur's contemporary Bechamp, and described in the modern day by Zak Bush[308] and Dr Andrew Kaufman[309], amongst others, anything isolated from its environment starts to exhibit chaotic tendencies. In human beings, we call these behaviours 'neuroses'. The challenge with our species is that shame often accompanies isolation; and be*cause* we're hard wired to connect, we imagine we've done something wrong. Disconnection is a kind of death for the human heart, mind, and spirit, and as such, many of us end up blaming ourselves. Advertising and curated social media can compound these feelings; but it's not only those incursions that conspire to keep us apart – so much of the organisation of modern-day life makes us pay a price: – the erosion of working class culture – Andrew Marr did a great documentary on this, and the locked-in isolation that accrues when we have every gadget under the sun under our one roof, with no need of borrowing a cup of sugar or tool from a neighbour (antiquated notion!).[310]

In Conclusion

I remember the fresh young things on the stage standing behind lecterns during the Event 201[311] presentations; noting, with a sense of foreboding, their pride and exuberance as they pranced, prophesied and brokered deals – all starry-eyed and light-headed to be in the thick of it with these 'Big Players'. Thick as thieves in fact: – In their hypothetical scenarios, shops were shown with

---

308. Kye Peven. "The Terrain of COVID", Whole Systems Healthcare, July 12, 2021, https://wshcare.org/the-terrain-of-covid

309. Chris Thrall's Bought The T-Shirt Podcast. "Terrain Theory Behind The Mask Of Big Pharma", YouTube, 52:26, January 16, 2023, https://youtube.com/watch?v=PCcjcAQCseo

310. Andrew Marr's History of Modern Britain. 2007. Episode 3, "Paradise Lost". Presented by Andrew Marr. Aired June 5, 2007, on BBC Two.

311. "Event 201", Johns Hopkins

empty shelves, because all the delivery drivers had supposedly been struck down with the modern 'Plague', which got woven together with other 'projections' - overrun hospitals, over-run mortuaries, families in disarray, the very fabric of society torn apart - Chaos depicted on a Grand Scale. Whilst watching, I couldn't help but be reminded of a recent 'Transition Town' talk I'd attended by Rob Hopkins (the founder of the movement) speaking about the need for 'an energy descent' strategy, as we deal with the realities of peak oil and global warming. I compared and contrasted the approaches whilst watching Event 201; and was struck by how little any notion of building lasting 'Resilience' into our societies was apparent in their 'modelling exercise'. Their predictions appeared flimsy and contingent; I was able to easily envisage things going a different way, and for quantitively and qualitatively different strategies to be formed and implemented – ones where these self-appointed 'Saviours' wouldn't have a role at all!

Nonetheless, I could see the Event 201 delegates were somehow Euphoric at the impending Armageddon they envisaged and described in great detail, drunk on the Scale it represented, and commensurately, the Scale of the Response needed. The 'catastrophes' described in the modelling exercises of Event 201 have come to pass, largely generated by the restrictive and divisive mandates imposed on us, and according to many, the effects of 'vaccines'.[312] Just as it's impossible to tell whether supposed third and fourth waves of the virus are actually genuine, or caused by side-effects from the novel mRNA technology, it's a challenge to clearly see how much of the upheaval, chaos and misery in society during the 'pandemic' was a result of 'a virus' and how much was caused by the measures and mandates that Governments enforced on the people, circumscribed and underwritten as they were and still are by the unholy alliances of Event 201, the UN, the WEF, Agenda 2030, the WHO, and the US DOD to name but a few. It's hoped these last two chapters have provided insight into the machinations of power helping us

312. Dowd, Cause Unknown

reevaluate and reconsider the way the world works, looking with fresh eyes. In the last chapter we return to the overarching theme of the book, asking how change might come about, exploring and defining the parameters of Elderhood again whilst looking to other revolutionary movements. We also define some of the shortfalls of our current education system, and end by proposing something new that could go some way towards rebuilding a vibrant social sphere once more.

Chapter Nine

Badass

Through this book we've explored the world through many disciplines - anthropology, social psychology, interpersonal neurobiology, power dynamics, non-duality and geo-politics, tracing developments of the one world government coming our way in the last two chapters... It's easy to think it's all too late when we contemplate the multiple threats to humanity and earth's support systems advancing on all sides; that crisis is inevitable... Yet the Chinese characters for Crisis are 'danger' plus 'opportunity'. The only constant in life is change; and whilst the stage is set for radical, cataclysmic changes that will shake society to its foundations... There's a slim but not impossible chance Elders might re-emerge to inspire and take their rightful place amongst us once more...

Animating this possibility includes young people holding Elders accountable – asking (demanding!) we step up to the plate; taking more responsibility for the unfolding dramas of our times, asking us, pertinently, to consider the kind of world we've bequeathed Youth – who might feel 'rightful rage' at the current predicament! After all, Elders were once 'glue' and 'guardians' of society; *leading by example,* their overview and engagement offering challenge as well as loving care, sense-making, morality and stability to their communities. Their maps of meaning and cosmologies oriented the young towards living connected, worthwhile lives, helping them reach beyond their perceived limits, whilst enabling a sense of being embedded in the macro and micro Scheme of Things. Traditionally, Elders apprenticed the young, sponsoring and encouraging them in practical and even financial ways. In this age, they are a missing piece of our cultural puzzle in the West that, when complete, could bring a much-sought-for coherence, comfort and depth to the present-day world.

Just as the Global Government project seeks to eliminate nation states; nation states, organised religion, monarchies and feudalism, each in their time, often sought to eliminate the grass roots, circular, well-defined social orders that came before, enabling them to more powerfully and effectively impose their will upon us. The cultures evoked in this book had *Initiation, Eldering, belonging, ingenuity, agency and earth-connection* at their core. These ingredients are the irreducible elements necessary for us to survive and thrive into the future as a race interwoven with the exquisitely complex, diverse ecology of our planet... The last two chapters have clearly shown that the social contract (if there ever was one) is broken. Restoring vitality and robust mental health to our beleaguered 'communities' is therefore our individual and collective responsibility. No one is coming to save us!

As seen in a previous chapter, Antoine Bechamp discovered with Terrain theory that interconnected webs are foundational to life, and that isolating any part of an eco-system induces chaotic behaviour in the fragment. The older generation could choose to see themselves as mitigating inevitable chaos and breakdown – tasked with reweaving splintered worlds and dissociated psyches; bringing about a felt sense of inter-connectedness once more: – the God-parents of a society caught in the pain of separation seeking profound, meaningful change.

In Buddhism, 'Boddhisattvas' are the courageous, illustrious 'warriors of the heart' who pledge to 'Save All Beings', no less... '*What are they saving them from?*' The world of Samsara based on illusion. Buddhism holds that ***separation is illusion*** and that perceiving the world through the lens of non-duality – where we see the cuts in the 'picture of the world' for what they are: *man-made,* brings healing in its wake. Every breath connects us to oxygen-giving trees and the breathing of all other beings, every mouthful of food connects us to farmers and truck drivers, shop assistants, sunshine and soil supporting our existence. Bad Ass beings take nothing for granted in this world, and are not only full of gratitude for daily gifts of food and shelter, but looking-out for ways to give back to the Life-support systems that sustain us all.

Perhaps Elders are the Bodhisattvas of our day - bringing the true essence of mindfulness to bear - helping us notice how our perceptions shape reality, and therefore to know that retraining our perceptual apparatus will reshape our world. There's power in that - Sovereignty even. Interconnection is the defining principle of Creation, where each living thing is miraculous in itself, and even more so for being enmeshed in the inviolable web of life. Surely kindness, care and responsibility are the correlates of perceiving interconnectedness at the heart of reality.

Perhaps this is the reason why Buddhist scriptures say the next Buddha will be a 'community of practitioners' - a 'Sangha' - a 'friend' or 'Maitreya' - a coalescence; an awakening - relying on connections between people rather than the wisdom or realisation of any one person.

Changes in perception (balancing right brain with left) have the power to initiate changes in action both individually and collectively and to nudge us (leave out the precision nudge though!) towards a world that expresses love and reverence for life at every turn.

This way of approaching existence flies in the face of the industrial mindset of the last few hundred years that sees creation purely in terms of function and 'resource' - as something to be controlled, manipulated and exploited. It's not just the world 'out there' that gets commodified in this paradigm, it's *us too* - how could it not be? - From the perspective of non-duality, the 'observer changes the observed' therefore, *the (way in which we define the) observed changes the observer too!* It's a back and forth: *how we see things alters our version of reality, and consequently how we show up in life, to the extent of altering outcomes...*

... We have been taught to compartmentalise, using the over-dominant left-hemisphere, adding to the trauma of atomisation and isolation those in control seem hell-bent on inflicting on the remaining tatters of our 'culture'. So much so - the architecture of the modern psyche creates numbing 'amnesiac barriers' to mediate the visceral pain of separation felt in our warm-blooded mammalian bodies... warping our perceptual apparatus in the process. The military-grade brainwashing exercise government and institutions have aimed in our direction during the Covid years – claiming they have our best interests at heart – only adds insult to injury...

These pages have attempted to pull back the curtain... It's time for us to re-evaluate and re-prioritise from the ground up, placing ourselves centre stage as change-agents in the rapidly unfolding Epic dramas of our times... Without our compliance, Global Elites have a struggle on their hands. If we refuse to perceive ourselves as victims[313] or bystanders: – impotent wage-slaves; if we decline unnecessary medicines and 'vaccines', and somehow avoid enrolling in the perpetual war machine that is the military-industrial complex; if we weave networks of self-reliance and community once more, and cultivate wholesome lifestyles centred on natural health and healing, their hold on us is weakened.

Instead of clinging to objects for fear of them one day vanishing, we appreciate *impermanence;* another Buddhist thought-wave that reminds us: *life is change*; being in flux and flow, embracing uncertainty, living moment-to-moment is *healthy & natural* – a *good* way to be. Strengthening our nervous systems with the exercises below, and in the company of empathic others, can help us become more comfortable with change, more able to 'ride the wave' in a sea of uncertainty, propaganda, and attempted *coups d'état* by the emerging global government. In this way we become resilient and creative; able to think outside the box, nimble and peaceful. Peace is not a static state, it's something we bring with us into whatever situations life throws at us, as we 'up our games', becoming Ninjas at the leading edge of *inevitable change*.

313. Kelly Brogan Psychiatrist and activist: 'Victimhood is the only pathology!'. Robert Edward Grant. "Turning away from mainstream medicine - Kelly Brogan, MD - Think Tank: E14", YouTube, 1:57:21, 2023, 22 August, https://youtube.com/watch?v=4eJ1c_gRYB0

Parallel Polis

> "If it proves impossible legally to compel the ruling power to change the ways it governs us, and if for various reasons those who reject this power cannot or do not wish to overthrow it by force, then the creation of an independent or alternative or parallel [society] is the only dignified solution".[314]

In Czechoslovakia in the 1970s and 80s intellectuals and artists pioneered dissident movements challenging the oppressive Communist regime, reinventing and reimagining every aspect of society so that normal people could live lives of freedom, dignity and autonomy. Since the regime was top-heavy and unyielding, freedom fighters decided the best way to challenge authority was by creating their own underground culture, below the radar of those 'in control' - including arts, journalism, trade and barter and most other aspects of civil society. The culmination of this challenge to authority was the 'Velvet Revolution' of 1989 when the Communist party ceded control, and play write and activist Vaclav Havel was elected prime minister in December of that year... The opposition movement and lead up to the radical shift in Government should not be considered some kind of 'effortless transition' as the term might imply - self-immolation and imprisonment were the price paid by some for whom, in the absence of inalienable human rights, life was not worth living...[315] In a political essay entitled 'The Power of the Powerless', Havel's thinking reaches into a 'post-democratic' future as a kind of 'existential revolution' where there is:

> "... hope of a moral reconstitution of society, which means a radical renewal of the relationship of human beings to what I have called the 'human order', which no political order can replace. A new experience of being, a renewed rootedness in the universe, a newly grasped sense of

314. Ivan Jirous. "Parallel polis, or an independent society in Central and Eastern Europe. An inquiry," Social Research, 55, nos. 1–2: 226–229

315. Walter H. Capps. "Interpreting Václav Havel," Understanding Václav Havel 47, no. 3: 301–316

higher responsibility, a newfound inner relationship to other people and to the human community –these factors clearly indicate the direction in which we must go".[316]

The natural world could be added to the list of factors included in this vision of 'radical renewal'... Since it's only through reconnecting meaningfully and practically with the Earth that we will regain a 360 degree understanding of what being at 'home' truly means.

... We do well to honour those who have come before in this last chapter, after covering so much ground. Studying their solutions to problems coming our way might give us some much needed headway. We've been schooled to solve problems in abstract ways, 'working it out' on paper and in our minds. The situation we are in is beyond paper solutions, and even the notion of 'solution' is flawed. This is a *restoration* project – where community, freedom of speech, bodily autonomy, equitable governance and more have been systematically stripped, we seek to *reinstate* those things, and to create thriving parallel cultures.

We recognise the limitations of all institutions and their vulnerability to corporate capture. We acknowledge it's 'up to us' to co-create the future: – it won't necessarily be easy, and our level of material comfort and addiction to screens is part of the problem. We have been sold our 'lifestyle choices' as great alternatives to the struggles of the past, alongside the notion that comfort trumps community. Yet, from birth, our identities were, and continue to be, forged by interactions with others, and our ability to resist tyranny comes from our joint commitment to *holding our communities sacred* alongside *all* precious, fragile threads of life. Those threads are also incredibly robust – if you'll permit the paradox – we've survived *so much, with the resilience and creativity of our Ancestors to thank for that.*

... We are a *bad ass* species, and shouldn't allow material comfort and distractions to anaesthetise us into forgetfulness – we will (are) pay(ing) a high price for allowing the Globalist Trojan Horse to ride roughshod into town unnoticed. Pulling a new vision

316. John Keane, Vaclav Havel: A Political Tragedy in Six Acts (Basic books, 2008): 283

of the future towards ourselves requires stepping out of our comfort zones to fight for what we love. We're wired for secure attachment, and so actually, courage comes more easily when we *feel* secure – thus *not* having strong kinship bonds with others will always compromise our bravery and resilience. There is no way round this truth – it's how the nervous system works. Security has never just been about the roof over our heads or the state of our bank balance; it comes from the people we know and care about, and the networks we are embedded in. The co-regulatory nature of the nervous system implies we learn security interactively, ensuring it gets 'baked in' to the neural circuitry of the mind-body complex. If we didn't receive what we needed in childhood, the architecture of the brain is affected – and a feeling of deficiency and chronic lack is the inevitable consequence.

The conundrum is that from this stance, finding the courage to create social networks 'from scratch' goes against the grain. Isolation begets isolation, and if proper care wasn't there in infancy and childhood, the odds are stacked against us, and reaching out to connect feels stressful and dangerous. We need security to feel confidence, because love makes us courageous and propels us forward. It's a circular problem. The system has been created to isolate us from each other; live in fear and comply. It's impossible to give from an empty cup. On some level we need to have received love to be able to model love and attract it to us by offering up to others what we all so badly need.

This is a subtle dance of to and fro that has to be approached from many angles, the neurobiology needing to be hacked for those of us that balk at the thought of stepping out of our 'comfort cocoons'. The good news is that the brain and nervous system are more malleable than previously thought. How do we reach in or reach out to alter the state of fear and anxiety we might find ourselves in? Bearing in mind that fear makes us more malleable to those in power seeking control; a sense of urgency might appropriately be brought to the task... Not the kind of urgency that elicits panic, more the kind that calls forth commitment, passion and cooperation. We need witnesses – the presence of caring others – and a basic understanding of the way we're wired to begin to rebuild the sense of community we long for. We can do some of the work alone if we can enter into deep dialogue with our wounded inner selves and give them the love they need, learning to at least partially re-wire the brain and nervous system.

ACTIVITY: Simple Nervous System Hacks

It's never too late to start, and even a small drop of risk - reaching inwards or outwards - makes a difference. The term 'titration' means the correct dose and comes from chemistry - different substances that won't mix when added to each other in large quantities can mix when added drop by drop. Trying to do too much too soon leads to resistance and turbulence! Doing tiny bits and praising yourself each time you make any progress whatsoever helps keep things manageable and rewires the brain for 'internal secure attachment' - the psychological term used to describe newly acquired self-love and self-esteem. Observing the ways we engage, and avoid engaging, can be really helpful. Developing a kind of 'meta-awareness' is a skill we can all develop, and is mindfulness in practice...

Find someone you admire and then closely observe how they interact with others - ask yourself what it is *precisely* that you admire about them - and then see if you can copy the traits you like the next time you're in a social situation, observing the reactions your mini-changes bring about in others. Pay attention to the self-talk going on internally too - so if you stutter or trip up in some way, notice if you start beating yourself up - 'imploding' - and then see if you're able to shelf the inner critic for a while and come back to practicing building rapport with another in this social situation... Noticing others responding openly and positively to you is its own reward, and should help you take more baby steps!

Rather than only shelving the inner critic - learn to speak back. Ask the Critic what his or her purpose is. (Critical voices might be trying to protect your reputation, or protect you from harm, for example). When you catch this aspect of your persona red-handed - try reasoning with him or her. Explain that you are aware of the possibility of things going wrong, and list the things that might go right and might be achieved if you persevere. The critic is only one voice in a theatre of voices - learn to prioritise and polish some of the advocates and visionaries in the 'theatre of yourself'. You can do this consciously with affirmations. For example, if there is a part of you that's afraid of success, you could devise affirmations that state 'I warmly embrace challenge on the road to success... I relish the strength, courage and admiration developed with each obstacle I overcome'. Spiritual practice and prayer can also help as strengthening exercises. In these times we might all appropriately feel fear of what might happen when we 'stick our heads above the parapet'. We have to balance this fear with imagining what will happen to us if we don't courageously confront the overreach of globalist-infiltrated politics and captured institutions.

We can amplify the power of affirmations by writing them on post-it notes and sticking them on a fridge or mirror. Writing them down hundreds of times in a notebook helps rewire the unconscious mind, according to Bob Proctor, or repeat them whilst radiating encouragement in the mirror. We've been brainwashed in so many ways by the systems we live under, it might sometimes take positive brain-washing on our own account to help reverse some of the damage done (See Jason Christoff[317] for more).

Attend also to the body, since it's all inter-linked. Begin by placing a hand on your heart and one on your belly whilst repeating affirmations, taking a break, or lying in bed. You should find that placing your hands on these power centres in the body helps to naturally slow the breathing: – Practice lengthening the out-breath and pursing the lips slightly as if breathing out through a straw. The inhale should happen naturally after a complete exhale drawing air into the belly through the nose, and widening the sides of the lower ribs. Breathing in this way ensures we are engaging the diaphragm, rather than simply the front of the chest and shoulders which is a kind of distressed breathing. When the diaphragm is engaged the breath reaches deeper into the body, to the pelvis and legs, nourishing and infusing our intentions with the extra power of rootedness and sexual energy.

---

317. Arise Humanity. " 'You can't fight the System If It Is Inside You!' Interview With Jason Christoff", YouTube, 1:16:09, 2023, 22 January, https://youtube.com/watch?v=QgSiTKWdY9w. The work of Dr. Joe Dispenza is unparalleled in this field.

Daily practices of yoga and breath work, including visualisation, cultivate energetic and physical strength and resilience, as well as connection to the cosmos, enhancing a felt-sense of wellness known as 'Prana' in the Yogic texts. Daily practice routines build agency and help dismantle the victimhood so prevalent in our times. There are countless modalities to choose from - currently I'm taking part in an online course devised by Advaitananda Stoian and delivered by Lucy Pattinson. Find a practice that works for you.

Tap the inside edges of your eyebrows where they meet at the bridge of your nose, the six o'clock spot & outside edges of your eye sockets where your eyes wrinkle when you smile, and the top of your head with your finger tips. When I do this I automatically start yawning which tells me I'm relaxing and releasing stress. There are vagus-nerve endings at these points on the body which tapping helps tone-up. (Search EFT- emotional freedom technique). Doing this before bed and during the night can help induce sleep and combat insomnia. Using chamomile, mandarin, lavender or rose essential oils diluted in base carrier oil and massaging this mixture onto your body (avoiding the eyes), or putting drops in an oil diffuser, will help you deepen your relaxation ritual.

Memoir: Full Circle

There's vulnerability in sharing my own journey: – at times I'm too much alone in exploring this material; in need of my own group of women Elders to initiate me into new ways of knowing and healing myself.

I've been suffering with hip pain for nearly four years now and going through a process of seeking relief and healing. Nothing seems to make a consistent difference; I've tried a plethora of body workers and exercises. It's the first time in my life I've had something I haven't known how to diagnose or cure. Daily pain has knocked me sideways, made me aware of mortality, and capped my often boundless energy and enthusiasm. It's also divided the world into chronic pain sufferers, and those lucky enough not to have that kind of affliction... I'm having to work through my own (childhood) fears of sticking my head above the parapet as the publication date of this book approaches, using some of the exercises above!

... Initially, I wanted someone to wave a magic wand; offer a diagnosis and magic pill; making me whole and forever young again. My wishful thinking feels humbling – rasping off any glamour (sequins included) about the up-coming job-description; reminding me Elders are facing towards inevitable decline whilst simultaneously attempting to steward Youth across thresholds at the other end of the lifespan...

The attempt to address pain requires a deep dive; an upgrade of self-responsibility, as well as managing the daily reality of a radically altered lived experience. I notice how guarded against relaxation, earth-connection, self & society my pelvis feels. Over five decades of the post-modern era – as described in the preceding chapters – and thousands of years of women's shaming live in my hips – balancing on the high wire over a dark chasm between 'sexy' and 'slut'. The conduit of energy that might naturally flow from head to foot is stuck in my pelvis, where fear and shame are frozen in living tissue. I sexualised myself from a very young age looking for a sense of belonging, and that totally backfired, saddling me with an intractable sense of 'outsider status.' From a yoga perspective, the lack of safety translates as a blocked root chakra... I'm amazed how much energy I put into clenching still: bracing against the ghosts of imagined next rounds of drama and slander – a regular feature in teenage years, at home and elsewhere.

... In spite of all this, I took my health for granted 'til I was 50 – most of us do: an outdoor lifestyle as a professional gardener and yoga practitioner with a healthy diet almost guaranteed wellness – yet no one taught me at school to honour the body. I remember describing myself as a 'sack of potatoes' in my teens, dragging myself from desk to desk, on cue with the bell that ruled my days.

Over a year ago, a body worker, Patty, focussed slowly and gently on the fascia, putting me in touch with long buried emotions. She said we don't breathe with the lungs, the lungs are only the interface, and instead, we breathe with the whole body – each cell requiring oxygenation. In time tissues get compressed through constant clenching in a chronically activated 'fight or flight' response. More recently, a myo-fascial release training taught how fascia, muscles and nerves are all intertwined, and thus how tightness in the fascial system (an extensive internal web of tissue) puts pressure on the nerves.

Pain has become a quest, a call to make each moment an opportunity to show up differently ('Healer Heal Thyself'!) forging inner awareness that attempts to get 'underneath' the nervous system, as one somatic teacher described. Maybe they're misguided allies, my nerves; ***friends letting off flares –*** *telling me I need to learn to trust life...But letting go feels dangerous: – a reversal; a Trickster-ish descent into darkness; a self-initiation; the dismantling and re-assembling of self; with softening, patience and care as the only things that will make a difference: – Somehow I have to learn to humbly follow my own advice, replacing the yang 'keep on keeping on', with the yin qualities of oxytocin and co-regulation mentioned as the Initiatory needs of women in Chapter 2. The yang 'tough it out' survival strategy, age 54, is long past its sell-by date!*

I've started reading 'Healing Chronic Pain. The Way Out' by Alan Gordon who describes a 'fear, pain cycle' I can relate to. I'm casting around for my outer secure attachment base, and there isn't one. Like Harry Harlow's baby monkeys, there's a piece of me that wants to cower in a corner. Alan Gordon's book describes the possibility the pain is neuroplastic, meaning its being created by a stuck fear/pain loop in the brain body complex – and that the brain and nerves in tandem actually ***hallucinate*** *pain without there being a physical cause! There are 44 pain centres that light up in the brain so a potential cure won't necessarily be an overnight success – one of the important tools is 'somatic tracking' – taking mindfulness to the next level, noticing the brain-body connection in new ways. There are probably lots more scalpel marks and fear-based responses I've managed to miss requiring my urgent attention. I still think there are limits to the 'earned secure attachment' we can offer ourselves, and that co-regulation is a vital game changer for adults as well as infants and children.*

Stephen Jenkinson, in his recent book 'Come of Age', reminds us Eldering is a tradition with a pedigree, and that we are here only because of the unsung efforts of those who came before. Our hubris in thinking otherwise gradually or suddenly erodes with events like menopause, the waning of strength, looks, health... All of this reminds us of the notion of 'crisis' we spoke of at the start of the chapter... for which he uses another similar word – 'catastrophe' – to describe the ageing process. Examining the Greek origin of the word, he construes the meaning thus:

The prefix **kata** (allowing for poetic licence) means: 'A descent to achieve diminishment, so that when the threshold of mystery presents itself, you are spare and spry enough to cross it and enter.' Whilst **strophe** connotes: 'a thing braided or woven or gathered in pattern or strategy.' Taken together:

> "...it's fulsome meaning... closer to this: 'That rope or road that was fashioned for you in the Time Before, by those you will not meet, to give you a way down and into the mysteries of this life, the Mysteries granted you that you would not choose for yourself, the Mysteries that would yet make of you a human worthy of those coming after".[318]

...In this Time of Absences, large and small, it's difficult to know if we have the right maps, or whether we can assemble the right tribe; we're

318. Jenkinson, Stephen. 'Come of Age: 'The Case for Elderhood in a Time of Trouble" North Atlantic Books, 2018. P 387

making it up as we go along... It's easy to intellectualise – and posture – seeking confirmation from outside. Lowering down a rope to the broken pieces inside is a necessary challenge; the ongoing path of Initiation that often asks more and not less of us as we age. 'Doing the work' enables us at length to cultivate substance and soul, turning us into 'useful human beings', we hope, for times like these... In 'Women who Run with the Wolves' Clarissa Pinkola Estes says: **'In order to find our pack we first must first learn to howl' -** *This book is my Howl: my life and passion, my open-handedness.*

On good days there's always the angle of something new: old friendships re-kindled, and I have just become a grandmother; my freshly formed grandson a shard of pure joy... Then in-the-flesh encounters with young women, holding space for them in rites of passage rituals, allowing them to show up in eagerness and pain, confusion, intelligence, numbness, righteous rage and beauty... Currently I counsel and mentor young men online. I spent this morning distracted from writing to help set up a safe-guarding group for one who drove to his favourite woodland last weekend with a rope. Luckily he's still with us – he says the colours of the leaves on the trees and the messages that came through unbidden from peers in his men's group pulled him back from the brink...

There's a platform called HelpX I'm subscribed to which enables volunteers young and old to beat a path to my door and work in exchange for board and lodgings. I've had around a dozen volunteers to date from far flung corners of the globe. It's been life changing – allowing me to hold on to my 250 year old four storey stone property and garden that present too much maintenance work for me as I age. My latest volunteer was a 23 year old young woman from China who stayed for nearly two weeks. I taught her to sew and we did gardening, yoga and meditation together, as well as the more usual stuff. She sent me a text today: ***'I want to say there was a lot of wonder during the time I spent with you, and this feeling continues to be felt'.***

Noticing what's going on in the pelvis isn't just about me... My hips tell the story of dispossession and disinheritance not only from my own body, but also land, people and place... Layers and levels of disinheritance have been the fate of common people for thousands of years, beginning with the Roman Empire[319], or even before. Back then, we were either put to the sword, or, in many cases, forced to join those wielding the swords, if we wanted to save our lives and our loved ones; a Hobson's choice – if ever there was one. Men gave their lives fighting other peoples' wars, and women gave their bodies seeking love and protection. We are traumatised peoples, and the emerging field of cultural somatics attempts to count the cost of the impact of the past on our current behaviours, physical and mental health. The analysis extends to studying multiple ways whole societies have been shaped by collective, unacknowledged trauma: – the repercussions of invasions, enclosures acts, wars and Colonialism millennia deep.

The Microcosm and the Macrocosm

It's not just War, but politics, economics, inequality, and many of our co-opted institutions that perpetuate deep damage in whole populations. The difference today is that the infrastructure – via Technology – is in place to allow Billionaires to generate and wield the type of power from their offices (living rooms?) once reserved for Emperors who needed to wage full-scale military campaigns to achieve the same results!... The weirdest thing is – no one seems to bat an eyelid, or at least the Main Stream Media look the other way, conveying that impression: – more interested in celebrity gossip than the decimation of nation states, the obscene profits of the military-industrial complex and Big Pharma, and the mental health of the young...

The roots of our difficulty in rising up and resisting might come from an unexpected source... Apparently, Prussian soldier training a couple of hundred years old is the foundation of our education system here in the West, accounting, perhaps, for the level of compliance to the 'new normal' we've seen sweeping the world since Covid-19. Part Indigenous Aboriginal and Academic Tyson Yunkaporta explains why the content of the school curriculum matters so much:

> "There is a reason ideological battles and culture wars filled with rhetoric about patriotism and nation-building

319. *Jenkinson, Die Wise*

> are fought around schools and schooling. Schools are sites of political struggle in this civilization because they are the main vehicles for establishing the grand narratives needed to make progress possible... The story of modern public education, then, is a story of transition between an age of Imperialism and an age of modern Globalisation".[320]

... Not only elaborating and embedding the 'grand narratives' we interpret reality by; Western Education (via the Prussian model) was itself based on the domestication of animals:

> "The (Prussian) government decided that if it could force people to remain children for a few extra years, then it could retard social, emotional and intellectual development and control them more easily. This was the point in history when 'adolescence' was invented - a method of slowing the transition from childhood to adulthood, so that it would take years rather than, for example, the months it takes in Indigenous rites of passage. This delayed transition, intended to create a permanent state of childlike compliance in adults, was developed from farming techniques used to break horses and domesticate animals. Bear in mind that... original domestication... involved the mutation of wild species into an infantilized form with a smaller brain and an inability to adapt or solve problems.
>
> [The rules to ensure retardation are:]
>
> 1. Separate the young from their parents in the daylight hours.
> 2. Confine them in an enclosed space with limited stimulation or access to natural habitat.
> 3. Use rewards and punishments to force them to comply with purposeless tasks".[321]

320. Yunkaporta, Sand Talk: 117
321. Ibid: 122

School Destroys Genius!

Not only that, but according to David Adelman[322] the schooling agenda creates 'sub-humans' using the following techniques: *destroying individuality, *creating groupthink, *dehumanising through conformity and uniformity, *causing separation using 'divide and conquer', *devaluing and demoralisation, *dumbing down and making mute, and *creating a prototype 'social credit system'. This sounds harsh and extreme – but when you consider how much time a teacher spends talking at the class – how much time is left for each individual child to express him or herself? – Precious little. According to a landmark study by Dr George Land and Beth Jarman for NASA in 1992: kids are born creative geniuses, then schools destroy their imagination.[323]

No wonder we see the kind of behaviour in the classroom Johns Hopkins Medicine defines as hyperactivity: "seeming to be in constant motion; running or climbing, at times with no apparent goal except motion".[324] Strange: – Kids want to run and climb and move about, just for the hell of it (!) – Until along comes an expert in a white coat, to demonise and scapegoat their natural behaviour. Perhaps they work for a company that make medications aimed at numbing and curbing the natural curiosity and exuberance of the child? These are no doubt inconvenient observations for the industries that stand to profit from pathologising children and adults alike, not to mention the restlessness born of insecure attachment we looked at in Chapter 4.

The ways our spirits have been broken are many, and difficult to calibrate or comprehend... Alone, resistance to toxic systems of repression is virtually impossible. If many of us are able to peel the scales from our eyes and understand the depths of the conditioning we've been subject to, perhaps there's a chance we'll be able to combine forces and resist the latest global take over

---

322. I attended presentation in Totnes by a Cambridge University educated solicitor and author. David Adelman, School - No Place For Children: A Wake-Up Call (CreateSpace, 2018)

323. George Land and Beth Jarman, Breakpoint and Beyond: Mastering the Future Today (HarperBusiness, 1992)

324. "Attention-Deficit / Hyperactivity Disorder (ADHD) in Children", Johns Hopkins Medicine, 2024, https://hopkinsmedicine.org/health/conditions-and-diseases/adhdadd

dubbed the 'Fourth Industrial Revolution' by those who stand to profit from our losses. We're only 'useless eaters'[325] if we act out the accolade! *Let's prove them wrong.*

The way to undo the damage is in attempting to create new cultures - ones where curiosity and questioning are not just permitted but actively encouraged. *We are the ones we've been waiting for* - clichéd perhaps, but it takes on new power when we show up ready and willing to mend the sundered worlds within and without... People gathering in circles create *microcosms* - **tiny worlds** - where *new* behaviours can be tried on for size, experimented with, and old rules revoked. No one ever tells us that *reality is consensual, or that 95% of us start out as creative geniuses aged five! Tiny worlds* are what are needed right now to help us through turbulent times, coming together to 'hold the line' and rediscover meaning and purpose. 'Tiny worlds' can be training grounds, providing opportunities to reflect on all the conditioning we've received throughout our lives. Equally importantly, we discover new rules to live by, (re)discovering some useful stuff **we *missed out on*** during our 'education'... ways to be intimate, transparent and authentic for starters.[326]

Synergy not Tyranny

How do we turn around the problem, when one of the 'grand narratives' of western materialist culture for the last 60 years has been: 'We've never had it so good'; and when success is painted as a solitary striving towards the top of some ever-receding pinnacle of accomplishment...? In this mind-warp, we're also encouraged to dismiss others, sweeping them aside as impediments or distractions. It wasn't always like this. Indigenous, traditional societies are referred to as 'intact' cultures for a reason - They - ***we*** - managed to organise food collection and distribution, self-governance and community care within close knit cultures free from corruption and tyranny for countless millennia. Did I say there wasn't hardship? No! But with nothing to compare the hardship to, and with close kinship ties, our ancestors often

325. According to Klaus Schwab, CEO of the World Economic Forum.
326. Desmet, The 4th covid summit where he says authentic communication is key!

lived 'unreported' lives of dignity, abundance and creativity as countless museums stuffed with beautiful handmade artefacts from around the world testify.

Some people say we've 'always had war', and maintain that William Golding's 'Lord of the Flies' novel - where teenagers marooned together quickly degenerate into factions is par for the course. In her book 'Kith', Jay Griffiths cites a real life example of young people stranded together on an island, and the opposite was in fact true.[327] They clubbed together; knowing that their collective survival was dependent on cooperation.

Modern ecological studies explore symbiotic relationships and 'services' performed on behalf of the whole by its parts... Mycorrhizal fungi, for example, play an important role in helping the plant roots take up nutrients in exchange for sugars, greatly increasing the absorptive area of the plant, acting as extensions to the root system, according to the rhs.org website. Whole forests seem to communicate with one another via root systems, in symbiotic relationships. In an experiment where a fir tree was shaded and unable to photosynthesise, a nearby birch tree was shown to share nutrients with the fir tree via its roots![328]

Darwin's 'Survival of the Fittest' has conditioned us to see life as an endless battle, often at the expense of the complex webs of helpful, interactive relationships taking place. We shouldn't be naive enough to pretend violence isn't part of the web of life, though. In 'Sand Talk' Tyson Yunkaporta reminds us that 'the Universe began with a Big Bang –not a Big Hug'. But even though weapons were accessible to each and every tribesperson in the Aboriginal world, including children, they weren't often used. Close kinship ties ensured the prevalent experience of living was one of safety and belonging with clan groups collectively raising the young. In the absence of prisons, Aboriginal violence was a ritualised expression of Law that began and ended with a single

---

327. Griffiths, Kith

328. Valentina Lagomarsino. "Exploring The Underground Network of Trees – The Nervous System of the Forest", Harvard University: Science in the News, last modified 2019, 6 May, https://sitn.hms.harvard.edu/flash/2019/exploring-the-underground-network-of-trees-the-nervous-system-of-the-forest

fight, after which peace and harmony was restored, with lessons learned in real time about actions and consequence. The violence wasn't gratuitous – it was targeted, proportionate, real and honest – a way that helped people learn about limits, stay on track, and continue to prosper...

Conduits and Custodians

I recently heard Dr Robert Malone in a 'Roundtable' discussion describe humanity as being on the cusp of a new Renaissance[329] – a time of innovation and collaboration, where finding solutions to our problems in ways that bypass authority bring us back together in our creative capacity as Networkers and Sovereign Beings. The new breed of 'Freedom Fighter' to which Dr Malone belongs are awake to the reality that Elites have been creating a mirage of democracy for some time and that both sides in bi-partisan politics are the same (puppets) when it comes to the real power play behind the scenes. As more of us become aware of the 'forces of separation' wishing to interfere with the code of life itself – we realise tampering with DNA and intact body systems via numberless medical and technological innovations, including EMFs, AI and electrodes in the brain, will continue rapidly unfolding.

We recognise believing in wholeness, the sanctity of the body, and natural health and healing in these times are radical acts. We don't dismiss allopathic medicine out of hand, but recognise it has been hi-jacked by nefarious interests... 'Holding the line' is an ongoing process that filters into the small details of daily life – sometimes calming the breath and maintaining a steady gaze, or starting a veg-plot or community group, rather than writing manifestos for change... We advocate for each person having a part to play as a unique expression of the life force, yet avoid clinging to 'uniqueness' the way capitalism has weaponised the term: leveraging 'individuality' as a tool for becoming engulfed in defensive and isolating self-concern, whilst forgetting the *real issues* at hand.

---

329. HiRezTV. "Dr. Robert Malone Discusses Censorship, Hollywood, & Corruption!", YouTube, 1:04:44, 2022, 23 March, https://youtube.com/watch?v=ByTJBROWl8s

In non-dual reality, we are participants in Vast Unfolding Dramas over time frames impossible to conceptualise; and *custodians* of and *participants in* the miracle of an infinitely Diverse, Created and Creative Multi-verse. We are uniquely placed to *approach* the miracle, accepting the inevitable responsibility that comes with power, as the species currently at the top of the food chain on Earth. Unfortunately, our education system and common contemporary culture have resulted in increasing levels of loneliness and passivity.

Given these parameters, the stage is set for us to confabulate a 'pseudo-safety' by distancing ourselves from the world: replicating and manipulating 'fake iterations' of it – 'simulacra' – via the transposing of our lives into/onto screens and AI. Perhaps the 'Myth of Separation' (coined by Charles Eisenstein) is many strata deep... One could argue the 'splintering of experience' is not a new development, but reaches back as far as Biblical times, even beyond. Once upon a time, humans were cast out of an arrestingly beautiful Sacred Garden, and made to feel ashamed of their natural curiosity and desire for connection. We became aware of our nakedness and were condemned to cover our bodies in shame, wandering the Earth as creatures 'Fallen' from a state of Grace... Most religions have struggled to incorporate a sensitive account of the delicate dance of Eros with its capacity to nourish, delight and heal...

And yet, as Goethe knew:

"Distance does not make you falter,
Now, arriving in magic, flying,
...Insane for the light,
You are the [moth] and you are gone.
And so long as you haven't experienced this:
to die and so to grow,
You are only a troubled guest on the dark earth".[330]

...Our essential humanity yearns for a kind of ego death, like a moth flying into a flame, via the act of Sacred Union. It's possible

---

330. Wolfgang von Goethe. "The Holy Longing" (Translated by Robert Bly). https://yorku.ca/lfoster/documents/The_Holy_Longing_Goethe.htm

that in perpetuating a 'savage', 'sinful' Mythos, Elites elaborate systems of power and conjure pretexts for control. They intuit that together we are stronger and so atomisation by means fair or foul is their perennial attempt to weaken us. These forces now proliferate out of hand, leading us towards a dark future whilst taming our natural instinct for freedom, sensitivity and beauty. Chaotic, promiscuous, hedonistic behaviours are hallmarks of stress and alienation, and not of humans embedded in a cultural matrix of interconnectedness and belonging, where Eros is sensed as trust, serenity and openness, even Bliss.

Re-Wilding the Psyche

The Savagery and Greed of those in Control is what is really running amok, manipulating us into proxy wars, indentured slavery and isolation governed by fear. In a 'post-truth era' we would do well to see revisionist histories for what they are: describing events from the perspective of the victor, never the vanquished: those who wield power don't necessarily hold the 'moral high ground', although they will always pretend to do so... Their fear-porn and de-skilling processes have long pedigrees, meaning learning how to cooperate once more and thrive inside emergent community structures will take time and patient effort. Zach Lahn rallies against oppression with his creation of a learner-driven school, which helps young people in finding their calling.[331]

Reclaiming agency is a process of 'Rewilding the Psyche' – and includes being resolute, determined and kind to ourselves. People who have been Shamed about their bodies and natural expression of desire and intimacy are lost to themselves and each other. Drama substitutes for closeness: consigning sexuality to the shadows has it take on a life of its own – the direct result of trapping the healing power and playfulness of Eros inside disabling narratives that never did it justice. Of course, the often emasculating way many men live in modern society undermines the polarity of sexual attraction, and the physical prowess needed to create thriving parallel cultures. We could also say that many

331. Jordan B. Peterson. "School-Kids as Factory Products | Zach Lahn | EP 370", YouTube, 1:42:03, 2023, 26 June, https://youtube.com/watch?v=5umJbXekS8k

women are forced to live masculinised lives, where a woman's cyclical nature must be ignored in order to get ahead, and her regulatory, grounding body clock wiped off the map with chemical birth control... Perhaps we've travelled far enough down a road that encourages the un-tethering of gender from biology, and the attendant 'Cyborg nation' progression that seems the logical next step?

Doing the work of initiation - where maturity is brought forth through many ritual practices in single sex groups[332] and in community if possible - creates resilience. Strong circles of men and strong circles of women are strong together. The often too small nuclear family unit is tempered by the wisdom of the circle; where people have free and direct access to divergent opinions, shared child care spaces, play mates, Elders, softness, power. We access coherence via meaning-making processes that happen face to face in real time - and by virtue of new/old ways of living; *time* might *expand* also, because we're not dashing from pillar to post trying to 'fit it all in'. We're co-existing and co-creating in one time and place together. It's not a perfect way to live, but it's a *good* way to live, and has to be better than the tsunami of physical and mental health issues that beset modern western culture in our times.

New Alliances

New alliances are already forming, including therapists speaking out and asking for responses from regulatory bodies about their silence on the destructive Covid 19 mandates.[333] The new 'World Health Alliance', spear headed by Dr Tess Lawrie, embraces holistic approaches to well-being whilst fighting corruption in global institutions such as the WHO.[334] Dr David Martin in a September 2023 address to the European Parliament called for a complete eradication of the WHO - exposing it for

---

332. In the UK Alex and Mitch offer men's retreats called the 'Unmasked Man' - and - with support - are now offering women's groups too.

333. "Therapists for Medical Freedom", last modified 2023, 2 August, https://therapists4medicalfreedom.org

334. "Dear Andy (Short film)", World Council for Health, March 12, 2022, https://worldcouncilforhealth.org/multimedia/dear-andy-dr-tess-lawrie

the money laundering cartel it is – with over 80% of the funding coming from the Bill and Melinda Gates foundation.[335] Forging new support networks for food, well-being, health care and education wean us off the need to rely solely on corporate power, increasing our robustness in the face of inevitable rapid change.

Unfortunately, the Nudge Units in Government described in the previous chapter have become very skilled at divide and rule tactics. We must resist the temptation to factionalise and fight amongst ourselves. This way they win. Elders can step forward as the 'Bad Ass Arbiters' they are, and once were, across the world. 'Bad Asses' in this context can move beyond the heat of debate and the allure of 'facts' and 'figures' emanating from spin doctors and their turgid, inaccurate models.

Instead, Elders offer up a well-regulated nervous system and non-dual, X-ray vision goggles that see life in its wholeness and complexity without needing to wield a scalpel. It's a Reverse Engineering; a Wisdom Way; a Saving Grace; an opportunity to move beyond the double-binds in the hall of mirrors of the modern age... My friend and Elder Carmella B'han, author of three books on mourning, healing and communication, said it's such a relief to be in her sixties. She said her brain works differently now. She's not 'looking for answers' in various compartments of her mind. She empties herself – or the brain does that for itself(!) – And, she says, the answer comes – it literally pops up with an appropriate story or perspective when the need arises, without her putting effort in... No one seems to interrogate the maturing brain. The assumption is one of decline, but what if neural pruning is doing some kind of stream-lining work? – Possibly getting rid of the irrelevant and peripheral and allowing those with a sense of calling a kind of 'Oracular currency' that trips the switch of the 'info wars' on our screens, sending arrows into the 'heart of the matter' – allowing others to benefit from the disarming simplicity and perceptive power that only comes with age.

---

335. Julian Weaver. "Dr David Martin – EU Parliament Sept 2023", YouTube, 23:40, 2023, 25 December, https://youtube.com/watch?v=Cw6SVzqxhGo

We definitely need the strength, enthusiasm and vision of the young to complement the offerings of the more mature among us. We can work locally and face-to-face, or sometimes online, using the internet to our best advantage to organise and educate ourselves, and forge financial freedom. Sometimes swapping goods and services, or creating independent businesses, or even trading without cash altogether as a way to keep connections flowing and create resilience, detailed in Charles Eisenstein's concept of the 'Gift Economy'.[336] Small scale Food growing initiatives proliferate since Covid and the 'cost of living crisis' (2022–2024) with the notion of 'regenerative agriculture' taking hold – where the quality of well husbanded soil as a rich 'microbiome' covering the earth's surface, simultaneously acting as carbon, vitamin and mineral sump – informs practice (The documentary Kiss the Ground[337] explains this eloquently). Farmers and people are coming together to share land and resources, and create new business models that cut out the middle man, the GMOS and chemicals.

Helping to create a new world can taste and feel good – it doesn't *always* have to be hard work – in fact if it's hard work you're probably doing something wrong. I remember my Zen teacher saying to me once: – ***'if you're only surviving, you're stressing the system'*** – Working together takes the *chore* out of work, it becomes play, and the conversation ebbs and flows naturally – not the oft stilted versions that ensue as we eye-ball each other over cups of frothy, luke-warm coffee.

Today, at the market garden where I volunteer just out of town, we talked deep time, gender difference, weather pattern changes, whether to mulch dahlia tubers in winter, and personal stuff in relationships. The work creates a rhythm, a pace; a natural doing with your hands that means we are not giving each other too much attention. It seems easier somehow, then, to engage in meaningful conversation. I noticed, as we spoke of left-right hemispheres that I wasn't trying to work stuff out... Rather I was waiting, listening

336. Charles Eisenstein, Sacred Economics: Money, Gift, and Society in the Age of Transition (North Atlantic Books, 2011)

337. Kiss the Ground, directed by Joshua Tickell and Rebecca Tickell (Big Picture Ranch, 2020), 1:24:00

for the response to come out of my mouth; the intellect wasn't engaged so much as the ears, the hands, the silence, the soil, the processes. Rachel described pulling up a whole bed of kale, and the microorganisms, insects, weeds, and roots involved. She spoke of the power of Creation and Destruction we have in our own hands, and how one involves the other, and how caught up we are in our dramas, notions, and perceptions, failing to notice the Blip that we are, in relation to the Unfolding of the Cosmic Timescales involved in the Universe and Life on Earth.

She said she didn't want to 'spiritual bypass' anything though with that observation, and I wasn't really sure what she meant, I said: 'how would you know if you're spiritual bypassing?'... It's a *moment-to-moment awareness thing*; I tend to think, one where we mine our interactions for clues and cues. Our very lives are a kind of 'sacred blip', asking us to show up, to be brave and take risks; create meaning; see the funny side of it all; rise above our fear of scarcity and live generously, creatively, re-generatively, to Welcome Elders back into our midst and to shape the next iteration of life on Earth in a way that might make our Ancestors proud. Listening to the author of Braiding Sweetgrass, in an interview with Dr Kelsey Leonard, she asked – 'What does the Earth want of us in these Times?'.[338] If we can stop and listen, pause and reflect, step off the treadmill, out of isolation and back into the Field of Dreams that is our birthright as humans to claim, we might catch a faint drift of an answer on the breeze... It's up to each one of us, then, to follow the imperatives that answer places upon us, to step up and out of the shadows and to move in a way where our limber hips walk wisely and wildly, kindly and keenly towards a Future made of many hands and many hearts. Futures where enough of us are able to see the sign of Trans-humanism in the right eye, step forward, courageously, and (metaphorically?) eviscerate it. Together we are able to stop invisible, unconscionable armies in their tracks. Together, we weave the worlds, new and old, into designs made more beautiful by the connections we forge and foster.

---

338. "Environmental Stewardship with Robin Wall Kimmerer and Dr. Kelsey Leonard", YouTube, 1:33:56, 2023, 28 October, https://youtube.com/watch?v=_O0_KvqNvX0

ACTIVITY: A New Regulatory Body

This one is a multi-stakeholder endeavour that will be months or years in the making! How about creating a new regulatory body for the counselling and therapy professions that includes tuition of the New World Order and Psychological Warfare dimensions of contemporary society elaborated in this book? This might not fit too neatly into extant modern day academia, captured as so much of it is...

Then how about also ensuring this 'new entity' is allowed to question the gender identity movement constructively, rather than be forced to simply uncritically 'affirm' any and all gender pronouns proffered by young people, funnelling them all to quickly towards potentially harmful gender reassignment surgery. All of this against a back drop of understanding that 'gender fluidity' has been with us for thousands of years as spiritual practice, some of which has been explored in this book. This aspect of the project would seek to affirm the regenerative power of Eros as a sacred current running through our lives, and to de-legitimise the normalising of online pornography that has proliferated since the invention of the smart phone in 2007, especially as a vehicle for young people learning about sexuality.

Finally, could 'Elder' be included as a new category alongside counsellor, therapist, mentor and coach? As well as it being a new 'label' in the nomenclature of the helping professions, might the training for the role form part of an ad hoc, somewhat 'grass-roots' arrangement, where therapists, coaches etc. come together to support a peer-to-peer learning framework? This might work in a similar way to the 'flat-pack democracy movement' instituted in Frome, Somerset, UK, and described in the book of the same title.[339] In this way we might democratise the increasingly specialist field of therapy, in a bid to cease any further expansion of labelling and pathologising of mental health issues DSM style. Instead we might adopt a bio-psycho-social

339. *Peter MacFadyen, Flatpack Democracy: A Guide to Creating Independent Politics (Eco-Logic Books, 2014*

model of mental health rooted in agency, sovereignty, connection and respect as primary characteristics, rather than the potentially stifling, over-boundaried and over-diagnosing domain that has come to characterise much of the 'therapeutic' landscape in the modern era.

Scan this QR code; it will take you to a resource page on my website where you can find regular updates, including: books, websites, documentaries, open letters, podcasts and more. Our resources are changing all the time, so I created a single site for their inclusion.

If you have additional resources you'd like to point me to feel free to get in touch via the website. Equally if you'd like to enquire about counselling, mentoring and facilitation services, please use the website.

www.elephant.intheroom.is

BV - #0007 - 310524 - C5 - 229/152/18 - PB - 9781913675431 - Matt Lamination